Implementing
Beyond Budgeting

Julienne,
Hope you
like it!
　　　Bjarte

Implementing Beyond Budgeting

Unlocking the Performance Potential

Second Edition

BJARTE BOGSNES

Published by John Wiley & Sons, Inc., Hoboken, New Jersey.
Published simultaneously in Canada.

For general information on our other products and services or for technical support, please contact our Customer Care Department within the United States at (800) 762-2974, outside the United States at (317) 572-3993 or fax (317) 572-4002.

Wiley publishes in a variety of print and electronic formats and by print-on-demand. Some material included with standard print versions of this book may not be included in e-books or in print-on-demand. If this book refers to media such as a CD or DVD that is not included in the version you purchased, you may download this material at http://booksupport.wiley.com. For more information about Wiley products, visit www.wiley.com.

Library of Congress Cataloging-in-Publication Data is available:

ISBN 978-1-119-15247-7 (Hardcover)
ISBN 978-1-119-22228-6 (ePDF)
ISBN 978-1-119-22227-9 (ePub)

Cover Design: Wiley
Cover Image: © Eugene Sergeev / Shutterstock

Printed in the United States of America

10 9 8 7 6 5 4 3 2 1

For Jeremy and Peter

Contents

Foreword

Bjarte Bogsnes's book is an important contribution to the transformation of finance from the controlling and bean-counting office to the company's value-creating office. Bogsnes describes how to transform finance's historical role of ex-post reporting and controlling into a new role that guides the enterprise forward for sustainable value creation. The transformation requires reexamining and, probably, abandoning some of the vestiges of finance's previous management control tools. In particular, several companies in Europe and North America have questioned their use of the annual operating budget, a management tool introduced at General Motors nearly a century ago by CEO Alfred Sloan and CFO Donaldson Brown. Although the operating budget was a great innovation at the time, today's dynamic and highly volatile environment has made an annual fixed operating plan an anachronism. The counterreaction to the high preparation cost, in time and money, of the annual budget and its inflexibility in light of rapidly changing external circumstances and internal opportunities has launched the Beyond Budgeting movement. Several academics and consultants have written articles and books, and led working groups of companies, about how to abandon the fixed annual budget.

The current book makes a major contribution to this movement. Unlike the previous writers, Bjarte Bogsnes has been there and done that. And not just once. Bogsnes was the intellectual and project leader at two transformational projects at major companies, Borealis and Statoil. The book draws on these rich experiences to offer practical advice about how to introduce a new set of planning and performance management systems that inspire both managers and employees to achieve breakthrough performance. This book is an essential read for anyone frustrated with the organization's budgeting process and looking to achieve the intended benefits from the budget with new systems that work better, faster, cheaper, and more flexibly. Bogsnes takes Beyond Budgeting to a new level by describing in detail the management system, "Ambition to Action," that he helped introduce to replace the budget system. Along the way, he provides vivid examples of the implementation process in the two large companies that enabled them to abandon and replace a strongly embedded management system.

Bogsnes was trained in finance and worked for many years in finance organizations. He does not, however, view finance just through its typical left-brain analytic lens. Rather, he is eloquent on the importance of incorporating right-brain concepts such as trust, empowerment, leadership, transparency, and communication when designing and implementing a new management system, especially with today's workforce and competitive environment. The book is a refreshing integration of analytic left-brain concepts, including activity-based costing, balanced scorecards, and performance objectives, along with vital right-brain sensitivities on motivating and leading organizational change.

I have heard Bjarte speak on many occasions. The enthusiasm, passion, and persuasion that he exudes in person come through well in his writing. Managers searching for new ways to motivate and evaluate their people will find him inspiring, refreshing, practical, and, even, entertaining, terms not usually applied to authors of management control books.

Robert S. Kaplan
Harvard Business School
Boston, Massachusetts

Acknowledgments

It has been said that if you want to travel fast, travel alone. If you want to travel far, travel together. I want to thank all my fellow travelers on this journey.

At Statoil, a special thank-you goes to:

Eldar Sætre, for creating the foundation, securing the green light, and staying rock solid behind ever since

Torgrim Reitan, for all the trust and support

Arvid Hollevik, Stian Flørenæs, Jone Solberg, and Toralf Rugland, for all our great discussions and for backing it all with a wonderful system

My other Finance colleagues and all of you out in the business, who have been taking this into your own units. I dare not list names, because there are so many of you. You know who you are!

My Human Resources colleagues. We are so much stronger together! A special thank-you to the wise and wonderful Siri Bentsen

My new friends in IT. Agile and Beyond Budgeting are a perfect fit.

I am deeply in debt to all my friends at the Beyond Budgeting Roundtable: Jeremy Hope (RIP), Peter Bunce (RIP), Robin Fraser, Steve Player, Steve Morlidge, Franz Röösli, Anders Olesen and Dag Larsson.

Thank you to Thomas Boesen in Borealis for a great job in Finance after I moved to Human Resources, and to everybody else on the Finance team, especially Gunnar Nielsen, Asbjørn Holte, and Anders Frøberg. I am also very grateful for all the support and patience from my HR colleagues.

A special thank-you to Bob Kaplan for the Foreword and for all the support since we first met almost 20 years ago.

A big salute to Katarina Kaarbøe and Trond Bjørnenak at NHH and their colleagues for introducing Beyond Budgeting to academia. Others will follow, but you were early!

And last, but also first, Svein Rennemo: Thank you for the challenge and for all your trust and support. Not everybody dares to ask for the unexpected. You did.

About the Author

Bjarte Bogsnes has a long international career, both in Finance and HR. He has been advocating Beyond Budgeting for more than 20 years and led its implementation at two large European companies, Statoil and Borealis. Bjarte is the chairman of Beyond Budgeting Roundtable (BBRT) and is a popular international business speaker. He is the winner of a Harvard Business Review/McKinsey Management Innovation award.

Introduction

"I may not have gone where I intended to go, but
I think I have ended up where I needed to be."

Douglas Adams

Many years have passed since I sat down in my mountain cabin in Norway and started writing about my Beyond Budgeting journey. The book I ended up with was conceived in the cold and dark of winter, but was written with a burning belief about a new and better way. I am both humbled and proud that the book found its way into academic curriculums, and that business schools around the world are teaching the Borealis and Statoil cases, which the book introduced.

Many have encouraged me to write a second book. I knew I would. There has been so much progress for Beyond Budgeting and so much learning for myself, more than I ever could have dreamt of when my journey started way back in the mid-1990s.

This wealth of new insights and experiences is, however, hard to share in isolation, without linking back to where it all started in Borealis and later continued in Statoil. I was therefore uncertain if I should update the first edition or write a completely new book. My publisher and many others recommended a revision first. I ended up with something in between. I hope returning readers will find it more new than revised.

My writing has been accompanied by countless hours of great music. A big thank-you to Neil Young, Bob Dylan, Van Morrison, Elvis Costello, Tom Waits, Warren Zevon (I have to stop here) and so many other great artists for providing the soundtrack to these words. Many musicians say about their best albums (Yes, I still use that word; I am a vinyl guy!) that they first took those songs on the road before going in to the studio. Without any further comparison, I can connect to that. All the presentations and workshops I have done since my first "album" came out have sharpened and improved old songs you may have heard before, but also inspired a number of new ones. I really look forward to sharing my new set with you!

When I first thought about writing a book about my Beyond Budgeting journey, my immediate reaction was "no." How could I possibly write 300 pages or more about something that actually should be nothing but common sense? So please bear with me that this book still is no brick. Maybe you don't mind. Maybe there are enough bricks out there. But thank you for spending a few hours on something that is less of a story about budgets and more of a story about leadership and what makes people and organizations perform and excel. The main purpose is not to get rid of budgets. The budget is only a *barrier* that must be removed, and certainly not the only one. The main purpose is *liberation* from dictatorship, micromanagement, number worshipping, bureaucracy, calendar periods, secrecy, sticks and carrots, and all the other management myths about what is best for achieving great performance in teams and organizations. This is the regime we have to overthrow in order to make the business world a better place. Welcome to the revolution!

I hope I did not lose you with this slightly emotional outburst. Please hang on. I promise to prove the case with sober evidence and lots of practical examples. Many will be uncomfortably familiar.

I am a finance guy by education. My first job was actually in Statoil's corporate budget department. Trust me; I know the budget game from the inside—not just from that job, but also from many later finance manager jobs. I have paid my dues, almost camping in my office during the frenzy of budget peak periods. Looking back, I did some incredibly stupid things during the early days of my career! Hopefully, it makes my criticism not only credible but also useful.

I am still with Statoil, in the role of vice president of Performance Management Development. I know it is an odd title, but it was the best we could come up with when an organization chart had to be finalized in a hurry back in 2007. Anyway, it is a great job!

For someone used to changing jobs every third year (and often country, too), it has been a surprising blessing to be in the same job and place for more than ten years now. My wife would probably disagree on "the same place," given my travel schedule. Fortunately, she is sometimes able to join me. She could probably step in and speak for me anytime and anywhere!

I am still actively engaged in the Beyond Budgeting Roundtable: more later about the amazing development of this network that started out in the late Nineties and is today stronger than ever.

Beyond Budgeting is about leadership more than anything else. I have been in leadership roles for almost 20 years, most of the time with international teams outside my home country. I sincerely enjoyed the leadership role. It is the most challenging and rewarding job there is after the ultimate leadership role, which always will be parenthood.

I also learned about leadership in the Norwegian Army, where I spent a year at an officer school before getting to practice it all in a second year. Much of my learning was, as I saw it, about how *not* to lead, enough to abort my plans about a military career and go for business studies instead. The army has fortunately changed since I got my overdose of command and control back in the 1970s.

I belong to the rather small group of finance people who have also worked in Human Resources (HR). I headed up an HR function for four years. I never learned more in any other job. That period gave me invaluable insights and inspiration for the next part of my journey. First, I realized something that should be obvious, but unfortunately isn't for most finance and HR people: Performance management cuts across both functions and neither will succeed without the other onboard. Second, the leadership side of Beyond Budgeting now gave so much more meaning.

I also have the practical experience of heading up two Beyond Budgeting implementations. Borealis was Europe's largest petrochemicals company at the time, while the energy company Statoil is Scandinavia's largest company. I have shared my experiences from these two companies at thousands of conferences and workshops across the world. I have met and had discussions with countless managers and professionals, and experienced overwhelming and heartwarming support, but also hesitation, confusion, and at times, outright disagreement.

I have always been curious about what lies underneath what we all observe on the surface. I have learned a lot from great stuff written on both leadership and management. This book is very much about the difference between the two. But I am also a practitioner. For me, the crossroads where theory meets practice is the place to be. When I studied at the Norwegian School of Economics (NHH), it was hard to relate to much of the organizational theory, and not only because I was perhaps not among the most frequent visitors to the study hall. I needed the painful but rewarding experience of trying it all out in practice, where theory hits the trenches of real life. This is a story from those trenches. Too often, the theory failed.

When I graduated and joined Statoil in 1983, it was a smaller company than what it is today. Most small companies want to grow. When preparing for the growth journey, many look to those who have already succeeded and become big. How are these companies managing themselves? Discovering their impressive menu of advanced management processes can be a daunting experience: scenario planning, strategy development, balanced scorecards, budgets, risk management, incentive systems, compliance, audits and controls, and on and on. The list is long. Sometimes management consultants are called in to help. It rarely makes the list any shorter! Then the company starts out, both growing and working on the list. New management processes are introduced one on top of the other.

Some succeed, not just in growing, but also in implementing everything on the list. They may even have become one of those benchmarks that small companies now look to with awe and admiration. Many will, however, discover that they have not only become big. They have also become bureaucratic, rigid, inflexible and slow, and sometimes also quite sad places to work. They have lost the agility and the "yes!" spirit they had when they were small.

The growth journey of organizations shares many similarities with the aging process of humans. As we grow older, we lose more and more of what we took for granted in our younger days: the agility and flexibility of youth. I am starting to get some personal experience here! As age takes its toll, some also get weary of life and lose their spirit and that twinkle in the eye. This development in the human body and mind is unavoidable and irreversible, at least the physical part. It can be delayed through a healthy lifestyle, but in the end, age takes us all. We have no choice.

Organizations, however, have a choice. They are not destined to become slow and sad because they grow and become older. If they do, it is mostly self-inflicted and cannot be blamed on destiny or age. Fortunately, the damage is reversible, although dismantling what was introduced during the growth journey will always be much harder than avoiding it in the first place.

The big question for big organizations should therefore be: "How can we find our way back to the agility and humanity we had being small? How can we be big *and* small at the same time, old *and* young, wise *and* brave?" The big question for small organizations wanting to grow should be: "How can we avoid ending up in the same place?" Most organizations are actually born Beyond Budgeting. They become something else because they think they have to in order to grow up. Of course, one cannot manage a big organization exactly like the small one it used to be. But could there be alternatives? Could there be other ways that better balance the benefits of being big, which of course are both real and important, with the benefits of being small?

For humans, older normally means wiser. For organizations, this is not necessarily the case, as many struggle to capitalize on a mountain of collective wisdom and experience acquired during the growth journey. The solution is often another new process: "knowledge management." Many employees experience instead a "dumbing-down" trend, as they observe more and more strange decisions being made further and further away from their own reality.

Many of the issues raised in this book have been discussed before in some shape or form. Douglas McGregor, for example, addressed many of the Beyond Budgeting leadership issues in his classic book, *The Human Side of Enterprise,* back in 1960. His "Theory X and Y" is spot on. What are your fundamental beliefs about people? Does your sympathy lie with Theory X? Do you believe that people generally dislike work and responsibility, have low ambitions, and prefer to be directed and controlled? Or do you instead believe in Theory Y, that people want to be involved, take responsibility, develop and perform, and make a positive difference? McGregor's book is timeless reading and is highly recommended.

The issue is not a lack of theory. There are thousands of other books and articles to draw from. The knowledge is out there. What we need is all of this theory to be put to work. We need to get all those managers who believe they finished their education at graduation to understand that they are at risk of becoming more finished than educated. We need to see radical change in the millions of organizations and teams where old-fashioned management is executed every day. Theory X is alive and kicking as if little has happened over the last 50 years.

One label for what this book is about could be "performance management." I actually don't like that phrase, despite having it in my title. "Performance" is great; it is the combination with "management" I struggle with. How do you feel if someone tells you they are going to "manage your performance"? I know what my response is. My defense system immediately goes on red alert. Nobody is going to mess around in my head! Nobody is going to pull my strings as if I am some kind of dancing marionette! In fact, I do not believe that performance really can be "managed" at all, at least not in the traditional way that so many management theories want us to believe. People are not robots, organizations are not machines, and the future is more unpredictable than ever. Managers can't just sit in the control room, pull strings, push buttons, and "manage" performance. You can't make a flower grow by pulling on it.

What we can do, however, is to create the *conditions* needed for growth and performance. We can create an environment of trust and transparency, of positive challenge and stretch, of care and support, where people perform because they want to, not because they are told to. But this is all we can do. People are not marionettes. They can choose to respond to these conditions, but they cannot be forced; they cannot be "managed." Many feel *over-managed* and *under-led*. They are hungry for good leadership: direction, inspiration, and support. Good leaders create *clarity, capability,* and *commitment*: direction on which mountain to climb, and the ability and wish to get up there. That is leadership in a nutshell, and also very much what *Beyond Budgeting* is about. It is not so much those budgets we are after. It is more the *mindset* and the myths and beliefs of traditional management we need to fight. It is the naiveté of believing that if we only describe the future with enough decimal places, then we know what will happen and can safely set sail. It is the blind belief that good performance is all about hitting those budget numbers. It is thinking that as long as we in great detail can explain why we once again got it wrong, we are in control. It is the myth that throwing money at people is the only or best way to motivate. It is Theory X again; unless people are kept on short leashes and are tightly controlled, they will all cheat and abuse.

You will still at times catch me using the phrase "performance management," because I have yet to find a better one. "Organizational behavior" could be an alternative. Unfortunately, many of those we need to reach with the Beyond Budgeting message immediately switch off when they hear such soft and nonfinancial words. Until we find a better name, I am afraid "performance management" will have to do. Please let me know if you have a better proposal!

There would have been no journey to write about if it weren't for Svein Rennemo, perhaps the best leader I ever worked for, among quite a few great ones. I was reporting to Svein when I headed up Corporate Control (*that* is a terrible name, and I even picked it myself!) in the newly formed Borealis back in the mid-1990s. Svein was the CFO and later the CEO.

"What do you expect from us?" That was the question I asked him back in 1995, when Borealis was undertaking a full-blown "business process reengineering," which is (or was) consultancy language for "Leave no stone unturned and look for a better way." I was asked to head up a part of this project called "management effectiveness," and I was quite uncertain about what content to put behind such a fancy label. So I asked Svein what he really expected from us. I will never forget his response. He looked at me with his mild and kind eyes, which I knew should never be mistaken for any lack of will or determination, "Bjarte, I expect the unexpected." That was all. So much challenge, and so much trust, in so few words.

Triggered by that message, some months later we had decided to abolish budgeting in Borealis. For me, those words from a great leader became the start of a long journey. You will learn much more about what we did and how we jumped without any knowledge at the time of anyone else jumping.

Before we get to this story, we have to start with the case for change, with all the problems caused by traditional management. We will do so in Chapter 1, where we discuss how traditional management has become more of a barrier than a support for great performance. The budget is one of the problems, but certainly not the only one. We discuss serious and often overlooked problems related to trust, cost management, rhythm, target setting, performance evaluation, bonus, quality, and efficiency. All sections are revised and expanded compared to how I presented these problems in the first edition. This didn't make them any smaller. On the contrary! I have also added a new section about "control," undressing some of the illusions of control that unfortunately so many believe in.

In Chapter 2 we move to Beyond Budgeting. First, we review the philosophy behind and the latest update of the 12 principles, before we visit the Beyond Budgeting Roundtable. The chapter has been updated with everything happening since 2009—a lot, actually. There has been significant progress, but also sad and serious setbacks.

We will then make the concept more tangible by taking a look at the famous Handelsbanken case. This Swedish bank made radical changes to its management model already back in 1970 and continues to be a great reference and source of inspiration. I have updated the story with new insights about this fascinating Beyond Budgeting pioneer.

We will also look at two new cases. Miles is an amazing IT company, a master of servant leadership with no budgets and no targets. The Reitan Group is one of Norway's largest companies with a vision of being "the most values-based organization." You have two wonderful stories to look forward to!

We then move to Borealis and Statoil in Chapters 3 and 4. The Borealis case is a story from the 1990s. If you read the first edition, this might be what to skip, as the chapter is relatively unchanged. Or could I tempt you back to those great questions and defining moments that turned out to be so incredibly important? Take that simple but big question from a very tired Borealis controller as we just had completed two budgets in one year during an extremely busy 1994 startup: "What if we don't budget at all?" Or the relief when we finally cracked it all with another simple question: "*Why* do we budget—what is actually the *purpose* of these numbers?" Those were the days!

The Statoil case is a field report from an ongoing journey, which keeps providing great learning even as these words are written. Much of the chapter is rewritten and also expanded as so much has happened in Statoil since the first edition was published in 2009. It was written during exciting merger times between Statoil and competitor Hydro's oil and gas business. I wrote this edition during equally special circumstances. The oil price collapsed once again. This time, the whole industry, including Statoil, has embarked on deep and fundamental changes not only on activity levels but also on operating models. The price crash that again took everybody by surprise clearly demonstrated the need for Beyond Budgeting agility, but it also put the model under pressure as some (so wrongly!) had assumed it meant that cost was not important. The skeptics came out from hiding, eyeing an opportunity for a return to the easier days of traditional management. I promise to come back to how this played out.

Chapter 5, "Beyond Budgeting and Agile," is new. Discovering the Agile community has been a wonderful experience, and not just because we have so much in common. There are so many warm and wise people in this amazingly vibrant community. Unfortunately, in most organizations where IT is not the core activity, those outside of the function have not yet discovered how Agile has revolutionized the way great software is developed.

I have significantly expanded Chapter 6, which addresses implementation, adding new insights from both inside and outside of Statoil. Today, there are so many companies on the journey that keep discovering new ways and routes. You will, however, find a wealth of implementation insights already in the Borealis and Statoil chapters.

There are also a number of new illustrations, especially in the Statoil chapter.

Before we move on, I need to issue a warning. Throughout this book, you will often find me shouting. You will probably feel that I from time to time make things quite black and white, when for instance criticizing the budget and the damage it causes. I do this on purpose and with no guilt, because I am convinced that something is fundamentally wrong. That starting point is non-negotiable. I just want to make sure that at least some of my worries and warnings about traditional management come through. If I succeed, I also want to offer help and a way out of the misery. As a minimum, I want to leave you with a feeling that perhaps there is something to this. I do, however, have high hopes. I believe most of you will agree with most of what I have to say, because it is nothing but common sense.

If you are a returning reader, I wish you a warm welcome back. Great to see you again! If you are new, I wish you an equally warm welcome to the fascinating world of Beyond Budgeting!

Implementing
Beyond Budgeting

CHAPTER 1

Problems with Traditional Management

"Most of what we call management consists of
making it difficult for people to get their work done."

Peter Drucker

Introduction

In this chapter, we take a closer look at the many problems with
traditional management, which I have only been hinting at so
far. This is where we have to start. If there are no problems, why
should we bother changing? Why fix something that is not broken? There has to be a case for change. Some of the problems we
will discuss are directly linked to budgets and budgeting. Others are more indirectly linked, but often rooted in the budgeting
mindset of command and control.

Let us start with the budget. It is not the only problem, but
still a major one. Over the last 20 years, I have asked thousands
of managers across the world (and many employees, too) what
they think of the budgeting process. It is just like pushing a
button. Everybody has a view. The vast majority is very critical,

and many are extremely negative. These are the problems they typically bring up:

Weak links to strategy
The strategy and the budget are developed in isolated processes, facilitated by different functions without much mutual respect and contact.

A very time-consuming process
Budgeting consumes a scary amount of time and energy, both when made and when followed up.

Stimulates unethical behaviors
The gaming, lowballing, and hidden agendas that normally would not be accepted are seen as normal and unavoidable in a budget regime.

Assumptions quickly outdated
Many, and sometimes most, of the budget assumptions turn out to be wrong.

Provides illusions of control
Most of the controls the budget offers are nothing but illusions of control.

Decisions are made too early
Decisions about activities, projects, and spending are typically made too early, without fresh enough information to make the right decision.

Decisions are made too high up
Lack of autonomy forces decisions upstairs, often making them worse, not better.

Often prevents the rights things from getting done
"I can't do the blindingly obvious, because it's not in my budget!"

Often leads to the wrong things being done
The flipside is people doing what they shouldn't, because it *is* in the budget: "Spend it or lose it!"

The world ends December 31

The budget year creates shortsightedness and a start/stop rhythm, which is often artificial from a business perspective.

A language ill-suited for performance evaluation

"Hitting the budget number" is a narrow and often meaningless way of defining performance.

That is a pretty long list of problems, representing a massive level of frustration. What I find just as problematic, however, is that while so many complain, the vast majority of organizations continue budgeting, year after year. When so many are so critical, why haven't more done something about it? Where is the revolution, when there is so much dissatisfaction boiling among people?

I have thought long and hard about why. I see only two possible reasons. Maybe managers see no alternative: "What shall we then do instead?" They haven't heard of Beyond Budgeting. Fortunately, this group is getting smaller as Beyond Budgeting finally has entered the global management vocabulary.

Those who have heard of Beyond Budgeting may not regard these problems as big enough to justify the long and hard change journey required. They are seen more as irritating itches than as symptoms of any serious disease.

They are dead wrong. These problems are much more than irritating itches. They are symptoms of something much bigger and deeper. The management technology "budgeting" was invented a hundred years ago, with the best of intentions, to help organizations perform better. It probably worked well back then and maybe even 50 years ago. Today, however, we are in very different times. Not only have our business environments become much more dynamic and unpredictable, but they are just as much about people: the birth of the knowledge worker and the demise of organizations as obedient machines. In this environment, budgeting has become more of a *barrier* than a support for great performance, something that instead *prevents* organizations from performing to their full potential.

This serious problem is not fixed by addressing budgeting only. The purpose of Beyond Budgeting is therefore not just, or not necessarily, to get rid of budgets. The purpose is to create organizations that are more *agile* and more *human*, because this is both good and necessary for great performance today. This requires radical change in traditional management. At the core of this kind of management we find the budgeting process and the budgeting mindset, which seldom can be left untouched and unchanged.

You might hesitate to buy into this massive attack on traditional management and budgets without supporting evidence. If you are skeptical, I hope we at least can agree that any process should from time to time be reviewed and pressure-tested. There is always a better way. So if your guard is up right now, the only thing I ask for is to let it down during the next pages, where we examine more in depth whether we have a problem. I promise to provide hard evidence. Maybe you won't be convinced. Fair enough. But please give me a chance!

Which Way in a New Business Environment?

What is it that really drives great performance in organizations? What is it that makes people get up in the morning, go to work, wanting to do their best? How do we release creativity and innovation? How do we sense and respond faster than the competition? Why should people work for us and not for someone else?

These kinds of questions have probably been asked from the very early days of organizations and leadership. The *questions* are the same. It is the *answers* that have changed. The old answers were quite simple and included strong doses of hierarchical command and control. Much of it probably did work well in the past. Today, there is so much more VUCA out there: Volatility, Uncertainty, Complexity, and Ambiguity. In addition, the expectations from employees, customers, shareholders, and society have also increased dramatically. So has the transparency of business. There are few places to hide anymore.

It is almost as if we have been through a "global warming" of the entire business climate. The "climate changes" are faster, more unpredictable, and more violent than in those reliable summers and winters we might recall from our childhood. Just look at the volatility of oil prices. Many businesses, not just oil companies, have the oil price as a key variable in their business performance. They try to make short- and long-term projections, and keep failing miserably, as the 2014 price crash once again demonstrated. Look at the pace of technology innovation. Making a five-year business plan for a record company today must be a nightmare compared to the days before digital formats, downloading, and streaming. And why should it stop here?

The real global warming still has its skeptics, but no one seems to dispute this one. The evidence of change is everywhere. We are almost overwhelmed with uncertainty. The only thing that has become *more* certain is that our predictions about what lies ahead most likely are wrong. "The future ain't what it used to be," as the American baseball player Yogi Berra once put it.

At the same time, life *inside* organizations has also changed dramatically. The massive difference between market and book value in most companies is tangible proof that something has happened. The value of human capital: innovation, creativity, passion, and people's desire to contribute and make a difference is often the only value that exists, and it can walk out the door any day. Actually it does, every afternoon, often becoming even more valuable as many then mobilize and reveal additional talents. Employees do not see themselves as "workers" in such organizations, and they cannot be managed as "workers." They have different and higher expectations than earlier generations. Traditional management struggles when people regard leadership as something that must be earned and not assigned through stars and stripes. I learned that lesson the hard way during my short military career.

Companies are not deaf and blind. Most do respond, but in very different ways. Some believe the answer lies in "even more of what we already do." Their response is to pull harder and tougher on existing management levers. They go for longer budget processes, more analysis, more number-crunching, tougher targets, tighter follow-up, and higher bonuses. The strategy is simple: more of the old answers in order to get back into the "control" they had or believed they had in the past.

This is a tempting strategy. It also represents a major paradox. The more VUCA out there and the more urgent need there is to break with the past and go for radical management innovation, the stronger the fear of letting go and leaving what is perceived as a safe and calm harbor in stormy weather, namely, those familiar and well-tested management practices, including the good old budget.

Some realize that there are problems with the old way, but they lack the insight or the courage required. The go for symbolic change only. This typically means no real change at all, just a bit of singing and dancing; hiring consultants to help introduce some of the latest music in the charts; simplifying the budget process by asking for a little bit less than last year; or maybe introducing a rolling forecast in addition to the inevitable reshuffling of the organizational chart.

Not everybody responds like this. A growing number of companies realize that the answer lies neither in increasing the doses of current medication nor in symbolic change. They realize that the disease is serious and potentially deadly and requires a radically different lifestyle. They believe that in this new business climate, people need more and not less room to move. They understand the need for a broader and more intelligent performance language. They appreciate that not all wisdom sits at the top. They understand that business is continuous, with individual rhythms that seldom match the calendar year. These companies understand that their leadership and their management models must be built *on* and not *against* human nature.

In the sections that follow, I will share which deeper problems these companies have identified and understood and why they are rebelling. Many of these go way beyond the budgeting problems we discussed earlier, as they address the much broader issue of traditional management. These problems are about:

- Trust and transparency
- Cost management
- Control
- Target setting
- Performance evaluation
- Bonus
- Rhythm
- Quality
- Efficiency

The Trust and Transparency Problem

Companies going in that opposite direction all have *trust* as a key ingredient in their leadership philosophy and their management processes. Trust is maybe the most important word in the Beyond Budgeting vocabulary. No one should consider leaving existing practices before being clear about where they stand here.

Where do you stand?

Do you believe that without tight controls and short leashes, detailed budgets and sharp instructions, the organization will drift into anarchy where people will do all kinds of stupid things and spend money like drunken sailors? If this is your belief, you do have a very serious problem, but probably not with your organization. If you hardly trust anyone and believe you are the only responsible person around, then maybe your problem rests more with yourself than with anyone else. By the way, who actually hired all these people that can't be trusted? Someone must have done a pretty bad recruitment job! If they on the other hand became so non-trustworthy only after they joined, then that is also something to reflect on.

Few would admit to thinking like this. Actually, I believe most managers do trust most of their people. So the starting point might be the right one, and also the only one you can have. But it doesn't help to have Theory Y leadership visions if there are Theory X management processes. All those nice words become hollow if the management processes have the very opposite messages, creating poisonous gaps between what is said and what is done. It doesn't help to talk about fantastic employees being the backbone of the organization—"You are all so great and we trust you so much" (but not that much); "Of course we need detailed travel budgets, if not ...."

Unfortunately, such gaps exist in most organizations. One reason is a lack of Finance and HR communication and cooperation. HR might be preaching Theory Y leadership while Finance is pushing Theory X management. The two are seldom aware of the inconsistency, as they seldom talk together, although they talk a lot about each other. I know, because I have worked both places! Out in the organization, however, these gaps are very visible as conflicting messages keep hitting frontline teams.

There are similar interesting gaps found also between society and business, between how people think about themselves as citizens or politicians in a free society compared to what they believe in as employees or managers.

Most of us would praise democracy as the best way of organizing and running a society fairly and effectively. Here, we take for granted that we elect our own leaders, that everybody has a voice, that having different views drives us forward, that information is open and free-flowing, that big decisions are taken in referendums, and that there should be full transparency around public spending and finances. We smile about the hopeless socialist idea of making centralized and detailed five-year plans instead of letting the market sort it out. It is a no-brainer that there cannot be a monopoly but rather a choice of capital sources open all year to fund new ideas and startups. This is what we preach and practice as members of a free and market-based society.

When it is time to go to work, all of this suddenly becomes unthinkable. Now, our beliefs and inspiration seem to come from very different places, from the very opposite ideologies. Traditional management has more in common with how the Soviet Union was run than with the principles and beliefs of a true democracy.

What about our private lives? Here, most of us face and make a number of big decisions as the years pass by. Which education? Whom to work for? Whom to marry? Buying a home? Having children? We neither want nor expect anyone else to make these decisions and take this responsibility from us.

But what happens when we put that other hat on? When we become managers or employees, none of this seems obvious anymore. On the contrary, we seem to leave behind or surrender at the company gate all our beliefs and values as citizens, and quite voluntarily.

Why does this happen? Why do we so easily give up on what we take for granted as citizens and in our private lives? Many seem to be on autopilot, stuck in the same traditional management pattern as their managers. Some do not like it, but accept it as inevitable. In many societies, democracy has a short history. The old regimes had perhaps less of this paradox, because the situation was much the same on both sides of the company gates.

All of this is changing, and not only in political systems around the world. Young people who question the old way now vote with their feet as they are drawn toward companies that dare to challenge the past, that want to tear down that Berlin Wall between how society and business is being run.

What about managers? Many are also stuck in tradition and old habits. Some might have built their career on mastering traditional management. They also get support for their beliefs from the behavior of *some* people in the organization. There are always people who are either too smart or too dumb to deserve or handle trust and autonomy. You have them in your organization, too. I am sure you can even name a few. Although we know they normally are few, and even if we do trust the large majority, far too often we let this small minority drive the design of our management models. The strategy seems to be preventive control on everybody instead of damage control on those few.

It cannot be this way. If we trust most of our people, that big majority must drive the design of our management models rather than the small minority. At the same time, we shall not be naive. The minority is a reality that must be faced and not ignored. We must be crystal clear on our values and performance standards, and we must act decisively when trust is misused. And I mean *when*, not *if*, because it will happen.

Our reaction must, however, *not* be a retreat back to the old way because "trust does not work." The pressure will come from the Theory X supporters who long for the simpler days of command and control: "We warned you! This trust thing doesn't work!" Do not let them push you. Deal firmly and swiftly with incidents, but do not let these drive you back.

Exceptions must not be generalized. In a democracy, we do not lock up everybody as potential criminals because someone did something wrong. Within certain boundaries we are all free citizens, but crossing the line has consequences.

If the entire management model reeks of mistrust and control mechanisms, the result might actually be more, not less, of what we try to prevent. The more people are treated as criminals, the more we risk that they will start to behave as such.

Those still insisting on a mistrust-based control approach are moving into a war with no end. People will always find ways of cheating if they really want to. Any control system can be gamed. People are smart. Their motivation to do so will be fueled by new controls. It is a vicious circle and a lose–lose game.

What kind of people are we talking about? In Statoil, it is, for example, people we trust with building or working on million- and billion-dollar machines: offshore platforms, oil refineries, and pipelines. It is people we trust with trading crude oil or handling currency exposures for millions every single day. Why shouldn't we trust them to also manage their own travel costs?

A good friend of mine is a pilot and captain with a well-known international airline. Despite the huge responsibility he is entrusted with, both people's lives and expensive airplanes, he still needs a written approval if he wants to change his uniform shirt more frequently than what is stated in the uniform procedure. For those working further back in the cabin, a "thumbs-up" used to be enough when tasks had been completed. Now, there has to be a signature. As a passenger, I am not sure if I feel much safer.

If we cannot trust these guys on the small things, how can we trust them on the big things? Could it be that we are more concerned about what we understand (such as travel costs or shirt cleaning) than about what most of us understand much less (such as building or operating offshore platforms, or flying airplanes)?

Some managers don't even seem to trust themselves and their own capabilities. Many cannot make decisions without calling in armies of management consultants because they do not trust their own judgment. They litter their language and communication with buzzwords and the latest management jargon because they do not trust the power of their own plain mother tongue. Try "Bullshit Bingo" next time you hear one of them rambling on!

Lack of trust often goes hand in hand with lack of transparency. If you do not trust people, it is logical to also restrict the information they have access to. "Need to know," as defined at the top, is seen as more than enough. Traditional management offers several effective ways of restricting information. The organizational hierarchy is one favorite—the deeper the better, and even better if there are no horizontal leaks over to neighboring structures as selected information is passed down the chain of command, filtered as necessary at each level. What is important is not what you know but what you know that others don't.

Then we have our management information systems, which sometimes come with more filters than governments have available for blocking the Internet. Instead of everything open, and closed only where needed, it is often the other way around. Much of the internal communication would also benefit greatly both in trustworthiness and usefulness by turning down somewhat the one-way "aren't we great" messages. The result is often the opposite—cynical employees laughing about all those polished corporate messages. Instead, we need much more employee-driven discussions and information exchange. Why are there, for instance, so few internal company blogs when the external world is full of them? We need more horizontal communication: sharing, challenging, and learning. But there seems to be a fear of people using these forums to speak up, voicing critical viewpoints that might fit badly with the image companies try to paint of themselves. Again, the parallel to totalitarian regimes is disturbing. It's mushroom management; keep them in the dark and feed them shit.

It is, by the way, interesting to observe how enterprise management software vendors mainly think about the transparency their systems offer in "drill-down" terms. They boast about how executives can drill down all the way into any thinkable detail: How many customer visits were made at the Italian sales company? How much gasoline was used? How many lunches were held? But why on earth does someone at corporate need such information? What we need instead is much more "drill-across"—people learning from each other—and "drill-up"—people seeing the bigger picture.

There is actually a major paradox here. Traditional management fears transparency because it threatens control. But as Jeremy Hope, cofounder of the Beyond Budgeting Roundtable, put it, "Transparency *is* the new control system." There is a reason why thieves and crooks prefer to operate at night (although in some businesses it seems to happen during daytime, too). The Swiss pharmaceutical company Roche did an interesting experiment on transparency. In a pilot, they kicked out the travel budget and most other travel rules and regulations. Instead, they introduced full transparency around travel cost. With a few exceptions, everybody could see everything. Where did you travel? Did you fly, sleep, and eat cheap or expensive? Everything was open for colleagues to see, and vice versa. Guess what happened with travel costs in the pilot? They fell, even though (or because) Roche tore out pages in the rulebook instead of adding new ones. It is a great example of transparency as a self-regulating control mechanism.

It is easier to talk about trust than to practice it. Some of you might not even want to go close to what is recommended here, because you are too uncomfortable with the implications, or maybe because you simply disagree. But do you actually have a choice? Think about the VUCA, the "global warming" of business environments, and the speed of change. The enlightened emperor making all decisions on behalf of the common people in the dark is not just old-fashioned thinking; it is simply not possible anymore. Whether you like it or not, you have to let go on more and more arenas where you used to be king of the road. You have to take the backseat more often and instead let frontline people drive; read the maps; find the quickest route; and do the turning, speeding, and braking. But do not worry; there is more than enough left for you to do in the backseat: setting direction, coaching, motivating, and assisting when needed. Just do not become a backseat driver!

In my parents' generation, there seldom was more than one driver's license in the family. Driving was a man's job. It would not have been easy for my father, or any other man of that generation, to let go if my mother had gotten a license as well. I do not think he was too comfortable the few times I drove, either, even if he never said so. But those were different days. Today, almost everybody can drive. You do not have to do all the driving yourself. Lean back, trust the driver, and *lead* instead!

The Cost Management Problem

According to French friends of mine, the word *budget* has French origins. They tell me that *bouge* is an old word for bag, with *bougette* being a small bag. That was the small purse filled with gold coins that the shipowners gave to the sea captains before sending them off to the Far East to buy spices and other goods to be brought back to Europe. It was a very physical constraint on available resources. Too bad if great unexpected purchasing opportunities popped up. When the *bougette* was empty, it was empty. The word later found its way into English, converted to *budget*. In 1922, James O. McKinsey introduced budgeting as a management technology: "Budgetary control is urgently needed as the basis for centralized executive control."

The *bougette* reminds me of a company where the Finance department literally deposits each department's budget in bank accounts. Again, empty means empty! Some years ago we did a workshop in Kuala Lumpur with a large Malaysian company. Their wise CEO opened the workshop. He described the cost budget as "... this cage we build. We know it will constrain us. When finished, we squeeze ourselves in, lock it, and throw away the key. It all happens voluntarily, no one forces us."

One of the most stubborn myths in traditional management is that the only way to manage cost is through detailed annual cost budgets, with a tight follow-up to ensure that no more is spent than is handed out. The many problems this practice creates are not necessarily among the most serious ones, but I have chosen to address them early as the consequences of removing the cost budget are definitely what worries managers the most when considering Beyond Budgeting. This is also where we find the two most common misunderstandings about Beyond Budgeting. First, many believe the concept only is about a different way of managing cost. Yes, it is, but it is also about so much more, as we will discuss in Chapter 2. Second, many think, "No budget means cost is not important and I can spend whatever I want." No! Cost is still important, but we need more intelligent and effective ways of managing than what traditional budgeting can offer.

"But we can't let things completely loose!" worried managers would say. "Maybe the cost budget has its problems, but isn't that a price worth paying for keeping cost under control? Our people are not mature enough for this!" It is the *trust* problem again. But beyond the trust issue, there are a number of *other* reasons why traditional budgets are no longer the most effective way of securing an efficient and optimal use of scarce resources. Let us take a look at these.

A cost budget is a *ceiling* we put on cost: "This is how much you can spend and no more." As a ceiling, it definitely works. It is simple to communicate and easy to track. Tight follow-up combined with a surprisingly high level of budget loyalty, given all the cynicism, typically results in actual cost coming in spot on or close to budget, year after year. Great performance! What is the problem? It works; managers did not spend more than they were given. We have cost under control, right?

Unfortunately, this is just half the story. That ceiling works just as well and often better as a *floor* for the same costs. Cost budgets tend to be spent, even when the initial budget assumptions changed (which they almost always do). Managers do not necessarily behave like this to cheat; they do it because the system encourages them to do so. This is simply rational management behavior in a budget regime. Managers see budgets as *entitlements,* meaning "my money." Nobody gets fired for spending their budget. Spending too much is, of course, bad, but spending too little is not good, either: "Why did you ask for more money than you really needed?" It is not very smart, if you want to protect next year's budget.

But Finance is happy. Executives are happy. The board is happy. Everybody is coming in spot-on budget! Aren't we great! What fantastic control we have! Well, really? The *only* thing we know is that everybody spent their budget, every single cent. This is, however, no guarantee whatsoever that it was the optimal use of scarce resources. Assumptions might have changed; threats and opportunities might have popped up. Some should probably have spent less and some more. I can hardly think of a bigger illusion of control.

When that bag of budget money is handed out each autumn, an artificial border of concern is created. As long as we are well within budget, we spend "our" money with a good conscience and few concerns. Why should we not? We got that bag from someone who is supposed to be a wise and competent person, our manager, did we not?

When we toward year-end start to see the bottom of the bag, the concern starts to creep in. Now we finally start asking ourselves: "Should we really do this? Is this wise use of money? Can we do it cheaper?" These questions, which seldom are heard in January and February when the bag is full, are far too important to be asked in November and December only. We should be concerned all the time on every single cent spent.

The problem gets bigger because not only *one* bag is handed out. There are a lot of smaller bags inside: "Of course, we cannot just give you one big bag of money!" We are talking about a huge mountain of bags, labeled *salary, overtime, travel, consultants*, and so on, often split further into even smaller monthly bags. There is actually some trust involved, because the organization is sometimes allowed to do monthly budget distribution themselves.

We end up with a budget close to or sometimes even equal to the accounting detail level (same cost item lines, cost centers, periods, etc.). Even in smaller companies with a few hundred cost centers and "only" 30 to 40 budgeted cost item lines, thousands of bags are handed out each year. In bigger companies, the number quickly reaches millions. Fortunately, no physical packaging is required!

There are, however, managers who love to be given detailed budgets, the more detailed the better: namely, those who don't like to make decisions (yes, they do exist!). Someone has then made all those decisions for them. They even have someone to blame if those are unpopular decisions!

There is a lot of work involved in negotiating the right size of all of these bags, which often stimulates behaviors bordering on the unethical. As the budget-approving manager, this is a game you are bound to lose. You will always have less information than those below you about the real need for resources, status on ongoing activities and projects, and the quality of new projects. There is serious information asymmetry, and not in your favor. "But I am the boss," you might say. "I can just cut the crap and decide." Yes, you can. But with all the uncertainty and with less knowledge of the business than those below, how do *you* know what the right number is? You can just add a percentage for inflation, you say? Yes, you can, and so can your secretary.

The budget might be too detailed and it might tie people's hands and feet, but at least it helps us to manage the cost pressure boiling in the organization, right? Well, really? What happens during the autumn budget negotiations? As the budget approving manager, you are presented with a long list of great new activities and projects. All of them seem so great that you feel like a butcher with bad conscience once you start challenging and cutting. What you do not get, however, is that other list, the one of finalized activities and projects that would have pulled the need for resources in the opposite direction. And then there is inflation and there are contingencies and more.

But if there are no surprises, no new opportunities, and no change in assumptions for the future ahead, the problem could have stopped here. But it does not. Combine the detailed pre-allocation of resources with the "global warming" and all the uncertainty about what lies around the next corner. How do we know, up to a year and a half in advance, exactly the right and optimal total cost level, and also exactly how much to put into each of all those bags? What kind of divine insight into the future do we think we have?

"But I can just reallocate between bags if things happen," you might say. Well, you are half right. You can give people more money, but just try to do the opposite; try to *reduce* the budget for someone during the year. You will be met with a thousand arguments why this cannot be done, and what kind of disasters will happen if you try. It is the entitlement effect again: "It is my money!"

When the year starts, it does not take long before the first applications for additional funds come in, backed by convincing arguments and strong business cases. But do we ever see the opposite take place—managers knocking on the door wanting to give money back because they got too much? Shouldn't the number of such budget adjustments generally balance? In practice, it is a one-way exercise.

To make sure that money is spent from the right bag, there is also the detailed monthly follow-up of actual costs against the year-to-date budget (the one we were trusted to make ourselves). Variances are spotted with accounting accuracy. Never mind the fact that our monthly reference point becomes more and more obsolete and irrelevant as months go by, assumptions change, and the real world moves on. We calculate and analyze, and then another illusion of control kicks in. *We can explain.* We know where the variances are and why. The more detailed finance people make the budget, the more comparisons can be made and the more they can impress executives with their detailed variance analyses. The controller is in control.

I used to be quite good at variance analysis. But when that backward-looking, explanation-and-excuse-oriented job was finished, there was seldom much time left for turning around and addressing much more important and forward-looking issues: Where are we heading and what do we do if we don't like what we see?

The word *cost* is interesting in itself. "Cost" is an accounting term for how a financial transaction shall be classified and treated. Cost is something negative; it is something we must deduct from revenues, reducing profits. We should, however, distinguish between two types of costs: *good* cost and *bad* cost. Good cost is actually investments, even though accounting rules require us to classify them as expenses. You spend but you get more back. As long as we have the financial capacity, good cost is something we want more of, because they create value. It is the bad cost we want to get rid of, because these are less generous; they destroy value. Frontline teams normally know the difference between the two much better than corporate.

The dominance of the cost budget often leads to a myopic way of managing. Take variable production cost. What is more relevant—how much we spend in total, or how much we spend per unit? Is it bad to spend more if we produce more? Would we not expect less cost if we produce less? Unit cost says much more about efficiency and performance because it addresses both sides of the equation, both input and output.

Another mantra is *low* costs. Costs should be as low as possible and cutting the budget is an effective way of achieving that. What we want, however, is not necessarily the *lowest* possible cost level. What we want is the *optimal* level, the one that maximizes value creation. How do we know what that level is? Of course, it is difficult to know. But turn it around. How do we know what the right *lowest* cost level is? It can hardly be zero. It is just as difficult to find that right lowest cost level as it is to find the right optimal one. But let us at least agree that it is the optimal level we are after, and that it is the bad cost we want to get rid of.

Let us move to a different resource issue. Our planning and allocation processes are based on the assumption that *financial resources* always are the main constraint. We have established a common and well-understood language for reporting on and managing this scarce resource. We are able to classify actual or planned spending down to the last cent. When new projects are evaluated, we can describe in detail how we believe these will first draw on and later contribute to our financial resources.

In an increasing number of businesses, however, this resource is no longer the main constraint, at least not all the time. Instead, *human capital* is often taking this role. Our processes struggle with this shift. Finance has spent decades developing and perfecting the financial language and process: common charts of accounts; international financial reporting standards; and systems for data capture, reporting, and audit. HR, however, is still in the very early days of trying to do something similar with human capital. There is no common vocabulary, and hardly any processes and systems to collect such information. Our records might tell us how many employees we have, their ages, education, and job history. But this is a pretty thin language for describing what we often claim is our most valuable resource. What do we really know about people's competence, about their skills, knowledge and potential? How can we talk about filling competence gaps when we hardly know what we have and struggle with describing what we need? In budgets and business plans, it is all often reduced to headcount only, and often we struggle even to get that counting right.

Some organizations are trying to establish common competence languages for their own workforce. The intention is good, but the result is often a range of functional languages, with limited possibility for a meaningful communication internally or with external stakeholders. Just imagine if the financial market had to relate to companies that all described their financial situation differently, through local languages developed in-house, without any common, agreed, and audited way of sharing the information. This is an area where Finance can help. The purpose must not be to reduce competence mapping to a detailed and mechanical accounting exercise, but some structure could probably be useful.

Let us finally address a question many of you probably have been jumping in your chairs to ask during these pages: "What if you are in a business where margins are wafer-thin? What if the financial situation is so bad that tight cost management is a question of life or death?"

Borealis was by no means a "rich" company. Red numbers were no stranger to us, and tight and constantly falling margins was the name of the game. Still, all the problems with traditional cost budgets that we have discussed were just as relevant in this type of business. The cost budget was just as much a floor as a ceiling. The concern questions were asked too late in the year. We spent far too much time, first on negotiations and later on follow-up and explanations. All these problems were actually even more serious because we lived on such thin margins. Doing away with cost budgets did not mean less cost focus and fewer cost discussions. On the contrary, we had many more, and these were better and more relevant than the old budget discussions. We also had them all the time, not just once a year. Costs did not explode when the budget was removed; in fact, they came down. This surprised even me, as we will discuss in more detail in Chapter 3.

But what if the situation is even more serious? Well, if I were running a company close to bankruptcy, where you have to turn every cent every day, the last thing I would do is to lock my spending for the next 12 months in a fixed and detailed cost budget. In such a situation, flexibility is needed more than ever!

Again, Beyond Budgeting is *not* about ignoring the need for good cost management. On the contrary, it is about *better* cost management, better optimization of scarce resources than what the traditional budget offers. In the Borealis and Statoil cases you will find practical and hands-on advice on how to manage costs without traditional budgets.

The Control Problem

Control is an important word in the management vocabulary. Some Finance people are even called Controllers. I recall the first time I got that title. I felt pretty good about myself!

When managers are asked about their biggest concern in abandoning traditional management practices, including budgeting, invariably the answer is "losing control." When asked to be a bit more specific, they all continue with "losing cost control." When asked what else they mean, everybody agrees the list is much longer but most actually struggle with providing specific examples for the controls they would be losing. Some talk about "avoiding variance"; they dislike the real world taking a route other than planned. Some mention avoiding people and making too many decisions on their own. Others might say "understanding what is happening," which makes sense. But generally, they struggle. They all insist that control goes way beyond cost control, but few can immediately name exactly how, even if this is what they fear to lose the most! I find this quite fascinating.

You might be struggling to put a finger on this as well, so let us sort this out right away. There is some control we want to keep and some control we want to get rid of. We still want to understand where we have been and where we are, through quality accounting and reporting. We still need effective processes with no waste and order in the house. We still need to understand when we are performing well and when we are not, and what might lie ahead if this is possible and useful to predict. These kinds of controls have nothing to fear from Beyond Budgeting; on the contrary, they are *good* controls. Transparency, as already discussed, is a great example of a good control mechanism. So is a strong, values-based culture.

There are, however, two other types of control that we want much less of. The first one is too much *controlling* of what people shall and shall not do, through detailed budgets, tight mandates, detailed job descriptions, rigid organizational structures, smartly constructed bonus schemes, and all other Theory X–driven control mechanisms. Some of these controls might seem real and effective, but are often nothing but illusions of control. People are smart, and any system can be gamed if people want to.

The second type of control we need less of is maybe an even bigger illusion. It is the perceived control of the future, the one we think we get if we only have enough details in our plans and forecasts. We try to cope with increasing complexity and uncertainty by adding on more and more. When we have that binder with a voluminous and single outcome set of numbers, it all seems less scary and more orderly and manageable. This perceived control of the future we carry with us when tomorrow becomes today. If we hit the numbers, we definitely feel in control, although it is no guarantee whatsoever that we got the best possible performance. If we on the other hand didn't hit because we once again got it wrong, we feel at least somewhat in control because we can at least explain in detail both where and why!

There is no problem with details when describing the past: where we have been and where we are. On the contrary, here they are needed and necessary to help understand how we are doing: results, value and cost drivers, and product and customer profitability. The problem starts when we carry the same or almost the same level of detail with us into the future. The big difference between the past and the future is uncertainty. The past carries none, the future a lot. The farther ahead we look, the more uncertainty there is, with obvious consequences for the relevant detail level. But the myth is strong: More details equal more quality. It does not look very professional or trustworthy if someone presents expected sales or cost developments as ranges, with a few numbers only and a simple what-if analysis, although often this would be more "right" and certainly more honest. Isn't there something suspicious about people presenting a few rounded numbers only? Are these people just guessing? Haven't they done their homework?

It is amazing how blind we can become to the stupidity of fine-tuning, for instance, the expected USD exchange rate 10 or 20 years out, while doing this within an uncertainty span of what kind of superpower the United States will be by then. Somehow, working on those details seems to shield us and make all the big and scary uncertainties disappear. William Gilmore Simms was a bit more forgiving: "I believe that economists put decimal points in their forecasts to show they have a sense of humor."

The budget variance analysis is another classical example of control illusion. Detailed explanations of the difference between actual and budgeted numbers might provide a comforting feeling that the past is both understood and well explained. The past is normally much better understood by using alternative methods for analyzing historical data and time series. One great method is the control chart, which reveals signals of importance in all the data noise generated by arbitrary variations.

There are more illusions: "If we don't manage performance, there will be no performance. If we don't develop people, there will be no development." Many Finance and HR functions seem to be built on such assumptions. Admitting they are merely illusions is of course hard. The famous Norwegian playwright Henrik Ibsen described it as, "Taking the life lie from man takes away his happiness as well." These illusions are, however, more than merely painful when undressed. They can also be dangerous as they can lead to wrong and even stupid behaviors and decisions. Most of us have been on the receiving end of one or more of those.

Some of the fear of losing control probably comes from the term *Beyond Budgeting* itself. The headline always runs faster than the rest of the story. As a standalone label, many believe the term stands for anarchy and unlimited spending. Most usually calm down when they get the full picture. When they understand *why* we are abolishing budgets and other worn-out management practices, and what we offer instead, most agree that it probably makes sense, even if many still have questions and concerns. Most people also relax somewhat when they understand that we will continue doing the things a budget *tries* to do but fails at so miserably. We will still set *targets,* provide *forecasts,* and *allocate resources.* We will even do all of this in a much better way. That doesn't sound like losing control, does it? Losing controls doesn't mean "losing control" when it is stupid controls we talk about. On the contrary, the result is *better* control: more about this in the "Quality Problem" section later in the chapter.

The Target-Setting Problem

A target is not necessarily "the target." What we *really* want and aim for is the *best possible performance, given the circumstances.* Setting targets is one way of achieving this, but not the only way and not always the best way. It is a performance mechanism that comes with a number of challenges and negative side effects.

It is hard to set good targets. We are trying to describe what good performance looks like at some point down the road, for instance at next year-end. If there is a lot of uncertainty around what we are trying to target-set, it can be quite difficult. We often need to make a number of assumptions: How will the market develop? What can pop up of threats and opportunities? Where is the oil price going? And exchange rates? If we move from macro to micro and individual goals, it isn't easier. When managers are setting goals for their employees, it is useful to understand their full performance potential. I don't think I will know mine before the day I pass away.

Key Performance Indicators (KPIs) are often used to set targets. As we will discuss later, we must remember what the *I* stands for. KPIs are trying to *indicate* if we are moving toward where we want to be, but they are not always able to reveal the full truth. They are *not* called KPTs, Key Performance Truths!

When using KPIs to set targets, these must always be seen together with the bigger and longer term objectives toward which we are trying to measure progress. These objectives are actually the goals we are trying to accomplish. KPIs and KPI targets are just there to help us.

You have probably heard about the SMART principle. Targets should be **s**pecific, **m**easurable, **a**chievable, **r**elevant, and **t**ime bound. It is a fair test, but be careful with making them too smart. Consider the example of a First Time Right quality target. Should we set it as "95.2 percent" or as being "first quartile" versus competitors? Applying SMART, the answer seems clear. There is no doubt that "95.2" is a more *specific* and precise target. But which one says more about performance? Is 96 percent great performance if all competitors made 97 percent or better? Precision does not always equal relevance. The more accounting oriented we are in our performance thinking, the more we tend to emphasize precision and sacrifice relevance. I will come back to the powerful concept of relative targets in the Borealis and Statoil chapters.

Targets are very often about numbers. Let us not forget the power of words. A well-formulated goal or objective can often motivate and drive performance much better than cold numbers. Many people are much more inspired by engaging messages about direction and ambitions than they are by hard numbers, including me. It is again relevance versus precision. Also here, we need to be careful with the detail level. Very specific and too action-oriented goals can easily become just as much a straitjacket as a detailed numerical target.

I can almost hear the reaction from some of my finance colleagues: "How on earth can we measure against something like that? It is only words!" Well, if this is what inspires people to do their best, then what is more important—good performance, or something to measure against? Let us not lose track of what performance management is meant to be about. Remember Albert Einstein's wise words: "Not everything that can be counted counts, and not everything that counts can be counted."

I recommend using the SMART principles with caution. Here is some advice to ensure they actually help and not hinder the ultimate goal, which is the best possible performance given the circumstances:

Specific—but not a straitjacket

Measurable—but do not forget words

Achievable—but do not forget Michelangelo (see below)

Relevant—do not forget strategy

Time bound—but do not leave it all for year-end

Someone once added **e**thical and **r**easonable to the acronym to make it SMARTER. Nice!

A target can easily create the same ceiling/floor situation we discussed on cost. After managers have negotiated and low-balled, they might strive to hit their targets, but they have normally few reasons to go beyond, especially if results can be lifted over to next year. Michelangelo expressed it like this: "The problem is not that we aim too high and miss, but that we aim too low and hit."

As with cost budgets, any target process can be cheated on if people want to and have a reason to. The solution is not to try to close another loophole, but to instead reflect on *why* people are gaming the system, and do something about this instead. The bonus system is often a good place to start (more about that later).

How targets are set is also important. There is a big difference between targets that you set for yourself, compared to those set for you. The assumption in traditional management seems to be that unless targets are set from above, ambition levels will always be too low. This is not necessarily the case. There are ways of achieving this great combination, for instance by using benchmarked or relative KPIs. Nobody likes to be a laggard!

Nothing beats ambitious targets that teams or people have set for themselves.

Most Finance people believe that all target numbers must add up exactly to the corporate target, and that this can be achieved only through top-down cascading. The fact that such cascading often destroys ownership, commitment, and motivation is ignored: "That is HR stuff, we work in Finance."

Top-down target setting isn't always dictatorial. There might be room for negotiations and bargaining, sometimes even starting with targets proposed from below. But which behaviors does such a process typically trigger? Lowballing, gaming, and sometimes even cheating and lying, all to get away with the lowest targets possible. We shouldn't be surprised. Again, this is rational management behavior. Finance can go on until the cows come home about the need for setting ambitious targets. For a manager, this only reduces the chance of hitting the target and reaping the rewards. It is Michelangelo all over again.

Do we always have to set targets? Could there be other ways of inspiring and motivating people to do their best, of achieving the best possible performance given the circumstances, while reducing or even avoiding the negative side effects? Is traditional target setting about leaders choosing that easier option, because inspiring and motivating is harder? Is it also about underestimating people? Do they not understand strategic direction? Have they no ambitions and no clue whatsoever about what good looks like?

I am not saying that we never should set targets, but we shouldn't be on autopilot. We don't have to set a KPI target just because we measure the actual development on a KPI. There are a number of organizations out there who have either dropped targets or radically changed the way they do it. There are some exciting examples later in the book.

In my own private life I have set very few targets, if any. I certainly have had my dreams and aspirations, and I know quite well what good looks like. When I many years ago was diagnosed with diabetes, I knew I had to lose weight. I never set any targets about how much and by when. But I changed my lifestyle, and I measured frequently that things were moving in the right direction, both weight and blood sugar. These are now where they should be. I am not saying that giving myself a target would have prevented that. If it on the other hand had come from my wife or my doctor, I am afraid I still would have been struggling.

As for measurement, nothing happens just because we measure. You don't lose weight just by weighing yourself. I tried that, too, with no success. I recall my wife's dry comment: "Bjarte, maybe you didn't stand there long enough...."

The Performance Evaluation Problem

The better the job we do on target setting, the easier performance evaluation is. But we can still get it wrong.

First, let it be clear that performance can be evaluated even if no targets are set. We normally know what good looks like when we see it, and there are always strategic direction and performance standards to relate to. As discussed, we probably set too many targets.

One of the problems with performance evaluation is that the process serves different and conflicting purposes, just like the budget does (more about that later).

These purposes are:

- Feedback and development
- Reward
- Legal documentation

There is tension between the three, especially between the first two. If the evaluation focus is on feedback and development, then not only strengths and achievements but also challenges and development needs should be at the center of the appraisal dialogue.

If instead the reward purpose dominates, it easily pulls the dialogue in the opposite direction. The rational employee might instead focus on "I'm so great" successes, and avoid anything that can taint the polished performance picture he or she is trying to paint. The manager's job becomes to balance the picture by emphasizing the opposite—not very motivating for any of them.

The legal documentation purpose isn't very motivating, either. It is about the employer needing to have the paperwork in case there should be a need for drastic action. The purpose is seldom the opposite: a legal justification needed for praise, promotion, or pay increase.

Of these three evaluation purposes, it is probably only reward that requires any numerical rating. Here, it could be argued that even without a rating, there will always be a number at the end when pay raises are announced. These would, however, not only be performance driven, but also reflect other reward issues like market level and career phase.

The development purpose requires no rating at all. The best appraisal dialogues I have experienced have been rating-free, with managers providing open, honest, and constructive feedback, focused more on my strengths than on my weaknesses. Rating can actually "dumb down" the dialogue because the number easily replaces or shortens the much more important words.

In the Statoil chapter we will discuss how this serious problem of conflicting evaluation purposes can be solved. There are as mentioned striking similarities with a very similar budget problem explored later in this chapter.

Performance evaluation and rating is something we encounter as early as school. Also here, different purposes are at play. Many argue that grading is needed for learning and development. Again, that is highly debatable. The justification is maybe stronger from a "reward/legal" perspective, where grades work as a *sorting* mechanism for further education.

Let us now move to another aspect of performance evaluation: the need for subjectivity and a *holistic* assessment, as opposed to a mechanical, metric-oriented, and seemingly more objective evaluation.

First, we need to remember that performance is not the same as results. A result is a measured outcome. Performance is the behavior and effort behind. When a runner completes a 100-meter sprint, there is a measured time, but this does not necessarily reflect performance. Performance is about how well the runner *executed* the sprint, how well movements fine-tuned through thousands of hours of training were applied. The *result* of that performance is a measured time, in both absolute and relative terms—how does it compare to the other runners.

Because of the target problems described earlier, we can't lean on measurement only—neither in absolute nor in relative terms. Before we conclude, we need to take off our measurement glasses and look at what measurement didn't pick up. We need to take into account hindsight insights: significant changes in assumptions, tailwind/headwind, and other information that wasn't there for us at target-setting time. Maybe values and behavior should also be taken into account. *How* were those results delivered?

We need a broader and more intelligent performance language than the old one of "within budget" or "green KPI." Is it always good performance to hit the budget? What if great value-creating opportunities were turned down because job number one was no cost budget overrun? Should we celebrate a project finished on cost and time if quality took the backseat? Should we call for champagne when we hit the market share target because a competitor unexpectedly went out of business?

Some leaders find this kind of more holistic performance evaluation too soft and also more difficult, because it involves assessment and not only measurement. They claim it involves too much subjectivity, and prefer to narrow it all down to "hitting the number," which they regard as much more objective.

This is an illusion. A performance evaluation can *never* be entirely objective. There will always be subjectivity. As we discussed earlier, target setting is about trying to describe what good performance looks like at some point in time, which is 12 months down the road in the case of annual targets. We do this surrounded by a lot of uncertainty, forcing us to make a lot of assumptions. Should the target be 80? Or 100? Or maybe 120? When we finally decide on 103.5 (a decimal or two makes the whole exercise look more thorough and scientific), it is a relief. Soon, all that uncertainty and all the subjectivity we just applied are behind us and forgotten.

But we have just been forced (we had no choice) to be very subjective at a point in time when it is actually quite difficult, due to all the uncertainty forcing us to make all those assumptions. Why on earth should we forgo the opportunity to be subjective also afterwards, when uncertainty has become certainty and there is so much more information and hindsight insights about whether hitting 103.5 was great performance?

True objectivity is therefore wishful thinking. There will always be subjectivity when targets are set. It might seem easier not having to go through it one more time. But again, leadership is not meant to be easy. If performance evaluation is reduced to only counting the number of green and red KPIs and making conclusions based on this alone, then the only qualifications needed are the ability to count and not be colorblind. Although I would pass the first test only, shouldn't we have somewhat higher requirements toward this important task?

I am no big fan of performance ratings, but when rating is also used in a forced ranking of employees we are entering the realm of stupidity. A number of companies are now abandoning this hopeless management practice. According to *Washington Post*, 10 percent of the Fortune 500 companies have now abolished the traditional annual performance appraisal, including Microsoft, Accenture, Deloitte, and Expedia. Even GE is experimenting with alternatives.

I am by the way pretty tired of those in HR banging on about managers having to use the full rating scale, and also their concern about too positive ratings. Most people are actually average! And what is really the problem with people feeling they are somewhat above and getting a somewhat higher score than "deserved"? People who feel good about themselves actually perform better! If the concern is pay, there is no need to pay more even if the average rating is higher. Reward is very much a relative thing: how people are paid compared to others.

The Bonus Problem

When presenting Beyond Budgeting in Europe, the first question I normally get is how cost can be managed without a budget? In the United States, the first question typically is, "What drives bonus if there is no budget?"

The smallest problem with bonuses is that they often are tied to delivery of budget numbers, which as we have discussed is a language quite ill-suited for performance evaluation. A much more serious problem is the negative effect on motivation and performance, which this section is about.

I have totally lost my belief in individual bonus systems. I am convinced they do much more harm than good. But I have to admit I was once a believer. In my HR career, I have been involved in both design and implementation of such systems. My skepticism grew over time. Again and again I observed not only how they failed to deliver what they promise, but also how much unintended damage they cause. There are few areas with a bigger gap between what research says and what business does. Fifty years of research almost unanimously discounts individual bonus as an effective way of motivating and driving performance in knowledge organizations. Despite this, bonuses are alive and kicking. But something is wrong. Satisfaction with the bonus system cannot be what causes companies to change it, on average, every second year.

Note that my criticism is directed at *individual* bonus. A common or collective bonus scheme is something very different, as I will elaborate on later. In the complex and interlinked reality we find in most organizations today, how individual is performance really? Isn't the Lone Ranger really something out of the past, riding into the sunset with a smoking gun having solved the day's troubles completely alone? Aren't most us highly dependent on others when doing our work and delivering on our goals, even when these goals have been set as individual ones? There is always someone behind or next to us, contributing directly or indirectly to what we too often herald as individual success.

The problem starts with economic theory and assumptions about the rational, economic man who is assumed to be driven solely by optimization of own well-being and benefits as measured in financial terms only. The employer–employee relationship becomes a "principal–agent" contract, where the main focus for both parties is to maximize their own gain and benefit. With these lenses on, there is an obvious conflict of interest between the two, and the relation is reduced to a commercial transaction that needs to be regulated in a detailed "performance contract," exchanging performance for money. If this is where we are coming from, then Theory X and traditional management absolutely makes sense, including the bonus practices to be challenged in this section.

I hear very much the same cynicism about bonuses as I hear about budgets, not just from employees but also from a number of managers. The vast majority seem not to believe they work as intended. The paradox repeats itself: With so much dissatisfaction, where is the uproar, where is the revolution that we are starting to see on the budget side? I am, however, optimistic. I believe that one day the idea of individual bonus will be driven out of town, shamed and undressed. But we need more little boys (or corporate rebels) raising their hand, shouting what everyone in the crowd also can see: This emperor has no clothes on. Let me explain why he is naked.

Most companies have a bonus system for two quite different and unrelated reasons. The two are often mixed when the system is explained and justified. The first reason has to do with *market,* the second with *motivation.* The market reason is about recruiting and retaining good people. I can partly buy into this one. Of course, we need to be competitive. However, are we too quick in pulling the bonus lever? Are we creative enough in looking for alternative ways of competing? If it has to be money, does it have to be individual bonus? Why can't a collective system be an alternative? Can sign-on fees sometimes be an alternative? Does it always have to be money? There are many other perks to compete on.

Are we also underestimating the value of the company brand (assuming it is a good company we work for)? The power of employees proudly talking to friends and neighbors about how great it is to work with us should not be underestimated. This creates a pull no bonus system can provide. It also attracts those we want to join, which hopefully aren't those who are only in it for the money. When Australian Atlassian decided to abandon their sales bonus system, they knew they would lose some of their salespeople. They did, but those they really wanted to keep stayed on.

Even corporate giants are on the move. In 2013, the pharmaceutical company GSK (GlaxoSmithKline) announced a new compensation program abolishing individual targets within sales. Instead, sales professionals who work directly with prescribing healthcare professionals will be evaluated and rewarded for "their technical knowledge, the quality of the service they deliver to support improved patient care and the overall performance of GSK's business." The purpose was clear: ensuring that patient interests came first, just like in Swedish Handelsbanken, where they want nothing that can create a conflict of interest with their customers. In Chapter 2, you will learn how this bank is able to attract great branch managers locally in the United Kingdom, despite offering no individual bonus in a market where this seems unthinkable.

What about the other justification for individual bonus: motivation? This is where my doubt started, many years ago. How could I argue (as I did) that individual bonus is a great motivator when it didn't work for me? I don't think I am that special. Asking my colleagues, almost all said the same: "I enjoy the money, but it is not what makes me tick." I then started reading and discovered 50 years of research, with quite unanimous conclusions. Here we go:

Individual bonus can be a very effective motivational mechanism for *simple work* where there is *little motivation* in the job itself, where the link between individual efforts and outcomes is *easy to measure*, and where *quantity* is more important than quality. So for picking fruit, catching rats, and similar simple, repetitive work, individual bonus definitely works.

But when moving to more complex tasks, where more cognitive skills and teamwork are required, research shows that individual bonus loses its power. For this kind of work, *purpose, belonging, mastery,* and *autonomy* drive motivation and performance: the great feeling of together being part of something bigger, the joy of mastering something challenging and not being micromanaged from above. Money is on the list, but further down. Interestingly, people often believe that other people have money higher up on the list than they do.

Most managers acknowledge this internal or *intrinsic* motivation as powerful. It might sound logical that we get more motivation by adding a dose of external or *extrinsic* motivation on top of the intrinsic, like for instance an individual bonus. Unfortunately, research arrives at the very opposite conclusion. Again, for simple work, it definitely works. More fruit is picked, more rats are caught. But for more complex tasks, external motivation typically has either no effect or a negative one, reducing the internal motivation. It is called the "crowding out" effect.

One explanation lies in "do this and get that." By introducing a bonus to get something done, the focus shifts from being on the task itself onto also what you get for it. A bonus can *undermine* the interest in the job itself and *reduce* the value of the task it pays for, even though the intention is the opposite. The message we send is that we do not believe people are sufficiently motivated by the intrinsic motivation coming from the job itself. Carrots are needed.

In his book, *Punished by Rewards*, social scientist Alfie Kohn tells a story about an old man who constantly is shouted at and insulted by a group of teenagers. One day he goes over to them and says, "I'll pay you a dollar for every insult you guys are able to come up with." Nasty words immediately come flowing. The old man duly pays up, and asks the youngsters to come back the day after. "Then I will pay you 25 cents for the trouble." The boys show up and the insults again come strong and fast. The old man pays what he owes, but then tells them that from now on he will only pay them one cent per insult. "One cent!" the boys respond. "Forget it!" And they never came back.

Beyond illustrating how you can kill interest by rewarding people for something they used to do without a reward because they thought it was fun, the story also reminds us that incentives do not create any lasting and sustainable change in behavior unless you keep paying up. We should also remember that although a bonus is intended to be a positive reinforcement, it is just as much a punishment because it is also something that can be held back. The carrot is also a stick.

Giving blood is a great thing to do. Experiments have shown that when hospitals have introduced financial rewards in order to get people to give more blood, the effect has often been the opposite. Donors feel that it reduces the noble act of giving blood to something closer to "selling body liquids."

Hundreds of studies on individual bonus arrive at similar results, across borders and cultures. There is probably no other area where there is a bigger gap between what research says and business does. How come? Is it lack of knowledge or pure ignorance? Or is it simply laziness? Dangling a financial carrot in front of people is undoubtedly much simpler and easier than motivating through great leadership. Money is so much simpler. But again, that old craft called leadership is not meant to be easy.

What about other types of extrinsic motivation, like a public clap on the shoulder or a new exciting assignment? Although these examples are in the extrinsic category, research shows that positive feedback does not cannibalize intrinsic motivation in the same way as money does. Could this kind of motivation be more effective than we think? Are we simply throwing money out the window?

Individual bonus is another example of illusion of control. By tailoring the system the right way, we believe we can almost program people into doing what we want them to do. We put a lot of effort into designing the nuts and bolts of the system: Which strings to pull and how hard in order to make the marionettes dance as we want? Which targets? Which weighting? Which thresholds and ceilings? Which triggers and funding mechanisms? There is a whole consulting industry out there ready to help out on these questions. Managers, however, quickly find ways of gaming the system. Imagine if all the energy and creativity spent on this could instead be directed toward simply performing better!

Journalist and author David Sirota sees it like this: "The main question for management is not how to motivate, but rather how management can be deterred from diminishing or even destroying motivation." Bonus systems can definitely be one way of destroying motivation, although there are probably those who find satisfaction and motivation in cheating the system. That is definitely not the motivation we want to stimulate, and are these the ones we really want on board?

There is another aspect of the motivation discussion that often is forgotten. There seems to be a silent assumption that there are no negative effects on those *not* included in the bonus scheme. Really? What about those just below? How motivating is it to work a certain body part off for your manager's bonus and get nothing yourself? The motivation effect is negative, not positive. Farther below the bonus borderline, the negative effect is probably smaller. It is more like an irritation, talked about around the lunch tables. People share stories and smile about how senior managers pretend they are not acting in strange ways because of the bonus scheme. The negative effect on each person around the table may not be that big, but the number of people being merely irritated is huge, because they make up the rest of the organization. Even if individual bonus should motivate those on board with the scheme, how much is left if we add up all these negative effects below the borderline, both the very pissed off and those merely irritated, and deduct from the possible positive effect? Is there anything left at all? Could it be negative?

By the way, if bonus is meant to motivate, how come the biggest dose is needed at the higher manager and executive levels? Is this where we find the most boring jobs? I just don't get it!

Even executives realize that something is wrong. Here is John Cryan, co-CEO at Deutsche Bank: "I have no idea why I was offered a contract with a bonus in it because I promise you I will not work any harder or any less hard in any year, in any day because someone is going to pay me more or less."

There are, however, a few camps in psychology that see things differently. The behaviorism theory of the American psychologist B.F. Skinner strongly advocates extrinsic motivation. The only small problem is that most of Skinner's supporting studies and experiments were conducted on mice, rats, and pigeons. The studies were about simple, mechanical, and repetitive tasks where individual results are easily measured—not exactly what life in today's knowledge organizations is about.

Alfie Kohn refers to more than 70 studies on people and organizations that all confirm the negative effects on motivation and performance. "This is one of the most thoroughly replicated findings in the field of social psychology," he says. "No controlled scientific study has ever found a long-term enhancement of the quality of work as a result of any reward system. For five years I have challenged defenders of incentive systems to provide an example to the contrary, and I have yet to hear of such a study," Kohn wrote in *Compensation & Benefits Review* in 1998.

Still, these insights do not seem to have reached much of management theory or many HR functions. I find this worrisome. One reason why so many managers and finance people are unaware might be that *any* knowledge and insight from psychology is met with suspicion and skepticism: "We are business people, not shrinks!" HR, however, has no excuse. This is supposed to be their home turf.

Maybe you are still not convinced, so here is my final argument. A bonus system is a combination of *targets* and *rewards*, often introduced at the same time. When we claim that it works, which part is actually working? Could the real driver behind the observed effects actually be the *targets*: the increased effort we put into communicating around performance, ambitions, and progress? Could it actually be all the increased attention that is delivering and not the bonus money?

As mentioned, my criticism has been directed at bonus systems designed as individual carrots. *Team* or *collective* bonuses are very different, as they are designed with a different purpose: hindsight reward for shared success. This is an important distinction. Individual bonus is intended to provide *both* up-front motivation *and* hindsight feedback. Collective bonuses are often criticized for not delivering that up-front motivation. But they are not meant to. Collective bonuses are meant to create a positive feeling around common efforts and shared success being rewarded in a *fair* way. Creating such positive vibrations has, of course, a positive *indirect* motivational effect.

A frequently used argument against collective bonuses is the "free rider," the person who never contributes but who loves to share the prize. Free riders are real. They exist in every company and in many teams. But they are still a small minority. Again, we cannot design our management processes based on minorities. We must use other mechanisms to deal with these guys.

There is, however, one challenge with team bonuses that shouldn't be ignored. The more interdependencies there are between teams, the more careful we should be. If one team is rewarded higher than another, and the latter feel they are part of the reason why the other team performed well, we are in trouble. The positive motivation in the first team is easily wiped out by the pissed-off feeling in the other team.

We have discussed two different reasons why companies have bonus systems—*market* and *motivation*. There is actually a third—*affordability*. It can be a cheaper way of paying people, because bonus is variable, not fixed. Could it, however, be that we still pay *more* than necessary because it is not the money that works? Would it have been cheaper to revive that forgotten old craft called leadership? Remember belonging, purpose, mastery, and autonomy? The Institute of Leadership & Management (ILM) recently did a study on the use of bonuses in British companies. It seriously questioned the business value of the £37bn companies spend on bonus annually, as only 13% of respondents said the bonus made them work harder.

A common bonus scheme like profit sharing does provide a much more precise affordability protection. It is also cheaper to operate because we avoid the huge and hidden cost incurred by all the problems with individual bonus described earlier. Talking about affordability, it is interesting how bonus money and especially executive schemes typically avoid scrutiny when companies look to cut costs. How often is "reducing bonuses" mentioned when the task is to come up with deep and radical cost-cutting actions? It is just as if bonus money is some other kind of money, a very different currency protected by Harry Potter's invisibility cloak. Often it is actually the other way around. Tough times are used as an excuse for increasing bonus levels, to motivate executives for all the difficult decisions ahead. As if it isn't their job!

Fortunately, there is management innovation taking place also here. Companies like Google, HCL, and Zappos are experimenting with peer-to-peer bonuses or non-financial rewards. The thinking behind is that colleagues and people you work with often have a better view of your performance than your manager. One model actually combines "common" and "individual." Everyone receives a flat share of a common bonus pool. No-one can keep it. You have to pass your share on to one or more of your colleagues. It is done monthly or event-based, and in some organizations the required justification is posted for all to see. There are already software vendors offering the full administration of such a process.

Let me close with a reflection on how the bonus process is normally organized in companies. This is not any criticism of good friends working on the reward side, just something I find a bit strange. Where in HR do we normally find this responsibility? Typically in the Compensation and Benefits department, together with pensions, employment contracts, union negotiations, and similar issues. We know why; it's about money. What is more logical than to place it with those responsible for all other compensation issues?

There is, however, an important difference between bonus and other pay issues. The smallest and simplest part of a bonus system is about market-related payout levels. The complexity lies in designing what should *drive* the payout. This is a very different area. If the company is big enough for HR to have a separate Compensation and Benefits unit, there would normally also be a Performance Management unit or similar. *This* is where such an important topic belongs, because motivation is a much more complex issue than compensation. The compensation and benefit role should be limited to providing data on market levels. If this had been the case in more companies, I am convinced there would be far fewer individual bonus systems around.

Wherever the responsibility is placed, the big question remains: Why should we have individual bonuses at all? A survey by the U.S. compensation and benefits consulting firm William M. Mercer sums it all up when concluding that "most merit or performance-based pay plans share two attributes; they absorb vast amounts of management time and resources, and they make everybody unhappy." Kohn recommends a simple way out of the misery: "Pay people fairly, and then do whatever possible to make them forget everything related to pay and money."

The Rhythm Problem

There once was a finance manager who met a fisherman. "Could you please tell me about your life and your work," the manager asks. "Well," the fisherman replies, "I am at sea for five months, then I am home for five months." The finance manager becomes very quiet and is thinking hard before his next question: "What are you then doing the two last months?" Something is wrong, five plus five is only ten! Yes, something is wrong, but not with the fisherman's work cycle.

It is amazing how the calendar year has been allowed to impose its stringent rhythm on so many aspects of business and organizational life. The fiscal calendar year makes sense for statutory accounting and tax purposes. Here, we have no choice, either. It creates few problems beyond quarterly short-sightedness. It makes, however, less and often no sense at all to organize all our forward-oriented management processes on the same rhythm. I once worked in Statoil's oil marketing and trading unit. Anything beyond three weeks was quite foggy for many of the traders. When I worked in Statoil Netherlands, it could take years from being awarded exploration acreage till we actually drilled. If a discovery is made, many more years are needed before there is any production. Why should we force businesses with such a different pulse into one and the same calendar rhythm?

Imagine a bank telling its customers, "If you want to borrow money for a new car or for refurbishing your kitchen, you better be here in October. The rest of the year we are closed." That would be a pretty stupid thing for banks to say, and of course they don't. But isn't traditional budgeting by the book very much like this? During autumn "budget time" we have to identify all activities and resource needs for next year. Of course it is *possible* to ask for money also during the rest of the year. Yet just one look at the application process is enough to realize that this is not something the system encourages you to do. One of my old core competencies, in addition to explaining budget variances, was to review such applications. We both loved and hated this. Although we felt quite important when even senior managers had to submit written applications for us to review, these also meant a lot of work. Why had these managers not thought about this earlier and just put it in the budget? That would have been so much easier for all of us!

Business would come to a standstill if we actually followed the budget book by the letter. Fortunately, real life in companies is somewhat more flexible. There is normally a small back door into the bank that can be used the rest of the year.

When Finance orchestrates the annual autumn ceremony of budgeting, events happening around us seem to fall into three categories. First, we have events that take place *before* the summer. These are quite okay. We would, of course, have preferred stability and as little new stuff happening as possible, because this makes planning easier. But we accept that we live in a dynamic world. We have time to include these events in our budget assumptions and reflect them in next year's budget in an orderly way. We have control. So far, so good! Then we have those events occurring *during* the budget process. There are many, given the increasing length of this process. We aren't too happy about these. Shall we include them or not? Maybe we have to issue revised instructions and assumptions. They mess things up! Finally, we have the stuff that strikes like lightning just *after* the budget is approved. These events we simply hate. Why could they not have happened earlier? Now our perfect budget is almost ruined, and our monthly variance analyses next year will need to explain again and again that "this was not included in the budget."

There is more we do not like in the real world. Projects and activities that run past year-end also mess things up. An approved project stretching over several years must be reap-proved every autumn. We need control!

We see many of the same problems on the HR side. Almost everything is organized around the calendar: annual goals, semi-annual and annual performance reviews, staffing budgets in the autumn, competence and deployment reviews in the spring. At the same time, in the real world, people change jobs all the time, projects and activities are assigned and completed as business needs them, competence and resource gaps occur and are addressed continuously. Somehow we cope, but more in spite of than because of the calendar cycle.

The traditional forecasting rhythm is another example. It almost looks like driving a car with a very peculiar use of the car lights, the low beams for the short range and high beams for the long range. We switch between the two in a fixed pattern that would create quite some attention in real traffic. During long autumn months we have the high beams on, not because it is a dark time of the year but because it is budget and planning time. They light up next year (budget) and also farther into the longer-term planning horizon. There is light all over the place. A lot is needed to catch all the details we want to see. Then we turn the high beams off and start driving into next year with low beams only. At the beginning of the year, these illuminate all four quarters ahead. As we drive on and the quarters pass, the low beams gradually get covered with mud and become weaker and weaker, covering a shorter and shorter distance. But we do not mind, as long as we can see until year-end. Finally they cover only one quarter ahead, the fourth. Then we stop and clean the lights, so that we again can see farther ahead, into the whole of next year (budget time again!). We also turn the high beams on for a couple of months; it is long-term planning time again. And the pattern repeats itself.

Is this a safe way of driving in the dark? Why do almost all "business cars" use their lights in the same way, even if some travel on well-lit highways, others on dark and bumpy gravel roads, and some off-road in the wilderness where no car has ever driven before?

There is an *accordion* rhythm to this way of forecasting, which seems to assume that the world ends December 31. One solution is *rolling forecasting*. Here, every time we update we always illuminate the same length ahead, for instance five or six quarters. This is definitely better than the traditional "against the wall" forecasting. However, if there is a broad variety in pace and rhythm between different business units, then other solutions might work better, as we will discuss in the Statoil case in Chapter 4.

One reason for having lights all over the place is because we want to *coordinate*. We want to make sure that, once a year, projects are prioritized and scheduled, resources are matched with planned activities, and sales and purchases are coordinated and reconciled. We want everything to hang perfectly together, at least once a year. I have forgotten how many nights I have spent trying to reconcile internal services budgets because those idiots could not agree on how much one of them should sell and the other one buy. In the real world, how many can demand that their external customers already in the autumn commit to all orders for the whole of next year?

I must however admit that I do miss that wonderful moment when everything was coordinated and reconciled, all the way down to the last cent. Pressing Enter for that last time was such a triumphant experience! Sadly, it was so extremely short. My fingers had hardly left the keyboard before something had happened somewhere, and all that beautiful coordination and synchronization was now out of synch. It would take another year before that magic moment would appear again.

It doesn't make sense. Why on earth should everybody be coordinated around *one* cycle that feels like tomorrow for some and is beyond any reasonable planning horizon for others? Coordination is about people needing to talk together. Some need to talk together every day about next day, some every week about the coming weeks, and some every month about the coming months. For some, once a year might be the right cycle, but those are probably a minority. For others, there can't be a predefined cycle, as they simply need to talk when things happen.

This is not an attack on coordination in general, only on the *annual* coordination stint. We need a coordination that is *continuous* and *customized*, where those who need to should communicate as they choose themselves, on a schedule and time horizon relevant for their business relation.

It is not easy to force the real world into our well-organized processes. We are trying to make order out of chaos. We struggle and fail, year after year. Maybe the time has come to do the *opposite* and adapt our processes to the real world instead. Imagine if we started from scratch, with no baggage or historical constraints, and designed a process based on business rhythms and realities. Would everything be squared into years, quarters, and months? Would everybody in the company be on the same rhythm? Would all targets have the same deadlines? Would all forecasting have the same time horizon? I doubt it. But we are on autopilot, stuck in historical traditions, comfortable with the convenience of doing things as we always have done them. "Change is good, but you go first."

Could there be a better way? Let us hold that thought until we reach the Statoil case.

The Quality Problem

"*Why* do we budget?" The answer to this simple question became the catalyst that got us started in both Borealis and Statoil. Most managers would list several *different* reasons for undertaking this massive process. Budgets are used for setting targets, mostly financial. At the same time, those budget numbers shall also reflect an expectation of what next year might look like. Finally, cost and investment budgets are a pre-allocation of required resources. We therefore want *three* different things from this process:

- Good targets
- Reliable forecasts
- An effective resource allocation

The three purposes are all important elements in a good management model. What can be more efficient than having it all done in one go?

There are some serious problems involved in trying to do just that. These three purposes do not go well together. They are in fact very often in conflict with each other. Trying to force them into one process that produces one number often hurts the quality of all three purposes.

Take the forecasting purpose. A forecast should be our best guess on the future, the expected outcome whether we like what we see or not. The purpose of a forecast is to get issues on the radar screen early enough to be able to take necessary actions. It is not necessarily about being right, but about being ready. My experience is that when it is relevant and possible to make forecasts (which often is not the case), people are reasonably good at doing so. They know their business and normally have a relatively good feel for which way the wind is blowing. They cannot make exact predictions, but they can make good enough indications.

The budget and planning process is, however, seldom the place to hope for any high-quality forecasts. Assume it is budget time again, and it is important for us to understand financial capacity and expected cash flow. We start on the revenue side with sales, asking our sales managers for their best sales forecast for next year. What happens, however, when the sales manager knows that the forecast number will come back as a sales target, and maybe with a bonus attached? We shouldn't be surprised if a lower number comes up. Maybe we feel this forecast is on the low side, but we are in busy budget times and we need to move on to cost and investments. Here, managers know this is their only shot at getting access to resources for next year, and whatever number they come up with, it will be cut. Last year it was 30 percent. What happens? This time numbers move the opposite way—up.

Every time I have this discussion with managers or finance people, there are both smiles and laughter. "Of course we know this is how the game works!" But this is not funny. It destroys the quality of the numbers, but even more worrisome is the unethical behaviors the process triggers. We should not necessarily blame managers. Their response is both natural and predictable. We should just as much blame our process, which is putting them in a difficult position.

It should also be quite obvious that an ambitious target can't at the same time also represent any expected outcome, unless we have very low or no ambitions. A target is what we *want to happen*; a forecast is what we *think will happen*, whether we like what we see or not. Forcing a target and a forecast into being one number in one process is almost guaranteed to result in either a bad target or a bad forecast or both, as we often negotiate and compromise and end up with a number somewhere in between that nobody is happy about.

As we will discuss later, it is hard to achieve any real quality improvement in target setting, forecasting, or resource allocation without first separating the three. A two-step approach is needed: *separate* and then *improve*. The Borealis and Statoil chapters will discuss in depth what this can mean in practice.

The Efficiency Problem

It is an indisputable fact that we spend an enormous amount of time and resources on budgets, first in making them and later when reporting against them. I have yet to meet anyone complaining about the opposite. According to the Hackett Group, companies spend on average 25.000 man-days on budgeting per billion USD in revenue.

I am addressing this problem last. Even if the resource waste is scary, this is probably the smallest problem. Compared to most of the others, this is more like a mosquito bite: very visible but merely irritating. It is no mortal disease, just a very costly one. Still, this is where many companies believe they have their biggest problem, and therefore where many budget reengineering projects start.

Why do we spend so much time and energy on budgets and budget reporting? One reason is the illusion of control that we discussed earlier. The more details and decimal places we churn out in our plans and budgets, the more control we believe we have, and the safer it feels to set sail in those treacherous business waters.

My first budget process in Statoil in 1983 was a manual one, with roll after roll of paper consumed by our calculating machines as visible evidence of hard work and long nights. I still have it in my fingers! Today, spreadsheets and software packages are an indispensable part of any budget process. What happened to all those promised IT efficiency gains? Though I do not in any way miss the manual days, we seem to have utilized technology to crunch more numbers, not to save time.

Since we are on this topic, here is a story about my first encounter with the PC. The first one came to Statoil late in 1983, to the planning department, which of course was separate from the budget department where I was based. It took the planning guys half a year to convince their boss to make this huge investment. It was probably not in their budget. The second one landed with us budget guys a few months later. It was a very early IBM model, with a double floppy disk station and no hard disk. Those floppy disks were just that, very floppy. Saving and backup was a slow and time-consuming effort, but I learned my lesson after having lost many hours of work for the third time because the cleaning lady pulled the plug to fire up her vacuum cleaner. "How should I know there are people in the office this late at night?"

The PC was located in a common area for everybody to use. The first couple of weeks a few of us had it almost to ourselves. Then the interest picked up, and we had to put up a booking list. I spent several months transferring a range of manual tasks into SuperCalc spreadsheets (anyone remember SuperCalc?). Then I started to harvest from my intensive effort. Apart from the cleaning lady, it was a great experience—at least for a couple of months. One day, a colleague came over, telling me that he had good but also bad news. "There is a new and much better spreadsheet coming, called Lotus 1-2-3. Unfortunately, it's not compatible with SuperCalc." I spent the next months redoing all my work. For a short period I was actually the company spreadsheet expert. I left that role many years ago, with no regrets. Today, my younger colleagues smile when I ask them for help on those rare occasions when I open Excel. Even my children tease me about my computer skills. I gently remind them that I was the one teaching them how to eat with a spoon.

Another fascinating phenomenon in the annual budget game is the "elevator rides." The bigger the company, the funnier (or more tragic) it is. It starts early, with the initial data production in the front line. The numbers are consolidated, level by level, week after week, until they one day reach top management. For corporate budget people, this is an important moment. The suit and tie is on, and the ceremony starts. After the CEO has thanked everyone for all the hard work through long nights and weekends, the inevitable message comes: "Is this really the best we can do? I had expected higher sales, lower costs, more of this, less of that. I want you back next week with better numbers."

And down again the numbers come. At the lower floors, people are almost waiting at the sliding doors. Everybody knows they are coming and what the message is. And everybody is well prepared. Of course there is something to give on costs, on staffing, on sales budgets. Some of the fat is sliced off; a few ambitions are increased, but only a bit. Up again the numbers go. This time the reception is slightly more positive. "Great work, but is this *really* the best we can do?" And down again they come.

In larger companies there will be many elevator round trips before the budget finally is approved. But everybody is happy: top management because they believe they have once again stretched the organization to the limit, line managers because they got away with it this year as well.

We might smile as we picture Dilbert on his way up the elevator. But it is not very funny. How many customers out there are really willing to pay for us spending time on such stupidity? Is there a better example of a non-value-adding activity, even before we include the negative effects on morale and motivation?

But the resource waste does not stop here. Now comes all the reporting against the budgets. Monthly detailed variance analyses explain down to the last decimal where and why we are off track. This is a core competence with many finance people. I have been there, too. I once kept track of different types of variance explanations we produced. On a top-10 list, there was one explanation coming out on top, year after year. "The monthly distribution in the budget is wrong." What a deep and insightful analysis from a highly paid finance guy! A great piece of advice to help a management team get back on track! It feels good to be able to explain, but it is too often just another of those very time-consuming illusions of control.

CHAPTER 2

Beyond Budgeting

"Simple, clear purpose and principles give rise to complex, intelligent behavior.
Complex rules and regulations give rise to simple, stupid behavior."

Dee Hock

The Philosophy

Everybody loves innovation. Don't we all dream of inventing something unique that would take us to the forefront of our industry and give us a leading edge? Innovators are heroes, and Silicon Valley is a wet dream for creative people from all over the world. Venture capitalists and customers are also eagerly waiting for the next big thing.

Our love of innovation is, however, not without boundaries. It seems restricted to *product* and *technology* innovation. The moment we move to *management* innovation, love is replaced with fear. Management innovation is scary. Now, the question is no longer how we can be unique. Now, we look for best practice, meaning "common" practice; what is everybody else doing? To be on the safe side, we might call in the management consultants, who are more than willing to sell what they just sold to our competitors. I don't necessarily blame them. Why should they push something no one else or very few are doing when the opposite is so much easier?

The management innovation arena is therefore not yet a crowded place, while the product and technology arena is in comparison very crowded. Everybody is here, as it is safer and much less scary. The likelihood of getting competitive advantage is therefore much higher in the management innovation area, something a number of early movers have discovered and proven. You will hear about some of these later in the chapter.

In Chapter 1 we discussed how traditional management, including budgeting, has become more of a barrier than a support for great performance. Let us for a few minutes reflect on that important word *performance* in a different setting than organizations and business. Buckle up, let's go driving!

In traffic, we also would like to experience great performance. For some, that might mean driving faster than everybody else. For most of us it hopefully means a *smooth* and *safe* traffic flow, as we try to get to where we want to go: work, home, kindergarten, meeting, or airport. I have yet to meet anyone who enjoys being stuck in traffic or being exposed to inefficient and dumb traffic controls. Traffic authorities would like exactly the same. They have no reason whatsoever to try to delay us, even if I have had my doubts a few times! By the way, I never quite understood why we talk about "rush traffic." There is no rush at all. On the contrary, those cars are all standing still!

My first reflections on this issue came to me when I was living in Copenhagen during my Borealis years. I was back from another business trip abroad during my early days in this wonderful city. Our home was located just north of the city center, opposite the airport. I always tried to drive myself instead of taking a taxi. Cost was important. I normally took the highway around the city. Arriving very late this night, I concluded that driving straight through the city would be shorter and faster, with little traffic this late. I was right on shorter but dead wrong on faster. Having reached the city center, it started to hit me. Not the traffic, as there was hardly anyone else around. What hit me was one traffic light after the other, signaling red, red, and red. "No worries," I thought, "I will soon hit a green wave and get home." There was, however, no green wave for me that night, as I stumbled through crossing after crossing in a deserted Copenhagen city, knowing I could have been in bed long ago if I had chosen my normal route. I couldn't help thinking back to my hometown Stavanger in Norway, where traffic authorities for years had been replacing traffic lights with roundabouts, preventing such horrible wastes of time.

What I experienced was one way of "managing" traffic to secure a smooth and safe flow. Let us take a closer look at this alternative: Who is actually managing, and which information is management based on? It's quite obvious, isn't it? It is the one who *programmed* the light that is managing, as we assume no high-tech sensors or similar. Where would that programmer be as you are waiting for the green light? I never checked, but I don't think there is anyone squeezed inside that pole. The programmer would probably be in the office, programming another light, or in bed, if you are out driving at night. The person would not be in the situation together with you, for obvious reasons.

Which information would this programming then be based on? The length of those red and green intervals would typically be decided based on historical and expected future traffic volumes and patterns. This would obviously not be entirely fresh information as you sit there waiting for the green light.

To conclude, performance is managed by someone who is not present in the situation, and decisions are not based on entirely fresh information. It is a simple, rules-based system. Green means drive, red means stop, although yellow sometimes seems to be open for interpretation. It is a centrally regulated system, with decisions made too early and too high up.

Let us then take a look at the *roundabout,* which represents a very different way of managing traffic, but with exactly the same purpose—a safe and smooth flow. Who is managing here, and which information are decisions based on? Now, we arrive at very different answers. Here, *drivers* are in control, and they apply *real-time information* to guide their decisions. They seize opportunities (opening in traffic), or react to threats (incoming car) based on observing the actual situation, not based on fixed and predefined instructions from above. Traffic authorities limit their involvement to the general principle of "giving way to those already in the roundabout." This is no very specific rule; it is much more directional and open to interpretation than the clear-cut "yes/no" from the traffic light. The principle says nothing about which speed to enter with, or which distance to keep from other cars.

Fresh information, and the authority to act on it, is, however, not enough (by the way, we do have access to fresh information in front of the traffic light, but we have no authority to act). Something else must also be in place. We often talk about "values-based" management, with "rules-based" as the opposite. The traffic light is definitely in the last category. If there is a "me first, I don't care about the rest" mindset among drivers waiting for the green light, it is not a big problem because such "values" would normally be overruled by the red light. In the roundabout, however, such a mindset is a big problem. Here, we are much more dependent on drivers having a shared purpose of wanting traffic to flow well. Drivers need to be more considerate and observant, as they try to understand the intentions of others as well as making their own intentions clear and visible. They need to honor, and they all benefit from the "zipper" or "every second car" principle (which maybe is not a roundabout rule, but more a gentleman's agreement). No single individual is "in control" in a roundabout, but there is still control because traffic is flowing, arguably more efficiently than it does with traffic lights (Exhibit 2.1).

Who is in **control**—based on which information?
Which is most **efficient**—which is most **difficult**?

Where are **values** most important?

EXHIBIT 2.1 Traffic Control

I hope we agree that this *self-regulating* approach can be a great way of managing traffic. It is more efficient because it is based on decision-making at the right level (close to the situation) and at the right time (as late as possible) in an environment of cooperation and courtesy.

We also know that it is much more *difficult* to drive in a roundabout than it is to relate to a traffic light. At driving school, my first traffic light was a piece of cake compared to entering that first roundabout. More mature driving skills are required compared to what is needed in the much simpler red/green situation. This competence only comes with experience. Just like in organizations, competence is key, and the good stuff is often more difficult.

The roundabout does not always work perfectly. Take the "zipper" principle. We have all been irritated when it was our turn and the other car refused to give way. We are all likely guilty of the same sin. But what should our response be when observing situations where values are ignored or violated? Whether in traffic or in organizations, the solution should not and must not be to give up because "this values stuff doesn't work, rules are much simpler."

What about the police officer in the middle of the crossing, whistling, waving, shouting, and pointing? Doesn't that person also make local decisions based on fresh information about the actual situation on the ground? Absolutely, but who really needs that middle manager and his command and control when a self-regulating system can do the job just as well and much cheaper? What about the risk of a roundabout gridlock? Fair enough. The two alternatives can, however, be combined, with the roundabout as the default and the traffic light as the backup solution for those few instances when the roundabout can't cope.

There is a fundamental difference between these two ways of managing. The label "performance management" is highly applicable for the traffic light alternative. That is exactly what traffic authorities are doing through a strict, rigid, and rules-based control system. In the roundabout, however, traffic authorities are not "managing." Their focus is instead on creating *conditions* for great performance to take place. They *trust* drivers to manage themselves under a framework that is more values- than rules-based. They delegate authority to those closest to the situation to make the right decisions, based on fresh, real-time information. The model is not chosen because it is the easiest, but because it is the best. *Transparency* is also critical. We need to be able to see the total picture of incoming traffic. As we approach a traffic light the only thing we, at least in theory, need to see and relate to is the light itself (although I must admit that I always check even if the light says green).

Here is a great story from the Netherlands. As in most cities, increasing traffic was a major problem in the city of Drachten. Traffic jams and accidents in the town center were steadily increasing, as did the doses of the standard medicine for this modern disease: more traffic lights and more signs to regulate and control drivers, cyclists, and pedestrians, the same medicine as any other growing city would chose to combat its traffic problems. However, traffic authorities found that increasing doses did not help. In 2003 the city council decided to challenge accepted truth. A bold decision was made to remove all traffic lights, signs, and physical barriers in the town center, based on a belief that people pay more attention to their surroundings when they cannot rely on strict traffic rules. Results were impressive. On the busiest intersections crossing times fell significantly, and accidents were reduced to almost zero.

Some years later traffic authorities in Poynton, Cheshire, in the UK made the same decision with equally successful results. Let us stay in the UK for another great, or rather, horrible, example. The Grovehill Junction in Beverley, East Yorkshire, used to be a well-functioning five-route roundabout. In 2015, traffic authorities decided that this wasn't good enough, and replaced it with a complex and probably expensive set of crossings involving 42(!) traffic lights. No wonder people called it the "Red Light District"! Results were not impressive. Traffic became slower and drivers more aggressive as they rushed to make the next green light. Not only were drivers unhappy, but neighboring residents also complained. One day, the whole system collapsed, with none of the lights working. But there was no chaos. On the contrary, drivers quickly reverted to old behaviors and treated all the new crossings as a series of roundabouts. Traffic immediately started to flow better!

Traffic authorities saw it differently: "Engineers are currently on site trying to fix the problem. We are looking at the issue of 'see through,' where a driver accidentally watches a set of traffic lights in the distance, rather than the set in front of them. A common way of dealing with this is to fit angled shields to the lights, and we are looking to see if this is feasible. We will also be adjusting the timing of the lights," the *Hull Daily Mail* reported. What a great example of not getting it!

British media quickly picked up the story. One newspaper ran a full page with the headline, "Should we scrap every traffic light in Britain?" More examples emerged. The Dome roundabout in Watford also functioned much better when traffic lights were turned off. The same was the case at the Wellmeadow junction in Pertshire.

I find these fascinating examples of self-regulation as an alternative to more traditional ways of managing performance in complex environments.

The "Shared Space" concept that Drachten and Poynton introduced was developed by the late Dutch traffic specialist Hans Monderman. In an interview in *The New York Times* in 2005, he explained: "To make communities safer and more appealing, you should first remove the traditional paraphernalia of their roads—the traffic lights and speed signs; the signs exhorting drivers to stop, slow down, and merge; the center lines separating lanes from one another; even the speed bumps, speed-limit signs, bicycle lanes, and pedestrian crossings." In his view, it is only when the road is made more dangerous, when drivers stop looking at signs and start looking at other people, that driving becomes safer.

Monderman believed in replacing regulated, legislated traffic with space that, by the way it is designed and configured, makes it clear what sort of behavior is anticipated and required. He did not argue for changing highway designs; his focus was on shared spaces where different players in traffic have to interact with each other. He had his own metaphor, which obviously couldn't be traffic. He compared his philosophy to an ice rink: "Skaters work out things for themselves, and it works wonderfully well. I am not an anarchist, but I don't like rules which are ineffective."

The Beyond Budgeting founders Jeremy Hope and Robin Fraser used *golf* as their metaphor for a self-regulating system: "Golfers keep their own score. There is a transparency; everybody knows each other's score. No one cheats on the course or misrepresents their score. To do so would bring disgrace and an abrupt end to their membership. Nor do golfers need anyone telling them what score to aim for. They already know their ranking whether it be a club or international competition. They know their handicap and what they have to do to improve relative to their peers. Their performance is continuously measured after each event and their aim is continuous improvement."

Let us move back to our organizations, where there also is a need for more self-regulating management models, for at least two reasons. The *first* is a business environment with so much more VUCA compared to when I started my budgeting career back in the early eighties. This has significant implications for how we need to design our management models. The *second* reason is about people. It is about asking ourselves what kind of people we generally believe we have onboard. McGregor's Theory X and Y provides a simple but useful framework for that discussion. Whether we mainly believe in X or mainly in Y will also have significant and very different design implications.

Traditional management seems to assume that the world is still a quiet and "plan-able" place, with no or little VUCA, and that most employees are firmly placed in the X camp. With those assumptions, it definitely makes sense to have a very rigid, detailed, and annual budgeting process, rules-based micromanagement, centralized command and control, secrecy, and sticks and carrots as the main motivation tools.

There was probably a time when these were sensible and right choices. There might still be places around where this is the case. For almost all organizations, however, the VUCA is for real, and few would admit that they did such a bad job recruiting that all their employees are X types, although the management processes they operate often signal the opposite.

The way out of traditional management is about radical change in *both* dimensions, both in leadership beliefs and behaviors and in management processes. On the *leadership* side, we need to be more *values*-based than rules-based.

This does not mean having no rules. It simply means that the stronger our values are, the fewer rules are typically needed. There also has to be more *autonomy*. Bringing all decisions nine floors up takes too long in a VUCA world and doesn't necessarily improve them. Often it is the other way around. We also need more *transparency*. As discussed, transparency can be a very effective control mechanism. This should be good news for the many managers who are afraid of leaving traditional management because they are afraid of losing control. The fear might be deep and heartfelt even if much of this control is nothing but an illusion of control. Finally, it is about focusing on the *internal* motivation instead of leaving it all to the simpler but less effective *external* motivation, as discussed in the previous chapter.

On the management process side, the *traditional budget* typically needs to go or at least be radically changed. *Relative targets* should replace absolute targets where possible and where it makes sense. The management process rhythm should be more *event-driven*, based more on business than on calendar rhythms, in everything from target setting to forecasting and resource allocation. A broader and richer *holistic performance evaluation* instead of only narrow and mechanical measurement should also be introduced.

This is what Beyond Budgeting is about: changing both leadership behaviors and management processes in a coherent and consistent way, with the aim of becoming more *agile* and more *human* (Exhibit 2.2).

In some organizations, the people and leadership discussion can be challenging. Especially finance people often struggle on topics like people, values, culture, and behaviors. Many of the steps in the management process dimension can, however, be implemented without touching the leadership side, like for instance making the process more dynamic. If the full potential of Beyond Budgeting is to be reached, however, there is no way around tackling also this discussion.

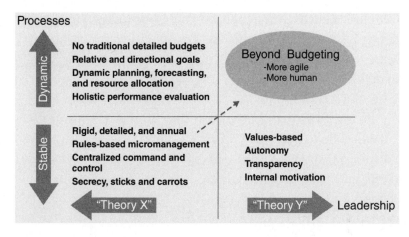

Processes

Dynamic

No traditional detailed budgets
Relative and directional goals
Dynamic planning, forecasting, and resource allocation
Holistic performance evaluation

Beyond Budgeting
-More agile
-More human

Stable

Rigid, detailed, and annual
Rules-based micromanagement
Centralized command and control
Secrecy, sticks and carrots

Values-based
Autonomy
Transparency
Internal motivation

"Theory X"   "Theory Y"   **Leadership**

EXHIBIT 2.2 We Must Change Both Process and Leadership

Maybe the purpose of Beyond Budgeting can be distilled and simplified even further into *defining performance* in the right way—broader, fairer, and bolder—and *creating the conditions needed* for people to perform in this way. That is simple, and yet so difficult.

Beyond Budgeting Roundtable

One day in 1996, shortly into the Borealis journey, I noticed a small ad in the UK *People Magazine*. An organization called CAM-I (Consortium of Advanced Management International) wanted contact with companies exploring alternatives to budgeting. I called the listed number and got Jeremy Hope on the phone.

That was my first contact with Jeremy, and soon also with Robin Fraser and Peter Bunce. We had a long talk, and I later met with Jeremy and Robin in Copenhagen as they wanted to write a case study on Borealis.

Jeremy started his career as a chartered accountant, moved on to venture management and business management positions, and later wrote several management books. Robin holds a degree in engineering and worked in various business roles before becoming a management consulting partner with PwC. Peter's background was also in engineering, with a PhD in manufacturing engineering. He managed several research programs for CAM-I.

Jeremy, Robin, and Peter also found other companies that had abolished budgets, leading to more case studies. These cases were all summarized almost 20 years ago in what they called the "final report." Jeremy later told us he thought the Beyond Budgeting Roundtable (BBRT) they established in 1998 wouldn't last for more than a year or so, because the final report had been written!

The BBRT is a great meeting place for companies, public organizations, academia, and individuals, where participants share their own experiences and learn from each other through case studies, presentations, and discussions. A great advantage compared to the conference circuit is the high trust level among members and the open sharing of both successes and failures. Member companies range from small to large, from those just interested to those well underway on the journey. They all have one thing in common: They realize that something is wrong with traditional management and want to do something about it.

Jeremy, Robin, and Peter ran the Roundtable for many years with Steve Morlidge from Unilever in a chairman role, which I took over in 2008 when Steve decided to leave Unilever to do a PhD. In 2010, Robin decided to retire. Both of them fortunately keep attending our meetings.

In 2011, we learned that Jeremy was seriously ill. He sadly passed away some months later. Jeremy was instrumental as a thought leader, writer, and speaker. He was also a great friend for all of us, and we wondered how we could keep it going.

Peter Bunce and I took on the job of giving it a try. After a few hectic years without Jeremy around, Peter started thinking about his own retirement. We discussed several transition alternatives. One thing was clear. It was not an option for me to take over, as I still had my full-time Statoil job. I found it important to be on the inside of an ongoing Beyond Budgeting implementation. The continuous on-the-job learning is invaluable. I also believe it gives me credibility when sharing Beyond Budgeting with other organizations, as they know I am in the middle of it every single day. I still wanted to be active in the BBRT, but there was no way I could free up the capacity to run the rapidly expanding network.

We found a great solution. Anders Olesen from Denmark came onboard. We had known each other since we both worked together in Borealis.

Anders stepped down from his CEO role in the Danish consulting company Basico to run our new London-based Beyond Budgeting Institute (BBI). In addition to supporting BBRT members, BBI also organizes open conferences and workshops and offers consulting support. A core team consisting of Anders Olesen, Steve Player, Franz Röösli, Dag Larsson, and myself provides direction and governance.

In 2013, it was Peter's turn. He was diagnosed with cancer and fought bravely for almost two years before he passed away. He kept his sense of humor to the very end. "I am afraid I need to pass on the next BBRT meeting," he told me the last time we spoke, shortly before he died.

Jeremy and Peter, this book is for you. I hope and believe we are moving on as you would have wanted us to. You are both sorely missed. I have lost count of all the times I wish you could have been here for help and guidance. You were such inclusive and generous persons, and our memories are strong and warm. Thank you for all the inspiration, for all the support, and for all those great discussions!

Now it was up to Anders and me, together with the rest of the Core Team to carry on. As membership numbers continued to increase, it became more challenging to provide sufficient local support to members and others. We therefore decided to establish national BBRT partners. These would be local focal points, offering both national meetings and conferences and also consulting support. This turned out to be highly appreciated by our members, leading to a further increase in membership numbers. So far, national partners are in place in UK, France, Ireland, Denmark, Sweden, Norway, and Iceland. Discussions are ongoing with candidates in several other countries. In North America, Steve Player has filled this role for many years.

I run the Norwegian BBRT in addition to my chairman role. I have always had a good overview of companies on the journey, especially in Norway. A few years ago I came across a Norwegian IT company without budgets, KPIs, or targets. I was thrilled. I love it every time a company embraces management innovation like this. But this was special. It was the first time I didn't know, and they even came from Bergen, where I grew up! The fact that I am starting to lose the oversight even in my own backyard is a strong sign that we are rolling! The company that surprised me was Miles. You will hear more about their fascinating story later in this chapter.

Not long after it happened again. I spoke at a conference in Oslo when a group of people from a big Norwegian real estate company told me they had kicked out the budget a year ago. Wonderful! I look forward to many more of these great moments.

Some members have stayed with the BBRT almost since the start. Others join for some years, long enough to learn and get started before they leave. Today, several hundred organizations have benefited from a membership. A good example is Schneider Electric, one of the early members. This French automation and energy management company has 170,000 employees in 40 countries. They left after some years, and we somehow lost contact. They reemerged at a Beyond

Budgeting conference in Paris in 2015 with a great presentation of their "budget-less" management model, which they had been running ever since those membership days.

France is an interesting example of how things might be brewing before there suddenly is an eruption. Beyond Schneider Electric we regarded France as quite dead. Then suddenly, within months, we were approached by Société Générale, Airbus, Michelin, Danone, and GDF Suez (now Engie). We have had several workshops and conferences in France and even held our autumn 2015 European members' meeting in Paris.

Beyond Budgeting in Iceland is also a fascinating story. There are more than volcanos brewing up north! Given its population of 330,000 people, no other country is showing a bigger interest in Beyond Budgeting. A number of Icelandic companies are on the journey, and several successful conferences have already been organized by the local partner.

The Beyond Budgeting Principles

The early observations and the first attempts in the BBRT to formulate concepts and models started where most companies also start: with the more concrete and obvious problems with budgeting. Research and new cases gradually led to an understanding that the budget problem was just one part of a larger *systemic* problem. The solution could not be found just in new *tools* and *processes* that could do the budget job in a better and more effective way. A set of *leadership principles* was also needed. Jeremy, Robin, and Peter observed many similarities in the organizations they had researched, both in philosophies and practices. These observations became the foundation for the Beyond Budgeting principles, six on leadership and six on management processes. The principles as they originally were formulated have developed over time, as we all have learned on our different journeys. Here are the principles as they stand today:

Leadership Principles

Purpose—Engage and inspire people around bold and noble causes, **not** *around short-term financial targets.*

Values—Govern through shared values and sound judgment, **not** *through detailed rules and regulations.*

Transparency—Make information open for self-regulation, innovation, learning, and control; **don't** *restrict it.*

Organization—Cultivate a strong sense of belonging and organize around agile and accountable teams; **avoid** *hierarchical controls and bureaucracy.*

Autonomy—Trust people with freedom to act; **don't** *punish everyone if someone should abuse it.*

Customers—Connect everyone's work with customer needs; **avoid** *conflicts of interest.*

Management Processes

Rhythm—Organize management processes dynamically around business rhythms and events, **not** *around the calendar year only.*

Targets—Set directional, ambitious, and relative goals; **avoid** *fixed and cascaded targets.*

Plans and forecasts—Make planning and forecasting lean and unbiased processes, **not** *rigid and political exercises.*

Resource allocation—Foster a cost-conscious mindset and make resources available as needed, **not** *through detailed annual budget allocations.*

Performance evaluation—Evaluate performance holistically and with peer feedback for learning and development, **not** *based on measurement only and* **not** *for rewards only.*

Rewards—Reward shared success against competition, ***not against fixed performance contracts.***

We have already discussed many of the themes these principles address. The Handelsbanken, Miles, Reitan Group, Borealis, and Statoil cases will provide a variety of examples of what the principles can mean in practice.

Coherence is key here: consistency between what is said on leadership and what is done in management processes. It doesn't help that we on the leadership side talk loud and warm about "us, team, and together" and "everybody in the same boat" if the reward process is about individual bonus only. This leaves a huge gap between what is said and what is done. A similar big gap is created if we talk equally loud and warm about "what fantastic people we have onboard, we would be nothing without you, and we trust you so much." But not that much: "Of course we need detailed travel budgets—imagine what would happen without!"

Beyond Budgeting addresses big and important issues, which for some can be scary. Many ask how critical it is to fully implement all 12 principles. The question is relevant, because each one can represent a big change project in itself. Being on a Beyond Budgeting journey can sometimes feel like eating an elephant. There is just one way to do that; it must be cut into smaller parts. This is not fast food, but as in real life, the results are also much healthier! With a more stepwise approach, each step must point in the same direction, and someone will need to keep an eye on the bigger picture and on a possible endgame. The principles do not, however, make up a buffet menu where we can pick a few here and there and hope for big change. The relative importance of each principle might vary depending on the specific situation. Most organizations on the journey have taken an evolutionary approach, but there are also more "revolutionary" cases out there. But even here, changes

in leadership behaviors took time despite radical overnight
changes in management processes. In Chapter 6 we will discuss more in depth "evolution versus revolution" and explore
different ways of getting started.

Some organizations never needed to change, because
they managed to stay true to the agile and entrepreneurial
way they started out. As discussed, organizations are actually
born Beyond Budgeting, but most become something else
because they believe (and are told) that this way of leading
and managing isn't good enough. Most end up as another big
company longing for the agility and humanity they left behind
on the growth journey.

The 12 Beyond Budgeting principles do not represent a
management *recipe*. They describe a management *philosophy*.
They provide ideas and guidance, but this is not "read the book,
tick the boxes." It is therefore not identical what has happened
in the many organizations that are on a liberation journey in
some form or shape (Exhibit 2.3).

The management models in these companies are not identical, as they are based on the specific business, history, and
culture of each one. That is exactly how it should be. I am
highly skeptical of management recipes, because someone has

EXHIBIT 2.3 Some of the Companies on the Beyond Budgeting Journey

done all the thinking for you! Your only job is to implement other people's thinking. I find that quite boring and also dangerous. For those who like to think for themselves, a Beyond Budgeting implementation has a lot to offer.

Some are frustrated about Beyond Budgeting not coming as a box with a simple instruction manual. In Statoil, a system documents all major processes through flowcharts. I was once asked to draw Beyond Budgeting as such a process. It can't be done!

We are often asked about what kind of organizational structure Beyond Budgeting recommends. There is no single, simple answer. The principles do advocate agile and accountable teams with a strong customer focus, but this can be achieved in many different ways. The organization chart seldom tells the full story. Reality can be much better or much worse.

Too often, problems are attempted to be fixed through "reorganizations." The process leading up to a new structure is often thorough and analytical, listing positive and negative effects of each alternative. The problem typically starts after the decision is made and the new structure is implemented. Now, the list of negatives is often forgotten, the one describing the disadvantages of the chosen model. The one we can forget, however, is the list of positives, because we get those benefits through our chosen structure. It is the negative consequences of the chosen structure that we can't forget. On the contrary, these require constant attention to minimize the disadvantages we identified. Unfortunately, this seldom happens. After a while, these problems materialize, first as sand and later as stones in the machinery. The response is typically another reorganization, with the same mistake being made once again.

Let us now explore what the 12 Beyond Budgeting principles can mean in practice, first in Handelsbanken and then in Miles and the Reitan Group, before we visit Borealis and Statoil in the chapters that follow.

Handelsbanken—the Pioneer

The most famous Beyond Budgeting case has long been
Handelsbanken, a Swedish bank that today operates almost 900
branches in 24 European countries and is the fastest growing
bank in the UK. What makes their story so fascinating is not
just the fact that the bank decided to kick out the budget as
part of a radical transformation of their management model
back in 1970. It is equally fascinating to observe how the bank
has performed since then:

- More profitable than the average of its competitors, *every*
  year since 1972
- Among the most cost-efficient universal banks in Europe
- Never needed a bailout from the authorities because they
  messed it up
- The strongest bank in Europe and one of the strongest
  in the world, according to financial information provider
  Bloomberg

It can't be a coincidence: such a consistently great performance and such a radically different management model.

The wise and brave man behind it all was Jan Wallander,
chief executive of Handelsbanken from 1970 to 1978 and later
chairman of the board until 1991. When he joined the bank in
1970, having the mandate to completely change the management model was actually a condition he set in order to take
the job. Handelsbanken had until then been managed more or
less like other Swedish banks, with very much the same mixed
results. It was actually crisis time when Wallander came in.

His vision was a radically decentralized management
model with simplicity, transparency, and self-regulation as key
principles. Wallander wanted to replace traditional controls like

budgets, hierarchy, centralization, and individual rewards with very different "controls." He strongly believed a new model would stimulate and drive good performance much more effectively, and deliver what he did *not* regard as conflicting purposes: high customer satisfaction *and* low cost. That is actually the bank's simple strategy, to create long-term value through higher customer satisfaction and lower costs than its competitors. Growth has no place in their strategy; it has instead been a consequence of great performance.

Wallander's bold steps included:

- Much greater branch authority—"the branch is the bank"
- A flat structure with only a few layers
- A focus on customers instead of products
- Transparent performance data
- No individual bonuses, only a collective profit-sharing system
- A strong values-based culture
- No budgets

Many see eliminating budgets as Wallander's main and bravest decision, but this was just as much a natural consequence of all the other things he was aiming for.

The explanation behind the bank's remarkable success lies of course very much in what it started doing but also in everything it stopped doing. It did not just put a new box on top of the ones it already had. The bank is thin on traditional management processes but strong on direction, values, autonomy, and flexibility. Beyond having no budgets, it sets no targets and does very little of traditional planning.

Each month, the head office in Stockholm provides the status on a few selected key performance indicators. These include return on capital, cost/income ratio, and customer satisfaction.

How are comparable branches doing on each one? These KPIs are not perfect but are accepted throughout the bank as good enough.

This is all Stockholm does. For branches coming out low, there are no instructions from above about increasing sales, cutting costs, more of this, less of that. The message from the head office is simple: "We can see that you have a problem. But it is your problem, and you know best how to solve it. You are closest to the market, you are closest to your customers, and you know your people best. We are happy to help, but your performance is your responsibility," Within a few boundaries, branches have the necessary authority to take all actions required. This includes not only wide lending authorities and all marketing activities (the bank runs almost no central marketing) but also the full cost side, including manning and salary levels. A famous expression in the bank is that "our chairs have no backs to lean on." If you make the wrong move, there is no head office to blame.

But who is comfortable with falling behind? Those at the bottom work hard to improve; those at the top work hard to keep their position. Everybody tries to improve.

This is just half the story. The purpose of the benchmarking is not only to drive performance. *Learning* is an equally important purpose. The bank wants branches coming out low to learn from those performing better. But why should you as a well-performing branch take those calls or agree on those meetings that the low performers are asking for? They might climb and one day maybe threaten your place at the top!

To make sure calls are taken and meetings set up, the bank has no individual bonuses (except in a small trading environment at group headquarters). All bonuses are collective, driven by how Handelsbanken is performing against other banks, which gives everybody a very good reason to share knowledge and best practices.

Everyone, branch employee or CEO, is onboard with this scheme that offers not just the same percentages but even the same amounts. The bonus is not paid out annually, but invested in an in-house fund called Oktogonen. This fund invests the bonus payout, much of it in Handelsbanken shares. Today the fund owns more than 10 percent of the bank. Shares are paid out earliest at the age of 60, so there are no short-term carrots dangling in front of anyone. If you had been with the bank since 1972, when the scheme was established, your balance today would be well above one million euros.

Stimulating internal knowledge sharing is not the only reason why Handelsbanken is shying away from individual bonuses. It is also very much about the customer. They want to make sure there is absolutely nothing that can create a conflict of interest when branch employees advise their customers.

Here is Anders Bouvin, chief executive in the UK: "Handelsbanken's current and future success in the UK depends on our clear focus on customer satisfaction. Our experienced branch teams have real power to listen to a customer's needs, use their initiative and local knowledge, and make decisions for long-term mutual benefit. We don't set sales targets or pay performance bonuses, which could distort this focus. Nor do we operate credit-scoring or remote call centers, because our customers have never asked for them."

With no individual bonus, how is the bank then able to attract and retain good people in a business where such bonuses are standard, at least on a manager level? Even in the UK, recruiting new branch managers is not a problem. "Actually, they call us, because they want to work for us," says Bouvin. "They like our philosophy and the way we work. Our management model is obviously attraction enough." He explains that when opening a new branch, they first recruit the branch manager and then move on with the rest, not the other way around.

It is an attractive bank not only for branch managers, but also for employees who appreciate the way the bank is run. In the UK, it didn't take long to reach a very high score on the "Great Place to Work" survey. Customers also love them. In 2014, the bank was rated top on customer satisfaction for the sixth year running in an independent survey of personal and business customers, far exceeding competitors both on customer satisfaction and loyalty.

Our Way is a household name for Handelsbanken employees. This booklet spells out the philosophy of the bank in a plain and down-to-earth language. You can't play Bullshit Bingo with that one! They have had it since Wallander's days, almost unchanged. Minor updates are typically made when there is a new CEO, meaning not that often. Although the bank is open and willing to share how they operate, they are for some reason quite secretive about the book. I once asked for a copy. The answer was a polite "no." I was, however, allowed to sit down and flip through it with a branch manager sitting next to me. I opened the book, and the very first words that hit my eyes were these: *We have an unshakeable belief in people and their will and ability to do good things well.* Those are wonderful words, but more than that. They are also reflected in the bank's management processes. There are no gaps between what is said and what is done, unfortunately the case in so many other organizations.

Jan Wallander's job experience prior to joining the bank in 1970 included public sector forecasting. This was probably why he arrived at his very logical but still unique view on forecasting. He writes in his book, *The Budget: An Unnecessary Evil*, about all the efforts put into forecasting sales of TV sets in Sweden and how they got it wrong, again and again. When he moved to the bank, he decided not to try even harder but rather the opposite. If things are stable and you believe tomorrow will be like today, why *should* you spend time on forecasting? You know what tomorrow will look like. The opposite is true as well: If times are turbulent and you have no idea what tomorrow will be like, how *could* you spend time on forecasting? You are most likely wrong, anyway.

Hearing and reading about how a company operates is one thing. Talking to people, especially on the front line, sometimes brings out different stories. I have met with a number of people working for the bank. The story they tell is very consistent. They all describe the same philosophy and the same practices. Some years ago I met a fellow student from NHH whom I hadn't seen for a long time. When exchanging career updates, he mentioned that he once had been responsible for starting up a new Handelsbanken branch. I immediately used the opportunity. Without any leading questions from my side, he confirmed everything I had heard: the autonomy they had, the power of the internal benchmarking, and all the other elements of the model.

Some wonder if the Handelsbanken model means a soft approach, with middle and top management shying away from difficult issues and tough decisions. Let there be no doubt: Difficult issues *are* being handled. But they are being handled where they occur. The majority of such cases will always take place in the front line, often related to customers or employees. One local branch manager explained how he replaced more than half of the team when he started "because they were not good enough in their current roles." He did not do this because he was told to but because he had to, in order to lift the performance of the branch. It should also be mentioned that those people went to other and more suitable jobs elsewhere in the bank. The bank has a long-term view not only on customer relationships but also on employment. It very rarely fires employees.

Handelsbanken is a fascinating case for many reasons: the radical but simple model, how long it has stuck to the same philosophy, and the consistently high performance. I have often wondered why competitors are not trying to copy. There are no secrets. The entire model is visible with no copyrights. Perhaps it does not come across as advanced enough? Maybe the other banks actually understand that this is a long journey and not a quick fix that will provide results tomorrow? Perhaps they lack the energy to get started or realize they do not have the patience to follow it through? Or, is the addiction to power and glory simply too strong?

Some are interested, however. The small Norwegian bank Sparebank Pluss actually copied the Handelsbanken model. It was no coincidence, as the chairman at the time, Trond Bjørnenak, is also a professor at NHH, a business school that is both researching and teaching Beyond Budgeting (more about this later). Results were impressive. Not only did the bank beat even Handelsbanken in Norway on cost/income ratio; bottom line improvements were also impressive. Another Norwegian bank, SpareBank1 Gruppen, also went Beyond Budgeting several years ago, again drawing on Handelsbanken and achieving great results.

The NHH research on Beyond Budgeting included a study of profitability in around 80 Norwegian banks, where around 10 percent said they operated without budgets. Guess which group had the highest profitability.

For those of us working in other businesses, there is a lot to learn from the Handelsbanken case. I disagree with those saying that because units in their business are not as comparable as bank branches, there is little to learn. The Handelsbanken model is about so much more than benchmarking. It is about trust, transparency, and simplicity. The benchmarking just makes it a bit easier.

Miles—a Master of Servant Leadership

Miles is a Norwegian IT company, founded in 2005 by Tom Georg Olsen and a few friends and former colleagues. The companies Olsen earlier had worked for had all been quite traditionally managed, leaving him frustrated but also with a strong belief that there had to be a better way. His frustration was about what he had seen of professional mediocrity and lack of passion for work, but also about a lack of focus on people. His concerns for both might have something to do with his education; he was trained not only as an engineer but also as a nurse. "Many big corporations seem to play Lego games with their people, treating them as inventory," he says.

Olsen and his colleagues wanted to build a company based on very different beliefs and principles. Values-based servant leadership, professional authority and warmth, and close to nothing of traditional management processes were to be the foundation. Processes would be introduced when only really needed, not just because everybody else had them. "There was no need for budgets when we started out, and ten years down the road we still don't see the need," Olsen says.

No targets are set. Some simple, high-level forecasts are made just to check that things are moving in the right direction. That is, there is one "target": to perform better than the competition. And they have, almost since day one. Miles has been growing by double digits almost every year. Growth was never a goal, however, just a consequence of doing well and being attractive. "Great Place to Work" has ranked Miles number one in Norway and number two in Europe in their category. It is still a small company, with just over 100 people and a turnover of around $20 million, but with margins almost in Apple territory. A public listing is off the table, as the market is seen as far too impatient.

Recruitment is probably the most important process in Miles. The company only recruits when the right people are found, and never in order to grow. There is no advertising. Many candidates come as recommendations from employees, who already know what it takes to be a member of the Miles family. The company is obsessive about taking references, normally not less than ten. Olsen and his small management team do not focus on IT competence when interviewing candidates. This is left to highly skilled employees already on board, who can veto any recruitment. No one takes this task lightly, as Miles only wants the best. The management interviews focus only on the candidate's personality, values, attitudes, and social and communication skills. "You normally can't change people, so we only go for those we believe will thrive on working in a company like ours," Olsen says. Not everybody does. He has several times recommended great candidates to go look elsewhere. "I did miss in my judgment a couple of times during these ten years, which made me work even harder on these crucial decisions for our organization."

Getting good people on board is important, but they also need to stay. As employees are out working with customers most of the time, Miles needed to find other ways of gluing people together socially. Enter "Smiles" or "Social Miles." Fifteen to twenty times a year employees get together on social gatherings, half of them with families included. I once had the pleasure of speaking at one of these events. I have seldom experienced more warmth and generosity; it beat even the best of all those great Agile conferences I have been speaking at!

It obviously pays off. Miles employees are attractive in the market. One of them once shared with Olsen a great external offer he had received: "We discussed it at home. My wife said no." The low turnover is something customers also highly appreciate, and is probably another reason for the strong growth.

Trust is a key component in the Miles model, and so is transparency. Both are put to work on cost management. The quality of your PC is obviously important in this kind of business. Employees can buy whatever PC they want and replace it as often as they want. Keeping your professional skills and competence continuously updated is even more important. Employees can attend any training they want, anywhere in the world, as often as they want. The only thing the company requires is that when the PC is bought or when the training is completed, the associated cost must be posted on the intranet, open for everybody to see. Employees are not abusing this remarkable level of trust. On the contrary, Olsen has only one small concern about this self-regulating control mechanism: Could it be too effective?

This unique approach does not mean that cost is not important. "We are highly cost focused and tight on a lot of cost types, but when it comes to our employees we are generous," Olsen says. When some of them were planning their travel to a conference in San Francisco, they were concerned about the high hotel prices in the city. Without any instructions, they were able to have the cost by booking through Airbnb. "Who needs budgets when everyone acts like a finance manager?" Olsen says.

He also stresses that the servant leadership he favors (both Olsen and his management colleagues have "servant" in their titles) is not about shying away from difficult decisions. "I practice servant leadership, but reserve 2 percent for being tough when required," he underlines. "That makes the 98 percent much more credible."

Miles does not operate with individual bonuses, but employees get a share in two different ways. There is a provision system where the employee gets a cut of the revenue he or she generates. They can choose the risk profile that best fits their private situation: high fixed or high variable. In addition, if the annual profit margin for their unit exceeds 10 percent, all employees with partners/spouses are invited for a weekend trip abroad. This model has worked well in the business segment where the company started: hiring out IT competence. Lately, the company has moved toward also developing complete IT solutions for their customers, making the provision model more challenging. "We will sort it out and find good solutions also here," Olsen says.

Miles is a great example of an organization that like most others was born Beyond Budgeting, but avoided the copying trap we discussed earlier by staying true to its beliefs. The curiosity about management and leaderships is still high. Olsen describes how early in his management career he read a lot, searching for the one right answer. "I have finally and luckily arrived at the conclusion that there is no recipe. It all depends. The more experience we get, the more confident we are about finding answers for new situations as Miles continues to develop and grow," Olsen says. "It was great to discover Beyond Budgeting, where we hope to find inspiration on how we can scale our model as we now are growing also outside of Norway."

I look forward to following Miles on their journey and to continue to learn from this amazing organization. Some of you might see similarities with the philosophy of Vineet Nayar as described in his great book about HCL Technologies, *Employees First, Customers Second*. There is of course a huge difference in size between the two, but in many areas I regard Miles as being even more radical on management innovation than HCL.

The Reitan Group—Values at the Core

"Those who only love money will seldom succeed." The words belong to one of the richest people in Norway. Odd Reitan is the founder of the Reitan Group (Reitangruppen), one of Norway's largest companies, with a turnover of around 10 bn USD and almost 37,000 employees across the Nordic countries and the Baltics, including franchises. Their business lies in four distinct areas: grocery, convenience, energy and fuel, and real estate. Customers know them through well-recognized brands like REMA, Narvesen, 7-Eleven, Uno-X, Pressbyrån, R-Kioski, and others.

Reitan was born into the retail business; his parents ran a small but successful grocery store in Trondheim, home of the group headquarters today. His experiences from what he describes as a great childhood through to starting up his own grocery store in 1972 continue to influence the way the company is being run, including what has become the vision for the Reitan Group: to be "recognized as the most values-driven company." The 15 people at the group headquarters have two tasks only: to develop a strong culture and to govern finances. Reitan focuses almost solely on the first job. Throughout his early years, he used to take brief notes on things he regarded as important. In the 1980s he collected all his pieces of paper, and the "Blue Book" was born, spelling out the company values and what they mean in practice:

- *We focus on our business idea.*
  Spreading your focus means losing your strength.
- *We keep a high business moral.*
  The company believes for instance that taxes should be paid with pride and joy.
- *We are committed to be debt-free.*
  Interest is seen as a fee on impatience. With a few exceptions, growth has always been funded with cash from operations.
- *We encourage a winning culture.*
  Delegation and believing in people is key. The company is famous for how it celebrates successes and great performance from people who thrive under the broad autonomy.
- *We have a positive and proactive mindset.*
  Reitan encourages his employees to be positive since everything was not better before. Much was actually worse!
- *We talk with each other, not about each other.*
  Reitan keeps reminding his management teams that loyalty is about speaking up, not shutting up.
- *The customer is our ultimate boss.*
  Customers must be more than satisfied; they must be delighted.

▪ *We want our work to be enjoyable and profitable.*

"If we have fun, it might be profitable, and always in that order," Reitan says.

Like Handelsbanken, the group is quite protective about the book. No one gets it before they have participated in a philosophy session held by Reitan himself.

Many organizations have similar value statements, but the way these values are brought to life makes the Reitan Group quite unique. "We can't have our values in a drawer, they must be in our backbone," Reitan says. It all starts with a sincere, positive belief in people. Decisions are pushed as far out as possible, with accountabilities clearly spelled out.

Shying away from debt as a value is not very common. The origin was seeing people forced out of business, strangled by interest payments. "I will much rather pay tax, which reflects what you earn. Interest doesn't," he says. A large acquisition once forced the company to take on debt. A stone outside the headquarters with the values engraved remained covered for three years, marked "Work in Progress" as the debt was repaid. The company runs its own "Values Academy," where Reitan himself teaches at most sessions. In 2012 The Reitan Group came out first among 1,600 European companies nominated for the Great Place to Work "Inspiring Pride" award. In the 2016 survey the company ranked as the most popular employer in Norway, ahead of almost 200 other companies with more than 500 employees.

Reitan hates bureaucracy: "I don't want processes, I want decisions and execution, and the distance between the two as short as possible," he says. He is no big fan of rules, either, but loves transparency. "Rules limit creativity, motivation, and enthusiasm. Transparency creates understanding and accountability." Their marketing slogan "Simple is often best" ("Det enkle er ofte det beste") has become legendary.

There is more he dislikes: "We don't want posh titles and fancy business cards. We want people with a strong backbone who have no need for stuff like that. Only when the job really requires it should there be a company car. People should earn enough to buy their own car." He doesn't want management teams bigger than six. "Anything more becomes a committee. Decisions shouldn't be made by committees." Bigger teams also dilute accountability; somebody makes a decision. "There is nobody called 'somebody'" is his clear message.

REMA, the discount food retail business area and the largest of the four, has a clear ambition of always having the lowest prices, while also being the "Rolls Royce of low price." Decisions are guided by and tested on how they can lead to lower prices for customers, followed by how they will contribute to store and group results. Cutting prices is a mantra. Reitan even invented a new word, *cuttism*, for the mentality he was after. It is not only about cutting sales prices; it is also about cost efficiency and cost consciousness on every cent. Beyond famous celebrations of success and great performance, the company is extremely cost focused. Reitan once made a worried call to his staff: Did the smileys he so often added to his text messages incur any extra cost? It goes without explanation that there is seldom business class or fancy hotels. *Kuttisme*, as it reads in Norwegian, has actually been formally endorsed in our language!

Privately, Reitan does admit to indulging from time to time. He has long had a passion for nice cars. One of them is a small sports car. Having given a lecture about company values for a group of store managers, he passed some of them as he took off for his next meeting. Realizing the potential double message, he stopped and rolled down the window; "Guys, this is 'cuttism' in practice. This car is half the size of a normal car!"

Autonomy does not mean anarchy. "Culture requires structure" is a mantra, and the group is very clear about spelling out the playing field. The REMA franchising concept describes for instance in detail the required grocery store interior and how products are to be placed and labeled and how local administration should be carried out. The cost efficiency focus does not mean cutting any corners on quality. On the contrary, high-quality processes and economies of scale enable the storeowners to focus their energy on "being on stage" in the store.

Reitan believes in dreams and big, hairy ambitions. When negotiating with suppliers during the tough early years, without much purchasing power, he was never shy of telling his counterparts they had better offer him a good deal, given how big the group was going to be. The growth was turbocharged when he, back in 1980, was asked by a journalist how big they would become. Caught off guard, his response was "a store in every place in Norway with more than 10,000 people." When asked about when, "by 1990" slipped out. He was able to warn his team and have them find out how many stores this actually would mean before the wild dream hit the front pages the next day. By 1990, REMA had grown from 30 to 185 stores. The party that followed is still remembered by those who can remember. Today there are more than 800 REMA stores in Norway and Denmark, and across all business areas the number is close to 4,000.

There are no budgets. "Many companies have big departments only doing budgeting, sending numbers up and down the organization, before they are presented to the board to give them something to talk about. A waste of time and energy! A forecast, however, is something very different. It gives us a picture of how things might develop. If we don't like what we see, it forces us to do something!" Reitan says.

The decision to drop budgets was both gradual and natural. When now-CFO Kristin Genton joined, there were budgets although these did not have a very prominent role. She started experimenting with both trend reporting and year-on-year instead of budget comparisons, and found this provided much better information. Reitan liked what he saw, and in 2006 it was decided to abolish traditional budgeting. Now, there is a lean four-quarter rolling forecast process, combined with an annual three-year forecast. When needed, the quarterly forecast is updated more frequently. At group level there is in addition a ten-year forecast, made mainly by Genton and her small team to avoid burdening the business areas.

Genton is not fond of the word *reporting*. She prefers the sports metaphor of timekeeping and coaching: the coach running next to the athlete, providing advice and fresh updates on status and performance. It is about supporting, not controlling. The company's view on control (*stålkontroll*) is about always understanding where you are and where you are heading. A good storeowner never leaves the store at night before knowing how the day ended.

At REMA, targets are partly coming out of a concept that could loosely be translated as "managing by percentages" (*PØS—Prosentuell Økonomisk Styring*). It is simple and self-regulating, not only helping fill the budget hole, but also helping in understanding and managing profitability. With revenue set at 100 percent, there are predefined percentage levels for each cost category like wages, wastage, and so forth. Based on the expected turnover, the storeowner knows how much should be spent on each category, without any detailed budgets. Higher revenues allow for more cost, more employees, and vice versa. A storeowner would only take on extra cost if really necessary, as they own and run their stores under franchising contracts with REMA. There is extensive internal benchmarking on these numbers to stimulate both performance and learning. The franchising concept, absent in the Norwegian retail business before REMA, is key to the Reitan Group concept. It creates all those local "profit centers" that allow for autonomy, benchmarking, and self-regulation, just as we saw in Handelsbanken. Here, this aspect is even stronger, as the franchisee owns the store.

"We believe in people's desire to create and perform, using their knowledge about local conditions. Our job is to make our franchisees good. If they do well, we all do well," Reitan says. "It is a balancing act, creating autonomy within a standardized and effective execution framework."

Reitan keeps dreaming. In his book, *If I Was President,* he not only describes what their simple but powerful management model means in business terms. He couldn't help also reflecting on how emphasis on people, empowerment, accountability, simplicity, and transparency is just as relevant and applicable when it comes to running a society.

CHAPTER 3

The Borealis Case

"*One* company, new, different and better."

From Borealis Values

Introduction

You have now heard about the many problems caused by traditional management practices, where budgets and the budgeting mindset play a major role. I hope those first chapters made you realize the seriousness of the problem we are up against and its systemic nature. We have been through the Beyond Budgeting philosophy and main principles of the model, and we have looked at Handelsbanken, Miles, and the Reitan Group as great examples of Beyond Budgeting in practice.

We will now move to Borealis and Statoil, the two implementation cases I know the best since I have headed up both. Neither should be taken as the right way or as mechanical recipes. They are both rooted in the specific business, culture, and situation of each company. Nevertheless, I believe they offer quite a range of advice that should be relevant for many. Feel free to borrow and copy. There are no secrets and no copyrights. Steal with pride!

As you will learn, neither of the two could probably be called full-fledged Beyond Budgeting cases, although Statoil is closer than Borealis. Together, however, they do provide a good illustration of what a Beyond Budgeting journey can be about.

Creation of Borealis

In the early 1990s, both Statoil and the Finnish competitor Neste were struggling with their petrochemical businesses. Statoil's activity in this segment was small on a European scale, as the company mainly was a producer of oil and gas and therefore a supplier to this business. Even after acquisitions in Belgium, Sweden, and Germany, lack of size was a major competitive disadvantage for Statoil.

Neste's petrochemical division had been in a similar situation, which had triggered an aggressive international expansion strategy. Within a short time Neste had acquired new capacity in several European countries, on a much larger scale than Statoil.

The petrochemicals business is extremely cyclical, with great peaks and serious troughs as a repeating pattern. The raw materials for this industry are petroleum based (naphtha, propane, butane, etc.); therefore, they have much of the price volatility of oil. Its products, various plastic raw materials, go into both consumer and industry segments where demand and prices typically are driven by other factors, at least short term. Being caught between such relatively unrelated markets has always been a major challenge for the industry.

The early 1990s was no exception. This time the market was down, after a period of solid margins. In Neste, the result was a serious cash squeeze. The international expansion had severely stretched the company's financial muscles.

For Statoil, the situation was quite different. The company was financially solid. The petrochemical business also served as a hedge for the oil- and gas-producing part of the company. Size was, however, still an issue.

The merger was announced in late 1993, and the new company started up in early 1994. The name was Borealis, after the northern light phenomenon "aurora borealis," honoring its Nordic roots. It became Europe's largest petrochemicals company at the time, with a turnover of around 2.5 billion euros and some 5,000 employees at 30 plants spread across Europe, from Finland to Portugal. To the surprise of many, the headquarters was located in Copenhagen, Denmark, which was "neutral" territory for both companies, a country with competitive business terms and a practical location with direct flight connections to the main production sites across Europe. Equally important, the country has a lot of bright people. This became a real strength for Borealis when expatriates from all over Europe joined forces with new Danish colleagues.

I came from the job as finance manager at Statoil's oil marketing and trading unit. Late in 1993, I started my petrochemicals career as head of Corporate Control in Borealis, responsible for financial control, accounting, and tax. Yes, I did pick that awful name myself!

It was a great time in a great company. There was a pioneer spirit flowing through the organization, inspired by the first of the four Borealis core values: "*One* company—new, different and better." It was a new start in many ways. To ensure we wore one hat only in the new company, members of the new management team had to resign from their respective mother companies. We were even required to buy and not rent accommodations in Copenhagen to demonstrate a firm and long-term commitment to the new company. None of this created much discussion. The enthusiasm was strong and real.

The Journey Begins

The new company started up in March 1994. It did not take long before the issue of budgets came up: "We need a budget for 1994. There will be no anarchy just because we are a new company!" Never mind that almost half the year would have passed before it was finished. It was a tough job. We had limited historical data on the new organization. Many were new in their positions, preparing budgets in parallel with a lot of integration tasks. We were all pretty tired, but there was little time to rest. Next year was approaching fast. Once we had completed the 1994 budget, we immediately started preparing the one for 1995.

When we finally could sign off the second budget made that year, we were completely exhausted. We decided to direct the minimal energy we had left into a "lessons learned" workshop. We gathered at a hotel outside of Copenhagen, with our minds focused on how to improve the budgeting process. The day was spent discussing peanut issues. Should we ask for this number instead of that number? Should we add a column here and delete a column there? Really important stuff!

There was one guy in particular who was completely knackered that day. Normally an active person with many constructive ideas, the site controller from Norway was surprisingly quiet. Then suddenly, out of nowhere, we heard from the back of the room: "What if we don't budget at all?" We all turned around and looked at him, and we all probably were thinking the same: "This guy needs a holiday." That was it. We shrugged it off and finished the meeting after having agreed on some completely unimportant improvements to the Borealis budgeting process.

Some months went by. The integration had gone well and spirits were high, even if the business was up for a rough ride again with rapidly declining margins. This also meant that our price and margin assumptions for the 1995 budget were completely wrong, just as they had been for the 1994 budget. Everything that built on these assumptions was now quite useless, and the year had hardly begun. But the budget was still our reference point, requiring long analyses each month explaining why we were off track. At least we could explain.

By now it had become clear that merger synergies were not enough. A radical overhaul of all operating processes was required to avoid falling behind and to prepare for a future where everybody expected average margins to continue their merciless downward slide.

This led to the birth of "Value for Money," a large business reengineering project. The message was simple: Leave no stone unturned and look for a better way. The consulting company Gemini was called in to support. The consultants were bright guys, although I was taken aback by the many young faces with rather soft skin on their hands. Young or more experienced, we later learned that challenging the budget was never on their mind.

I was asked to head up a part of the program called "Management Effectiveness." This cryptic title led to my simple question to CFO Svein Rennemo: "What do you expect?" You will recall his response: "Bjarte, I expect the unexpected." Backed with such a mind-blowing mandate, we went to the task really fired up, wanting to make a difference. The whole company was in change mode. Other functions and units went to work on their own processes, but no one had the kind of mandate we had received.

It did not take long before that crazy comment from a few months earlier came back to us: "What if we don't budget at all?" Of course we knew that budgeting was a flawed process. That was an old insight, not just from the two budgets we made the year before, but also from many years of previous budgeting experience in the team. "This is it!" we said. "Let's blow up the budget!"

We immediately went back to Svein, glowing with excitement as we shared with him what we wanted to do. When the obvious question came about what would then replace the budget, we had to admit that we had no clue, not yet. "Maybe you should go and find out" was his short and simple response, again with that little smile on his face.

It would take quite some time before we could answer his question. We moved on by spelling out more clearly what we wanted to achieve. That list was short on words but high on ambitions, as shown in Exhibit 3.1.

Shortly after, we spotted an article in a Swedish magazine. The title read "Volvo drops budgeting." Wow! There *is* actually someone trying this! Beyond Budgeting and the BBRT were still years ahead, so there were no conferences to attend and no books on the topic as far as we knew. We were actually far down the road before we heard about Handelsbanken, even if the bank had been operating without budgets for 25 years, and was headquartered only some 100 miles away!

We immediately went to visit Volvo and came back with some new insights but also somewhat confused and uncertain about how much the company really had done. But inspiration hit again when somebody showed us the famous Jack Welch quote: "Budgets are the bane of corporate America!" If *he* could say this, we must be onto something!

◪ **BOREALIS** _____

Why shall we abolish traditional budgeting?

We want to:

- Improve our financial management and performance measurement
- Decentralize authority and decisions
- Simplify the process and reduce time spent

EXHIBIT 3.1 The Vision

◤ **BOREALIS** _____

Traditional budgeting has many weaknesses....

- Conflicting purposes—target setting versus financial forecasting

- Not only a ceiling—also a floor for costs

- Promotes centralization of decisions and responsibility

- Inflexible to changes in planning assumptions

- Tends to make financial control an annual autumn event

- Absorbs significant resources across the organization

EXHIBIT 3.2 The Case for Change

With no solution or alternative in sight, we continued with describing what we saw as the problems with traditional budgeting. That was not a difficult job. The problems came pouring out of the project team, and very soon the list looked like Exhibit 3.2.

Actually, the initial list looked *almost* like this. The first point about conflicting purposes only came to us a month or two later. That insight turned out to be key to finally discovering the alternatives to the Borealis budget.

The period before we arrived at that understanding was a time when our enthusiasm started to fade, gradually replaced with a feeling of resignation and failure. We *knew* the process was flawed, that was not the issue. But how could we find this one single great tool that could replace the budget and solve all our problems? Had we been too arrogant when we declared war on the budget?

We discussed and we searched. "Searched" meant something very different back in 1995. There was no Internet and no Google there to help us. Searching was about calling people and going to the library. We searched and searched and could not find anything. The writing was on the wall. Svein Rennemo's great mandate did not sound that great anymore. We were close to giving up.

But then we finally asked ourselves that simple but important question that cracked it all: "*Why* do we budget? What is the *purpose* of those budget numbers?" We simply had not thought about it from that angle before. It was another magic moment. Just like pushing a button, answers came pouring out: target setting, forecasting, cost/investment management, and delegation of authority. It soon became clear that many of these purposes were not that closely related. A few were even in conflict with each other. We also realized that the answer did not lie in that one great new tool we had been dreaming about. Instead, we understood that we had to look for a set of *tailored* tools and processes, each one dedicated to one of the different budget purposes.

We went on to define and design these individual tools, purpose by purpose. This was yet another great exercise. The new solutions suddenly became blindingly obvious for us: rolling forecasts, balanced scorecards, activity accounting, trend reporting, decision authorities, and so on. We were almost disappointed. Could it really be this simple? We later learned that it was not. The challenge was not to find and implement these new tools; it was to demolish the old budget mindset and replace it with a very different kind of leadership.

One of these new tools was already under development right under our noses, the balanced scorecard. We decided to use the scorecard for target setting and performance monitoring. Other tools needed to be designed and built, but at this stage we could already see quite clearly how the tools would work and how the whole process would fit together.

Then our next picture was ready. We knew not only what we wanted to achieve and what the problems were, but also what would replace the budget. (See Exhibit 3.3.)

BOREALIS

We can achieve what the budget does in a better way

The budget was used for:	We achieve the same through:
• High-level financial and tax planning	✓ Quarterly rolling financial forecasts
• Target setting	✓ Targets on the balanced scorecard
• Controlling fixed costs	✓ Trend reporting ✓ Cost targets where and when needed ✓ Activity approach
• Prioritizing and allocating investment/project resources	✓ Small projects—trend reporting ✓ Medium projects—varying hurdle rates ✓ Major strategic projects—case by case, the budget was never a tool
• Delegation of authority	✓ Use existing mandates/authority schedules

EXHIBIT 3.3 The Budget Alternatives

All illustrations in this chapter are, by the way, originals from the Borealis days. These are the pictures we used to explain the model to the organization and later to the outside world.

The Borealis Model

Let us take a closer look at the different elements in the new model. First, I want to remind you that the Borealis case was mainly an attempt to solve the more tangible in-your-face problems with budgeting. I am still proud of our courage and what we achieved, but I do not think any of us at the time fully understood how this could fit into a larger organizational context, as building blocks in an alternative leadership model. Personally, this was before my days in HR and before long hours of discussions with friends in the BBRT and good colleagues in Statoil.

However, it was not only about tools. We clearly sensed that there was something more to what we were embarking on. It was no coincidence that our second purpose read "Decentralize decisions and authority."

The reaction in the organization was much more positive than I had expected. I do not think too many fully understood where we were heading, or all the new tools, but we got a lot of positive feedback just for *daring* to attack the budget monster. It also helped that the company was in change mode. All over the place, the mantra was "New, different, and better." I have never experienced a value statement being so powerful, giving people so much direction and energy.

Exhibit 3.4 shows the way we explained how the new processes would not only cover what the budget had done for us but also give us a lot more. "More for less" was an expression

BOREALIS

The new tools cover what the budget did, but also a lot more

Rolling Financial Forecast	Balanced scorecard
- Quarterly update - Rolling five quarters outlook	- Non-financial targets and measurements - Link to strategy
- Annual outlook	- Financial targets and measurement

Budget

- Limited cost understanding	- Annual plan
Activity accounting and product costing	Investment management
- Improved cost understanding - Product and customer costing	- Trend reporting and five quarter outlook - Decentralized decisions - Frames if needed

EXHIBIT 3.4 More for Less—the New Model in a Nutshell

we often used. Again, Svein Rennemo had been gently pushing us: "We need *one* simple picture that summarizes what this is all about." (See Exhibit 3.4.)

Five-Quarter Rolling Forecasts

"For high-level financial and tax planning, we need reliable financial forecasts. These do not require a lot of details, because the purpose is not cost management. And why should a forecast stop at year-end? This is not an accounting exercise. A five-quarter horizon updated every quarter makes sense," we concluded in one of our project meetings. That was it! The Borealis rolling forecast was born.

We had a mental picture of what the new forecasting process should feel like. It should be so simple that we could write it out on the back of an envelope. Although we ended up using a few more envelopes and a simple spreadsheet, it still was a very lean process, where quality meant "roughly right." If we got it wrong, it only lasted a quarter, anyway.

Another reason for choosing a five-quarter horizon was the Borealis owners. Both Statoil and Neste had traditional budgets and needed numbers from us. With a five-quarter horizon, we could use the forecast we made in the autumn as the budget they requested. We simply carved out next year, renamed it "budget," and shipped it off. Fortunately, both owners were reasonable in their follow-up and did not demand too much reporting against these numbers. They were happy, and we were happy.

Today, the five-quarter rolling forecast has almost become a standard in Beyond Budgeting implementations. Some people even believe that Beyond Budgeting equals rolling forecasting, one of many misunderstandings about the concept. At Statoil, we did not implement a five-quarter rolling forecast. I will explain why and what we did instead in Chapter 4.

Balanced Scorecard

One of the new tools came to us through a recommendation from Gemini Consulting. The balanced scorecard was introduced by Robert Kaplan and David Norton in an article in *Harvard Business Review* in 1992 titled "The Balanced Scorecard: Measures That Drive Performance."

I assume you are reasonably familiar with this concept, so I will not explain it any further. If not, I recommend one or more of the Kaplan and Norton books. None of these were written in 1995; the article was our only theoretical guidance beyond the consulting support we got. We found the article and the thinking behind it fascinating. We were especially intrigued by the key performance indicators (KPIs). Finally, we would get full insight into all the different drivers behind our business results. We did not yet see the relevance of the balanced scorecard for the other and, for us, much bigger question: What could replace the budget?

A scorecard project group was established. The Executive Committee was very enthusiastic and heavily involved. There was a textbook start, with several long workshops with this key group of people. The only problem was that it turned out to be more difficult than we had expected. Looking back, we clearly searched too hard for the perfect scorecard and sacrificed simplicity and clarity on the way.

Then came the day when we cracked the issue of the different budget purposes. As you will recall, target setting was one of these. It immediately became clear to us that our budget targets should get a new home. We would simply move financial targets from the budget over to the financial perspective in the scorecard.

From Absolute to Relative Performance

It was not enough just to move financial targets over to the scorecard. We also had to do something with the way we set these targets. You will remember that one of our three objectives was to decentralize decisions and authority. Our traditional way of setting budget targets had been very much the opposite. Not only did we tell the business units what kind of financial performance we wanted. We also told them *how* to achieve it, through detailed sales, cost, staffing, and investment budgets.

We got out of this simply by limiting our financial target setting to improving "return on average capital employed" (RoACE). This KPI measures the return a business is able to make on invested capital. Which levers to pull to lift RoACE would, within some limits, be up to the business units themselves to decide, whether it was revenue, operating cost, working capital, or investments. We were well aware of how this KPI potentially could hamper growth by discouraging investments. We balanced this by also introducing such KPIs as production and market-share growth.

There was another problem: the cyclicality of the petro-chemicals business. Veterans in the company claimed there was a seven-year cycle between boom and bust in the industry. That might have been the case historically, but we experienced a market where prices and margins were on a much faster rollercoaster ride, with no sign of any seven-year cycle. (See Exhibit 3.5.)

How could we set meaningful RoACE targets in such an environment? What is good performance when prices are extremely volatile in a commodity market you cannot influence? No wonder we got our price assumptions terribly wrong in both the 1994 and 1995 budgets.

The solution we developed was the *relative* RoACE. This was not RoACE benchmarking between Borealis and competitors, or between Borealis business units. Instead, we calculated the historical relationship between market conditions and RoACE both for the company and for each of the business units. For most units, the relationship between the two was quite linear. Low market margins resulted in low RoACE and vice versa.

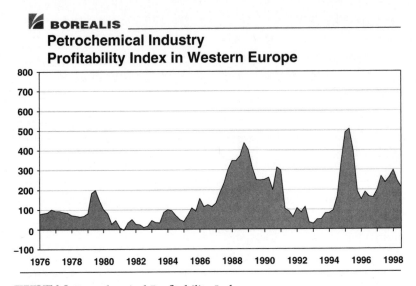

EXHIBIT 3.5 Petrochemical Profitability Index
Source: Chem Systems

Performance had nothing to do with riding up and down this line depending on market conditions. Performance was about *lifting* the RoACE line independently of a strong or weak market. This became the new way of setting targets. All the levers that could improve RoACE were available for the business units to pull:

- Invest in profitable projects.
- Divest nonprofitable assets.
- Optimize working capital.
- Optimize fixed cost.
- Optimize variable cost.
- Increase margins versus market.
- Increase volumes.

Exhibit 3.6 illustrates the concept. Relative RoACE was a tangible and effective way of saying goodbye to micromanagement. The business units were suspicious in the beginning.

BOREALIS

We must improve and measure our financial performance independently of market cyclicality

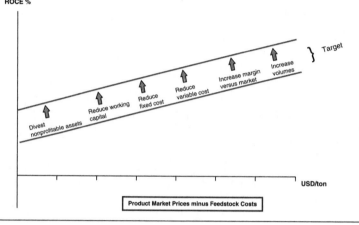

EXHIBIT 3.6 Relative Financial Performance

Do we really have this freedom and authority? And no budget constraints? Our answer was a clear yes, within certain boundaries. These included first of all the Borealis values, where no compromises were accepted. We also had a set of common decision criteria and clear decision authorities expressed in a mandate structure. These were wide enough to allow units to make most decisions themselves, although all larger and strategic investments were still to be brought to top management for approval.

Financing was still centralized. So were most of our IT solutions and other support processes. It was *business* freedom we wanted to provide, not the freedom for anyone to go out and buy their own accounting system. This distinction is important. It is possible to be centralized and decentralized at the same time: centralized on common processes and support operations, and decentralized on business decisions.

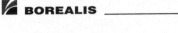

ROCE follow-up—a report example

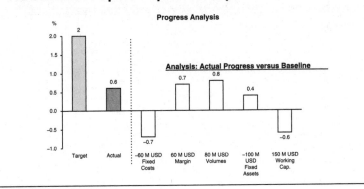

EXHIBIT 3.7 Business Follow-Up

Exhibit 3.7 is an example of how we reported against relative RoACE targets. This illustration reflects a unit that so far has achieved an improvement of 0.6 percent against a 2 percent target. The analysis explains which levers the unit has pulled. Note the "negative" development in fixed costs. This might actually have been "good costs," for instance, sales costs that lifted both volumes and margins more than the increased sales costs. We wanted to give the business the freedom to decide on the optimal trade-off between all these different levers for profitability.

Benchmarking was another important part of the model. Production plants across Europe benchmarked their own operational performance with similar plants inside and outside the company. It was amazing to observe the power of such comparisons. For those coming out low, there was always the initial denial phase: "This can't be true. We are different. The data is inaccurate." But when a unit came out low not only in one but in several comparisons, and not just once but over and over again, the message tended to sink in and trigger some remarkable effects. I recall some of our plant managers, famous for their cost budget negotiation skills (perhaps why they didn't do well on cost comparisons). When they finally accepted that there was some truth in these rankings, something clicked as their competitive genes woke up. Now, they wanted to move from bottom to top almost overnight. Our job became to hold them back on a somewhat more realistic improvement schedule. That was a new experience, both for them and us!

Trend Reporting

Like much in the Borealis model, trend reporting was nothing new. We wanted, however, to use trend reporting as a way of breaking the calendar-year dominance. We accepted that statutory reporting still had to follow the calendar year, but that should no longer be a straitjacket for everything else. Nothing but tradition stood in the way for taking this step. We introduced trend reporting on costs, on production, on smaller investments, and other places where it made sense. We looked at periods ranging from 6 to 15 months, depending on the area.

We then added on a small feature that turned out to be much more effective than expected. To help the reader better understand trendlines, we added the actual "% change" number in the graphs. We experimented with different periods, mainly using the last 12 over the previous 12 months. This information was especially useful on costs. In the petrochemicals business, average margins are steadily declining, and production unit cost has to follow. A cost trend constantly growing at 1 percent is a serious problem even if the line in the graph looks quite flat.

Budgeting and budget reports, in comparison, tend to blur such realities, first by allowing for higher costs during budgeting and later by "hiding" the increases. Even if everyone knew that costs had to come down, the budget negotiation always included a number of convincing arguments for the opposite. The result was often higher budgets instead of lower ones.

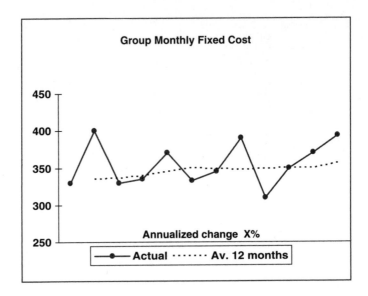

EXHIBIT 3.8 Trend Reporting Example 1

You know the game. But as soon as we started reporting against the new budget, things looked okay. No worries, we are within budget!

This constant reminder of being on a rising trend when we should have seen the opposite did something that we seldom saw with traditional budget reporting: a much stronger focus and urgency on costs. One year it even triggered the top 40 managers to forgo part of a December salary as a symbolic contribution to help break a cost trend moving in the wrong direction. (See Exhibits 3.8 and 3.9.)

Activity Accounting

Managing costs without budgets was by far our biggest concern. We were torn between a strong belief that everything would work fine and a nagging concern that refused to go away: Could we risk the opposite? Would costs explode? They did not; they actually came down.

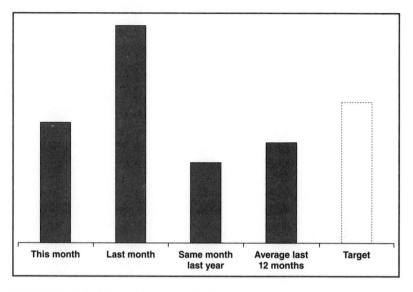

EXHIBIT 3.9 Trend Reporting Example 2

But before we had jumped, we were concerned. We there-fore felt that we at least had to *understand* our costs better. We needed that understanding to help with better and more rele-vant discussions on *actual* costs, when we no longer could lean on budget comparisons. What were the drivers and purposes behind the costs we incurred? We found the answer in *activity accounting*.

Activity accounting is about understanding the *purpose* of costs, not just the *type* of costs (accounts or cost items) and *where* they occur (cost centers). When we discuss costs, we often do it in the activity dimension: We talk about marketing, maintenance, training, and so on. But when asked if we can provide accounting data in the same dimension, we are lost. We have details down to the last cent on cost types (travel, consul-tants, steel, power, etc.) and on cost centers; who has spent the money? But when asked *why*, we are quite blank.

Exhibit 3.10 shows how we explained activity accounting in Borealis.

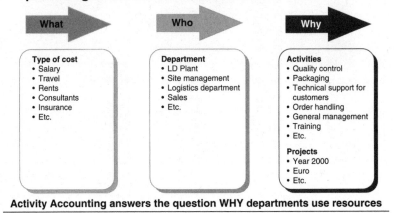

BOREALIS

Activity accounting introduces a new dimension providing more useful information

Activity Accounting answers the question WHY departments use resources

EXHIBIT 3.10 Activity Accounting

Thinking in activity terms was something that had fasci-
nated me from my early Statoil days. I first heard about activity
accounting from the late Danish professor Vagn Madsen. Thank
you to my then–Statoil colleague, Audun Berg, for pointing me
in this direction. As early as in the 1950s, Madsen described the
need for accounting in dimensions that better reflect business
realities. "Every action has a purpose and every cost can conse-
quently be attributed to an objective," he wrote. He called the
concept "variability accounting." I once got a lift with Madsen
after a conference he had been speaking at. He was a fascinating person, with driving skills way behind his accounting
insights. He spent most of the trip through half of Denmark
turned toward the two of us in the backseat, enthusiastically
explaining his thinking while puffing away on his pipe.

Robert Kaplan revitalized the activity thinking and took
it a long step forward with activity-based costing (ABC). By
identifying the *drivers* behind the activity costs, these can be

allocated to the *products* and *customers* generating these costs, providing a much better picture of true profitability from both. The concept is great. The challenge is that we normally have very limited activity cost data in our accounting systems. This is why activity-based costing often is interview based. Accounting by interviewing is an approach we hardly would dream of practicing in our statutory accounting. Imagine accountants walking around at year-end, asking people how much they believe they have sold and how much they have spent. I am not sure the auditors would be thrilled. Of course, we do not need accounting precision on all activity and driver data. But if this dimension is important for us, more quality and efficiency is required than what can be achieved through interviewing and similar manual data collection.

Before implementing SAP, Statoil had a Swedish accounting system called *Horisonten* (Horizon)—a great name: The farther you travel, the more you discover over the horizon. I was heading up the implementation project back in the late 1980s, working with a great project team. The system had been developed by finance people with information technology knowledge, not the other way around. That makes a huge difference. It is the best finance system I have ever worked with. The philosophy and functionality was simple: Model your business into the system, not the other way around. You could add on as many independent dimensions as needed beyond accounts and cost centers, such as activity, project, profit center, or customer. On each of these dimensions, as many flags, or sorting criteria, as needed could be defined. This functionality covered any need for building multiple and parallel hierarchies or any other additional sorting of information. If you believe today's dominating accounting systems can do the same, forget it.

Activity accounting was an important element in the model we configured in Horisonten. In Chapter 5, I will share both great learning and painful experiences from this project, where

I without realizing it had my first encounters with something that much later became known as Agile.

Vagn Madsen was way ahead of his time. In the 1950s and 1960s, no accounting system was able to handle the multidimensional concept he was describing. That all changed with a new generation of Swedish systems emerging in the 1970s and 1980s, such as EPOK, EPOS, and later Horisonten.

The Borealis business was different from Statoil's, including a much stronger need for integration on transaction level from production to customer. Due to this and other reasons, SAP was selected as the Borealis system. Statoil made the same choice a few years later.

As mentioned, the trigger for introducing activity accounting was a need for better *understanding* costs as there would be no budget. We started off by designing a common "chart of activities" to complement the chart of accounts. That turned out to be more difficult than expected, and it took us quite some time to agree on which activities to include, as well as their definitions. We finally succeeded in describing our total costs base through around 100 generic activities, in addition to specific projects. This included activities such as order handling, maintenance, quality control, training, and so on. Take training. Costs had traditionally been recorded by organization and cost item only, such as conference fee, travel, and consultants, with no possibility of tracing their original purpose. Now we would also code and register the activity, in this case training.

We got a major challenge when we tried to build this third activity dimension into SAP. We managed somehow, but not in a very elegant way. The nightmare began, however, when we also wanted the system to charge the activity costs further onto products and customers. The theory was simple, as illustrated in Exhibit 3.11. Practice was not.

This second step became so complicated that we had to back out again a few years later. I take full responsibility for that

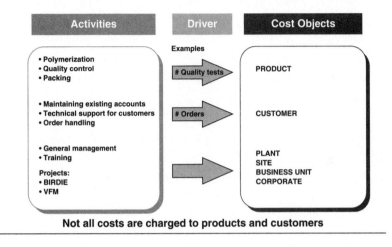

EXHIBIT 3.11 From Activities to Drivers

mistake. Nevertheless, activity accounting was still useful for us. During my years in HR, I managed the function's group-wide HR cost through a report that listed our costs across 15 to 20 activities and projects. The report also showed where costs had occurred, and on which accounts, but the main focus was activity: *why* costs had been incurred.

I still do not understand why companies put so little emphasis on the important activity dimension. Maybe it is another example of the external statutory accounting mindset setting the scene for how we organize our internal finance processes, just like with the calendar year.

Investment Management

Capital allocation without annual budgets was almost a no-brainer. The starting point was the relative RoACE, with profitable investments as one of several levers available for the business units to improve their performance. We created three investment categories:

1. **Small projects** were treated more or less like operating costs, even if accounting-wise they classified as investments.
2. **Medium-size projects** were decided case by case. The hurdle rate (the "interest" that future cash flows are reduced with because a dollar tomorrow is less valuable than a dollar today) was meant to be the lever to pull if we needed to take down the total investment level in this category. In practice, this mechanism was never used explicitly. When money was tight, there were simply fewer proposals coming forward.
3. **Major strategic projects** had never been managed through annual budgets. These projects could be acquisitions, new plants, or other major capital commitments. Such decisions seldom fitted any autumn decision scheme. They were made as needed, using the best and most recent information we had on commercial assumptions, financial capacity, and the project itself.

When a project was approved, the investment number used in the project valuation became the cost mandate or budget for the project. So even if we still had project budgets, we abandoned the annual investment budget.

The rolling financial forecast gave us a continuous and updated view of our shorter-term financial capacity while a longer-term forecast was made annually. The investment forecast was a combination of approved projects and projects in the pipeline. When the forecast signaled capacity constraints, the actual and planned investment level was reduced by delaying or turning down projects.

Evaluation and Rewards

We were convinced that for the new model to work, we had to connect it all the way to evaluation and rewards. At the time, I still believed that individual bonus was good for motivation and performance. My belief in what KPIs could do for us was also much stronger than it is today. This is probably where I have had my longest journey since the Borealis days.

We chose a simple approach, which at least was easy to communicate and operate. Bonuses were connected to the scorecard through the number of green KPIs. "Percentage green" became a new expression. The target was typically set around 80 percent, with a sliding scale around the target value with threshold and ceiling values. Initially there was no weighting, but after a while we introduced "golden KPIs," which counted more than others.

As expected, the bonus link focused a lot of attention on the new scorecards. But quite soon we experienced the KPI problem. The effort put into developing strategy maps and strategic objectives was not always the best. The more "activist" oriented the teams were, the more they hurried past what they saw as an academic strategic objectives discussion and into the more concrete KPI discussion. KPIs dominated, in target setting, follow-up, evaluation, and rewards, causing many of the negative side effects we discussed earlier. The emphasis on strategic objectives did improve later on, but I do not think the model ever fully recovered from our initial myopic KPI focus.

Implementation Experiences and Lessons Learned

Even if the Borealis case was not a full-blown Beyond Budgeting implementation, what we did was quite radical at the time. Aside from the Handelsbanken case, I think few other companies our size have jumped into the unknown the way we did. Given how early we moved, and how few others we could learn from, I am proud of what we achieved. Of course, we had a great starting point. It was a new company with strong values, an open-minded CEO and CFO, and a strong finance team.

Still, there are things we should have done differently. First of all, we could have articulated our vision more clearly and broadly, especially on the leadership side. We could have aimed even higher. But this is hindsight wisdom. Beyond Budgeting now provides a framework that did not exist when we started out.

I also wish we had involved the HR function earlier. We did so later, when we linked the scorecard to bonus. Yet HR should have been with us from day one, and in a broader role. Bonus was not where we should have started our collaboration. I will elaborate on this later in the book. My own days in HR were still ahead of me. I must also admit that at the time, I believed in some of the rather negative things said about this function.

The relative RoACE KPI was abandoned after some years. It lost out in the battle between relevance and precision, but it was also complicated to operate. It was replaced with more absolute financial targets, but these were still set at a high level without a lot of detail.

A consequence of being an early mover on balanced scorecards was the lack of any supporting software. The process in Borealis was very much a manual one, supported by numerous spreadsheets. The fact that the scorecard survived without much system support shows how strongly anchored the concept was.

A key lesson learned came as quite a surprise to us: *Don't design everything up front.* The issues and challenges might pop up in the most unexpected areas. Design to 80 percent and jump, and sort out the issues as they occur. In hindsight, this should have been obvious to us, as it actually is what Beyond Budgeting is very much about. Everything cannot be planned. You have to sense and respond as you go.

At the time, our philosophy was to design as much as possible before we jumped. We felt we had to, because there were so many questions coming from the organization: "How will we now do this and that without a budget?" We felt we had to answer all these questions properly in order to get people on board. Most were obviously related to cost management. Because we were quite concerned ourselves, we spent a lot of time developing activity accounting, trend reporting, mandates, and other mechanisms.

What happened? Cost had come in above budget both in 1994 and 1995. Then we abolished budgets, but costs did not explode. They actually came down. I do not think this happened only because of our thorough work up front. Also, I am not crediting the cost reduction only to the fact that we took away budgets. Obviously integration costs were disappearing and synergies were kicking in. But I do believe that what we experienced had a lot to do with people being more responsible than what traditional management assumes.

So the first challenge did not occur on cost management, as we had expected. We got it in a very different area, in *investment forecasting*. For us, the rolling forecasts had been a no-brainer. We had explained again and again to the organization that a forecast should reflect the expected outcome and nothing else. It should *not* be an application for funds, because this would be handled in a separate process. Everyone nodded and agreed that it absolutely made sense to distinguish between these two very different purposes.

Then came the big day when we had consolidated our first rolling forecast. It was an important milestone, and our excitement about what the numbers would look like was sky-high. It all seemed okay, until we came to the investment forecast. That number was two or three times higher than any previous investment level ever seen in the company, and way above our financial and organizational capacity.

It was not difficult to understand what had happened. Our message had been understood but not really believed. On the way up, everybody had as usual added on a bit to be on the safe side. This time, no one had taken anything away. We had asked line controllers to be careful with challenging the numbers, to avoid giving an impression of just another budget process. What we had in front of us was therefore not a forecast, but a massive and unfiltered pile of investment proposals.

We now had two choices regarding which numbers to take to the Executive Committee later that week: We could go back to line managers and negotiate the numbers down to a more reasonable level. They were all waiting for us, because they knew they had sent off inflated numbers. We knew what the reaction would be: "You are coming to cut our investments? So much for a new process!"

We therefore chose the opposite tack. We took the inflated numbers with us to the Executive Committee without any adjustments. The response came fast from CEO Juha Rantanen: "Bjarte, this is nonsense!" "We know," we replied, "but this is the forecast we got from the business areas sitting around this table." The room became dead silent, and we noted some blushing faces. Later, we simply adjusted the total numbers, without telling the organization. The next quarter almost the same happened, but this time with somewhat lower numbers. It took four rounds and four quarters before the organization finally had internalized that these numbers were about forecasting only, not about investment proposals and funding. It only happened because the organization experienced a new and different behavior from our side, and not just once, but again and again. We did not come to cut those numbers, as everyone out there had expected.

Abolishing budgets turned out to be an even more positive experience for the finance function than we had expected. In addition to all the benefits for the company, we also enjoyed less number crunching and much more interesting work. We also experienced a remarkable effect on our *image*. It used to be similar to the image of most finance functions out there. There was not much respect for our processes or our ability to add value. When we first proposed to kick out the budget, many were actually quite suspicious about our motives. "Why would these guys want to give up their number-one power instrument?" they wondered. What was our hidden agenda? When they realized that there was no hidden agenda, and that our only goal was to make Borealis a better company, our standing and image got a major boost. It took us a big step forward toward that business partner role that most finance functions strive so hard to achieve.

Borealis Today

The Borealis years were a fantastic experience, and something I am extremely grateful for having been a part of. It was a great time with great people in a great company. Borealis was a real pioneer, driving change in a number of areas, not just within performance management.

There were more changes to come. In 1998 Neste sold out as part of a strategic reorientation. Austrian OMV and IPIC of Abu Dhabi came in. OMV had its own European petrochemicals business, PCD, so now it was integration time again. Svein Rennemo took over as the new CEO. I was asked to head up the integration project and took a leave from my finance role. Although on a much smaller scale, the project had some similarities with the Statoil-Hydro merger ten years later. The Borealis name was kept, but the intention was a true merger between equals, even if PCD was a much smaller company. The integration work included a completely new organizational structure with new management teams at all levels, especially in sales, marketing, logistics, research and development, and other areas with significant overlaps and synergies. There was a lot of positive feedback on how the integration was executed from both old and new Borealis colleagues, even from many of those who had to leave the company. For me, this was another major learning experience, which continued when I was asked to head up HR after we had gone live with the new organization.

There was, however, tension brewing between old and new owners. This went well beyond the discussions and occasional disagreements between Statoil and Neste. Svein Rennemo left Borealis in 2001. I left half a year later. I have a lot of respect for the new CEO's drive and the ambitious goals he set for the company, but we had different views on too many things. "I need a stick in the ground" was his response when I explained the relative performance concept.

Statoil divested its Borealis shareholding in 2005. The company has now moved its head office from Copenhagen to Vienna and has also sold its Norwegian assets. Today Borealis is firmly under the wing of its main shareholder OMV, which again is partly controlled from Abu Dhabi. The Nordic roots are not that visible anymore.

The company has taken some steps back on its Beyond Budgeting journey, although not all the way back. Many of the processes still exist, such as the balanced scorecard and the rolling forecasts. My impression is, however, that there is now more of a traditional management culture compared to how the company was run in the 1990s. Why this happened is probably a book in itself. I believe it had much to do with the high number of new external recruits to the Executive Committee, starting with the new CEO. These were all bright guys, but they had not been part of the original journey. Without that history, perhaps they found it difficult to understand and fully appreciate the underlying philosophy and intentions.

It is obvious that the greater the changes in top management a company goes through, the longer a Beyond Budgeting model must have been in operation to survive. This is especially true if few in the new team are from the company's own ranks. It takes years for these kinds of process changes to find their way into the hearts and minds of people and to be reflected in behavior and leadership. The transformation was well under way in Borealis, but the seven-year-long journey may not have been long enough to balance the effect of so many new guys at the top.

How long does it then take for Beyond Budgeting to take root, to become so strong that it survives the kind of changes that Borealis went through? I do not think anyone knows yet. There are few old cases that can tell us how long it takes before the walls are thick enough to resist a few earthquakes. Handelsbanken has of course been going since 1970 and seems to have a rock-solid foundation. Still, if something similar had happened in the bank after seven years, perhaps things would have looked quite different today. Fortunately, Handelsbanken has a policy of recruiting top management from within, which makes a big difference.

It can be argued that the Borealis model primarily addressed the *process* side and less the *leadership* side of Beyond Budgeting and that this made it less robust against later management changes. I partly agree. It is true that our starting point was the budget itself and the problems that most directly originated from this area. But we clearly saw and addressed leadership implications such as autonomy, transparency, and values. For instance, the value focus was extremely strong from day one.

Talking about values, let us close with a wonderful little story. A few years after I left, the new CEO wanted to update the original values. A group of people from across the company was asked to develop a proposal. Coincidentally, none of them had English as their mother tongue, as opposed to most of the new executives. When the first proposal was presented, one word in particular got special attention. Both nimbleness and simplicity had been important themes in the discussions, and the group believed there was a word that captured both: *nimblicity*. After a lot of laughter, the executives realized the brilliance of this new and nonexistent word in the English vocabulary. Today, nimblicity is one of the Borealis values. The company even has it copyrighted. Wonderful!

I still have many friends in Borealis. I wish you all the best wherever your journey has taken you since then. Together, we made a difference!

CHAPTER 4

The Statoil Case

"The *way* we deliver is just as important as *what* we deliver."

The Statoil Book

Introduction

Sharing the Statoil case is quite different from sharing the Borealis case. First time around compared to getting the chance a second time makes a big difference. I am very grateful for that opportunity. The Statoil journey actually made me understand the Borealis journey better: what we did, what we didn't do, and what we could have done differently. Back then, there was no Beyond Budgeting guidance to help us put things in perspective.

The Borealis days are long enough behind to allow for the necessary reflection and learning. The Statoil case is still a work in progress. Although we have been on our Beyond Budgeting journey for more than ten years now, we still are as I write and probably also as you read.

Statoil was established in 1972 as a national oil company following the discovery of significant oil and gas reserves on the Norwegian continental shelf in the late 1960s. Norway is among the very few countries in the world where huge natural resources have been a blessing and not a curse. Even the Dutch messed it up when the country discovered big gas reserves many years ago. Wise Norwegian politicians have not only secured a fair distribution of the new wealth, they have also resisted the temptation to spend it all. The Government Pension Fund now has close to one trillion dollars invested around the world, almost USD 200,000 per Norwegian.

Statoil hit the ground running and grew fast during the 1970s and 1980s. International activities were turbocharged through an alliance with BP in the 1990s. In 2001 the company went public with a listing in New York and Oslo, although the state kept a majority shareholding. Statoil quickly became an attractive investment due to a track record of combined growth and profitability.

In 2007 Statoil merged with the oil and gas division of Hydro, a Norwegian competitor. The new company was named Statoil-Hydro to underline that this was meant to be a merger of equals, although Hydro's oil and gas business was much smaller. The name was also meant to defuse a potentially heated discussion. After a few years it was quietly changed back to Statoil without much reaction from ex-Hydro employees, a great confirmation that the merger had been a success.

Statoil is today Scandinavia's largest company with more than 20,000 employees in well above 30 countries across the world (Exhibit 4.1). Turnover and market cap is around $100 billion, varying of course with the oil price. The company is the world's largest offshore operator, the second largest gas supplier to Europe, and a leading international oil marketer. Statoil is also involved in renewable energy, mainly through

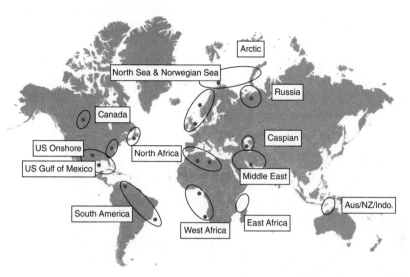

- Turnover approx. 100 bn. USD

- 22,000 employees in 33 countries

- World's largest operator in waters deeper than 100 meters

- Second largest gas exporter to Europe

- World leader of crude oil sales

- Listed in New York and Oslo

EXHIBIT 4.1 Statoil in Brief

offshore windmills where we can build on our offshore competence.

The Statoil story does not have the same speed and defining moments as we experienced in Borealis. Statoil is a much larger company. Although still a youngster compared to most competitors, it already had a history and a legacy that the newborn Borealis, with its key value of "One company—new, different, and better," did not have.

On May 9, 2005, Statoil's Executive Committee formally decided to abolish traditional budgeting. Up until this point, the journey had been one of gradual and steady change.

Throughout the 1990s, brick by brick had been laid onto a foundation that finally was robust enough to carry the weight of more radical change. From here on, we accelerated the building activities significantly. Our vision of what we wanted to build also became more ambitious as we moved on.

Creating the Foundation

During the 1990s Statoil took several important steps that together paved the way for the 2005 decision. Most of these took place under the guidance and leadership of Eldar Sætre, who held several key finance positions before becoming CFO and in 2015 CEO, after heading up one of the business areas for some years. I reported to Eldar in my first management job in Statoil back in 1984, heading up the budget department, where I had joined the company a year earlier.

I was busy in Borealis when many of these changes were taking place. The steps taken ranged from culture and competence to process and systems. A strong and professional finance network was built. The network was glued together with common and group-wide finance systems and processes, regular network meetings and conferences, functional competence development, and a strong corporate involvement in key finance role appointments in the line. An important step was to redefine the controller role toward an active business partner, adviser, and challenger to business teams. To support this new role, most transactional tasks were moved over to Global Business Services, Statoil's shared service center. The line controllers no longer had to deal with data production and much of the basic data analysis.

In 1997 Statoil went for a large-scale SAP implementation. At the time, it was one of the largest SAP projects in Europe. Compared to many other similar projects, it was a success. It also created something that became crucial for later developments: a common set of both financial and non-financial business data in the SAP data warehouse module.

Already at this time there were thoughts about doing something with the budget process. For different reasons, the effort ended with some simplification only and little real change. The budget problem was not yet fully understood. Few other companies had declared war on the budget. There was also a corporate balanced scorecard initiative that did not really take off as intended. It was a manual process, focused on group and business area levels. It was a start, but initially not a success. The budget also survived very much intact. "We were simply not ready yet," as Eldar Sætre put it. In 2000 another scorecard exercise started, this time in a very different place. At one of the offshore production units, the gigantic Troll field, there was a strong wish for better information and support around daily operations.

This line-driven project became the start of Management Information in Statoil (MIS). It is an in-house application, a web interface built on top of the SAP data warehouse. The main purpose at the time was to provide frontline teams with better information, primarily on operational indicators, and help them manage their own business with faster and more relevant data, with less dependence on outside staff.

Most scorecard implementations start at the top and are cascaded out into the organization. They are mainly about translating and communicating group strategies. The earlier corporate scorecard initiative was in this top-down category. The idea of less central control was not very prominent. Reports to the Executive Committee and the board included KPIs but could hardly be called a full scorecard. The original good intentions of this project had slowly faded away.

MIS was more of a *bottom-up* phenomenon. The Troll implementation was a big success. Rumors spread, and other units came onboard. After some time the whole "Exploration and Production Norway" business area decided to implement MIS. It did not take long before other business areas followed. Soon all of them used MIS. In 2004, the obvious decision was made that MIS would be a common group system, a natural consequence of the successful growth from the front line up.

At the same time, the scope of MIS was growing. A vision emerged to make this the "management portal" in Statoil. New reports and information were continuously added: benchmarking data, action planning and follow-up, and miscellaneous monitoring reports.

Along the way, Ambition to Action was born. It started out as a place in MIS to document strategic objectives, KPIs, and actions for local units. It was a "dead" document and a voluntary exercise, aimed at helping teams develop their KPIs and document the work. This was not used in any subsequent follow-up and was not brought to full life until several years later. You will hear a lot more about Ambition to Action shortly.

My colleague, Arvid Hollevik, was the driving force behind the MIS system. He was everywhere in the organization, preaching, teaching, pulling, and teasing people onboard the thinking and the system. He also drove the broadening of the system functionality, always one step ahead, seeing new opportunities and areas where the system could be used. We could never have taken Beyond Budgeting to where we are today without the MIS platform and the work done by Arvid and his team. We worked closely together. People say we are quite different, which is probably why we complemented each other so well. No one has challenged me harder on making a simple picture that explains what Beyond Budgeting is all about, on one page only! Arvid has now retired from Statoil, but is still busy out there challenging the status quo. Thanks, buddy!

After several years of continuously building and strengthening the performance management platform, the situation in 2004 was a strong one:

- A competent and united finance network
- Common data definitions across the group, from chart of accounts to KPIs
- A group-wide and common SAP system
- A scorecard process built from below over several years, supported by a great MIS system
- An emerging Finance/HR alliance
- And last but not least, a Statoil organization with an open culture and strong values, including my personal favorite: "Challenge accepted truths and enter unfamiliar territory"

The last point is important. Statoil has always been a values-driven organization, although these values were not put on paper before the end of the 1980s. There have been a few updates since then, but all versions have emphasized transparency, trust, and autonomy, combined with strong encouragement for change and improvement. These values created an environment where challenging the status quo is both expected and accepted.

Statoil has a history of giving people wide responsibilities and challenging tasks at a young age. It was simply a necessity, because the company hit the ground running. Within ten years, the young and rapidly growing organization had taken on challenges many other oil companies have spent much longer mastering. The trust and autonomy from those early days have been instrumental in shaping the Statoil culture. I believe it also made the company better prepared for a Beyond Budgeting journey than many of its peers.

In 2004 a new CEO, Helge Lund, came onboard (42 years old at the time). He picked Eldar Sætre as CFO. A new head of HR, Jens R. Jenssen, was also recruited. The platform was in place. Statoil was ready to take its management processes to the next level.

Starting Out

I returned from Borealis in 2002 and started as Corporate Controller (*this* title I didn't pick myself!), based in the CFO organization but working toward the International Exploration and Production business area (INT) with Eldar Sætre as my manager once again. It was a great job and a great time, despite the title. Statoil's growth had to take place internationally. The Norwegian continental shelf is a relatively mature oil and gas region. Here, holding the fort and maintaining current production levels is job number one. INT was therefore charged with realizing the growth ambition. The business area had already secured substantial international acreage and production through the now-terminated alliance with BP.

INT was very much a project-driven organization, chasing growth opportunities around the world. My job was about challenging and advising on new projects and business opportunities. I was also coordinating the budgeting and planning process between the corporate center and INT. Compared to its sister unit responsible for the Norwegian continental shelf, INT operated in an even more dynamic and unpredictable environment. This provided us with a wealth of great examples and evidence of why traditional budgeting and planning is a flawed process. INT was not afraid of aiming high and taking on challenging targets. Securing access to capital and internal resources had a high priority. It definitely influenced the proposed budget and planning numbers, and in one direction only.

I recall one year, when the first inputs on long-term production profiles and required investments were sky high. We all knew these numbers were not even close to reflecting any expected outcome. As a challenging ambition they made much more sense, by stretching and firing up the organization. But the process allowed for only one number to represent both an ambitious target and a realistic expected outcome. It was simply impossible. Not surprisingly, the result was a negotiated compromise, an "in-between number" that nobody was very happy about.

Another favorite discussion was country office cost. At the time, most country offices were cost centers, a "hotel" and a service provider for the various businesses with activity in the country. All business units wanted country offices to be managed tightly through detailed cost budgets, because they were picking up the bill. A lot of time and energy was spent each year negotiating the cost budget and detailed allocation keys, often with executive involvement from the "hotel guests."

Then the year started and reality hit. Suddenly a business opportunity emerged. These often came out of the blue, and seldom could they be planned for. I was always impressed with how quickly and professionally the business grabbed these opportunities, which often involved significant costs and activity peaks also for the actual country office. Now, last year's budget negotiations were completely forgotten. The focus was where it should be: on making the right and necessary efforts to secure the deal and create value, even if doing so had cost implications beyond agreed budgets. But when autumn came, it was back to the negotiation table, quarreling about next year's budget and allocation keys.

Another favorite of mine was the exploration budget. Exploration is about finding new oil and gas reserves. Before I share this story, I want to underline that I am not criticizing the Exploration management team. They were (and are) great people, and I highly respect the job they do. I am criticizing the system we asked them to operate under. They did not invent it; we did.

The list of arguments for why next year's Exploration budget had to be bigger than last year's was always long and convincing. But more as a rule than an exception, the unit came back at year-end, announcing that it was "giving money back to the company." The budget the team had fought so hard for had not been spent. As you will recall, we also had balanced scorecards at the time. These were very much KPI dominated. An important KPI on the Exploration scorecard was "Exploration costs versus budget." Even I, who struggle with colors and separating red and green, was able to see that this KPI was almost always shining green. The scorecard was also connected to the bonus system: the greener the KPIs, the higher the bonus.

It was not difficult to understand why the exploration budget had not been spent. It was not necessarily bonus driven. It was often about not being able to enter new exploration areas as planned (which can be expensive) and about delays in exploration drilling. None of this could really be called good performance, although some of the reasons were outside of their control. Still, we managed to turn all of this into good performance through that not-very-meaningful KPI, "exploration costs versus budget."

My colleagues brought similar stories from other business areas. We spent more and more time discussing what we observed and also *why* all this happened. In these discussions, I often referred to what we had done in Borealis. I should have stopped doing that much earlier. It must have been both irritating and tiring for my colleagues to listen to me banging on about the Borealis story, a company they had little relation to. Looking back, I realize how patient they were. I forgot an important principle: Everybody needs their own journey. If roles had been switched, I probably would have asked the guy to shut up, or even kicked him out if I could. So again, thanks for the patience. We had some great discussions, though!

All of this continued throughout 2003 and 2004. Gradually, a shared understanding emerged about the underlying problems and also sketches of possible alternatives. The appetite for addressing the problems in a radical way was increasing. The team became more and more confident that there was an alternative, a different model that actually would work. In early 2005 we were ready to go to the Executive Committee.

Our proposal was twofold: First *separate* and *improve* the different budget purposes, as we had done in Borealis. In addition, we would let the scorecards introduced from 2000 to 2004 become the new cornerstone in the management process, under the name Ambition to Action. The latter definitely created comfort and helped to secure a *yes*. There would not be a big black hole where the budget had been. The proposal would also solve another problem, the conflict between scorecards and budgets. As we will discuss in Chapter 6, there are often conflicting signals coming from the two. Almost always, the budget wins, undermining the importance of the scorecard. Letting the budget go and continuing with scorecards, but in a new and better way, turbocharged the whole concept.

On May 9 we got the green light with strong backing from the CEO and CFO. Eldar Sætre was, of course, very comfortable with the proposal as he had been instrumental in building the platform and had actively participated in our discussions. It was a bigger leap of faith for the new CEO, Helge Lund. He demonstrated a lot of trust, both toward his CFO and toward us and the rest of the organization.

Some years later Helge shared his thoughts at the time, as he was opening a Beyond Budgeting research project at NHH (more about this great project later). He described how he had arrived at Statoil with a pretty long to-do list. "The last thing I need is one more thing on that list" had been his immediate reaction when we tested with him the idea of kicking out the budget. He, too, knew it was a flawed process. He didn't necessarily understand all of how things would work (neither did we!). "But the ideas appealed to me," he said, "so I decided to give it a chance." Thanks, Helge! With a less trusting and courageous CEO, this chapter of the book could not have been written.

Shortly afterward, I moved into a full-time Beyond Budgeting implementation role. Steve Morlidge, who once held a similar role in Unilever, claims that there were only three of us in such roles at the time. The third one was in the World Bank in New York. Thankfully, that number now is significantly higher!

The Statoil Model

Introduction

Before we move into the Statoil model, I want to remind you that what follows is a description of the model as it is intended to work. All is decided and described in what we call the Statoil Book. The board has not approved a budget since 2005. That does not mean that all of it has reached every head and every corner of Statoil. Many managers find the new model quite demanding, especially from a leadership perspective. How far we have come depends on which glasses you put on and where you are in the organization. We still have managers with one foot in the old world and also those with their entire mind and body still firmly rooted in the past. This does not necessarily mean that they are not using the new tools and processes. It is the *way* these are used that sometimes resembles traditional management more than Beyond Budgeting.

I will therefore not share a sanitized story where everything is solved and everything is perfect. Those cases might exist in polished case studies and in glossy conference presentations, but seldom in the real world. Still, compared to most other companies, or compared to where we started out in 2005, we have come far. I also want to emphasize that what you now will hear about is *our* way of implementing Beyond Budgeting. It is not *the* way. Other companies have found different ways.

When people hear that we have abolished traditional budgeting, the immediate question is often, "What do you do instead?" I do not like to answer before I have had a chance to explain what we wanted to get away from and, more importantly, the philosophy behind our model. It can be fully understood only if that background and also the Beyond Budgeting ideas are understood.

In Chapter 1 we identified a long list of budget problems: weak links to strategy, a time-consuming process, unethical behaviors, outdated assumptions, illusions of control, decisions made too early and too high up, budgeting as if the world ends December 31, and budgets ill-suited for performance evaluation. At Statoil, we could tick off every single one, and we wanted to solve them all. We needed, however, more than problem lists; we also needed to describe the principles of a new model, preferably on a one-pager, as Arvid had challenged us to make.

One of our attempts is shown in Exhibit 4.2. Ambition to Action, which you will hear more about later, is our version of the Balanced Scorecard and also the name of our management process.

You will recognize the thinking behind many of these statements, and also the inspiration from Beyond Budgeting. "Do the right thing" is about making the room to act and perform bigger, but not without boundaries. There are still solid walls

Ambition to Action—Key Principles

- Performance is about performing better than those we compare ourselves with.
- Do the right thing in the actual situation, guided by the Statoil Book, your Ambition to Action, decision criteria and authorities, and sound business judgement.
- Within this execution framework, resources are made available or allocated case-by-case.
- Business follow-up is forward-looking and action-oriented.
- Performance evaluation involves a holistic assessment of delivery and behavior.

EXHIBIT 4.2 Ambition to Action—Key Principles

in the room. We call it the "Execution Framework," shown in Exhibit 4.3.

The *first* wall in the larger room is the Statoil Book, a booklet given to everyone in the company. It is about who we want to

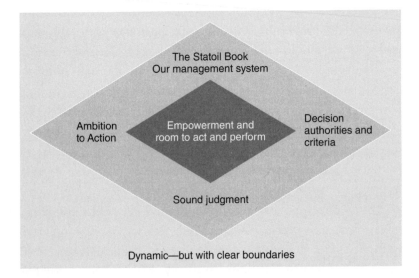

EXHIBIT 4.3 The Execution Framework

be and how we do things in Statoil. It starts out where it should start, with values and leadership principles. Then it describes our Operating Model, including the Ambition to Action process. The book also includes some key corporate policies, but it is not a huge instruction book. It provides guidance and direction, not microinstructions.

There are in addition a number of corporate work process requirements. These are developed by process owners responsible for design and standards within their own process, and documented in the management system Aris. You will hear more later about how these have been radically simplified, and responsibility moved to the line.

Making a printed version of the Statoil Book to make it stand out from everything else that can be found online turned out to be a wise decision (Exhibit 4.4). It is wonderful to see how many have the book lying on their desk. "The Statoil Book says . . ." is often heard in meetings and discussions.

The *second* wall is each unit's Ambition to Action, which provides more concrete guidance and direction through strategic objectives, KPIs, and actions.

EXHIBIT 4.4 The Statoil Book

The *third* wall consists of a set of both financial and non-financial decision criteria, combined with a set of decision authorities stating how big an individual decision a manager can make before having to go one level up. This wall has been there all the time. What is new is that we no longer have "double decision making" with regard to also approving, for instance, annual investment budgets.

The *fourth* wall is sound judgment. The power of common sense should never be underestimated. I mistrust any model lacking this important component.

Within this framework, resources are made available or allocated case-by-case. All principles will be explained more in detail later on, including dynamic resource allocation, forward and action-oriented business follow-up, and holistic performance evaluation.

You may find our model disappointingly simple, with many elements that perhaps already exist in your own organization. Much of the difference lies in the way we operate what might be seen as standard components in a management process. For instance, having a balanced scorecard is not unique at all. The way it is implemented and operated, however, makes a big difference. A scorecard can protect and reinforce a command-and-control regime, or it can do the opposite. Too many companies are in the first category. We aim to be in the second.

The way it all hangs together and how we have integrated the different steps in the management process also make a difference. The parts are not unique, but they are well connected, from strategy to people, from corporate to front line.

You might still be disappointed. And fair enough, because there is no rocket science involved, just a lot of common sense and also hard work over many years.

As already mentioned, budget purpose separation and the introduction of Ambition to Action were the two steps that got us started. Let us first look at the separation.

Separating the Budget Purposes

In earlier chapters we discussed the different purposes of a budget—target setting, forecasting, and resource allocation— and why combining the three causes serious problems. Let us quickly recap.

One by one these do not represent a problem as long as each one is done in a meaningful way. The problem emerges when the three are combined in one process allowing for only one set of numbers, the budget numbers. This management "Kinder egg" might seem very efficient: three things at the same time! This efficiency comes at a big price, as the three have different and often conflicting purposes. Take targets and forecasts. A target is an *aspiration,* what we *want* to happen. A forecast is an *expectation,* what we *think* will happen. A good sales forecast can't also function as an ambitious sales target. Forecasts that also are applications for resources tend to carry a systematic "too high" bias, as managers hoard and secure room to negotiate before the axe comes out.

As we learned in Borealis, there is fortunately a very simple solution. We can and often should continue with these three management activities, but in separate and different processes, allowing for different numbers. We can even do them at different times and with different time horizons.

Once the three purposes are released from the straitjacket of having to be one number produced in one process, huge improvement opportunities open up. Working each purpose separately, we can now let business and people realities inspire and drive our design. We can take reality seriously, and not just as a VUCA world. We should also let our beliefs about people saturate our design choices. If that is Theory Y (hopefully it is), there are significant consequences. Here are some key questions that now can, and should, be asked:

How can we set targets that inspire and motivate people, that stretch without anyone feeling stretched? How can we set targets that are more robust against all the VUCA out there?

How can we quickly get on the table a set of unbiased forecast numbers, without a million details, that we know we can trust because we have removed the reasons for gaming the numbers?

How can we find more effective and intelligent ways of managing cost and optimizing scarce resources than what the traditional budget offers?

You might recall the picture we made in Borealis to explain the separation of these purposes (Exhibit 3.4). At Statoil, we tried to further refine and sharpen the message. Exhibit 4.5 shows what it looks like today, reflecting where we now are on the journey.

How far organizations go in exploring improvement opportunities varies, as it should. Some do little beyond the separation, which still brings major benefits. Others go further and find they can radically improve each process. Some go for the ultimate simplification of setting no or only a few targets, and also dropping forecasting. Again, there is no one right answer, but a lot of great alternatives to choose from or still to be discovered. Many also find that they get braver along the way, and go for more radical change after a period of operating with separated numbers only.

Here is one way of separating target setting and forecasting: Do target setting first, based on an outside-in perspective of what is possible. What have others been able to do? What does

Start of the Statoil journey—solving a serious budget conflict

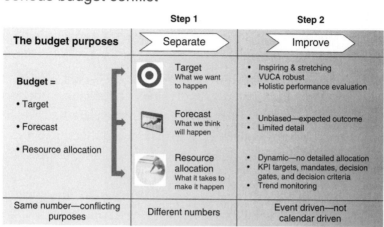

	Step 1	Step 2
The budget purposes	Separate	Improve
Budget = • Target • Forecast • Resource allocation	**Target** What we want to happen **Forecast** What we think will happen **Resource allocation** What it takes to make it happen	• Inspiring & stretching • VUCA robust • Holistic performance evaluation • Unbiased—expected outcome • Limited detail • Dynamic—no detailed allocation • KPI targets, mandates, decision gates, and decision criteria • Trend monitoring
Same number—conflicting purposes	Different numbers	Event driven—not calendar driven

EXHIBIT 4.5 Separating Budget Purposes

great look like? It is all about high ambitions, stretching, and what we want to happen. Once this is in place, we can start thinking about how to deliver on these targets. This is about action planning and trying to understand consequences of our actions through forecasting. Will they take us to our targets?

The Statoil/Hydro merger was an example of applying this principle. When the merger was announced in December 2006, it was promised that the new company would be up and running by October 2007. There was no plan at that point showing how this could be done. We were hardly allowed to talk together back then. The plan came later, driven by this ambitious target. But we made it. If it had been done the other way around, with no startup commitments made before a full master plan was ready, we might still have had an October startup, but probably in 2008 instead.

I cannot emphasize enough how important and effective a separation of the budget purposes can be for getting started on a Beyond Budgeting journey. The improvement discussions that follow often lead to bigger and more fundamental discussions, where the Beyond Budgeting principles provide guidance and advice, but in a less scary way. The focus is initially on management processes, but flows naturally to the bigger issues of people and leadership.

The separation also calms the scared. There will always be managers who are frightened by the idea of abolishing budgets. By separating and then improving, we can assure these managers that we will continue doing what the budget tried to do for us, but in much better ways. That doesn't sound too scary, does it?

Let us now move on to Ambition to Action, the process where the three activities take place, and much more. We could have merely separated and still have harvested significant benefits even without Ambition to Action, as is the case in many Beyond Budgeting companies. Ambition to Action adds important new dimensions to our model, making it even more powerful.

Ambition to Action

Ambition to Action is a combination of Beyond Budgeting and the balanced scorecard. Although it might look like a standard balanced scorecard, there are at least four reasons why Ambition to Action has something more to it than the typical scorecard:

1. We did not just put it on top of what we already had. We also took something away. The budget was a serious competitor, which almost always won when the two concepts collided. When budgets were removed, it was a strong signal to the organization that we were serious about Ambition to Action, because that is all there is.

2. We have worked hard to make Ambition to Action a process that helps teams manage their own business, and not just another command-and-control tool at the top.

3. When initially introduced, scorecards in Statoil were about KPIs only. A tired cynicism was emerging around these KPIs, because we promoted them more than they deserved. By lifting up strategic objectives and actions alongside the KPIs, we got a broader and more meaningful performance language. We became less dependent on KPIs, and Ambition to Action became a process that better reflected business realities and how the organization actually works.

4. We have used Ambition to Action to build bridges, not just toward the strategy process but also toward HR and the people process. The focus on *integrated* performance management has been very well received in the organization, again because it better reflects reality of how things actually work in the line. This integration has brought synergies well above our expectations. Ambition to Action is now a household term both in Strategy and HR.

Exhibit 4.6 shows Ambition to Action in a nutshell.

Ambition to Action—purpose and process

- Translating strategy from ambitions to actions
- Securing flexibility—room to act and perform
- Activating values and leadership principles

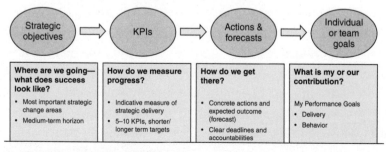

Strategic objectives	KPIs	Actions & forecasts	Individual or team goals
Where are we going— what does success look like?	**How do we measure progress?**	**How do we get there?**	**What is my or our contribution?**
• Most important strategic change areas • Medium-term horizon	• Indicative measure of strategic delivery • 5–10 KPIs, shorter/ longer term targets	• Concrete actions and expected outcome (forecast) • Clear deadlines and accountabilities	My Performance Goals • Delivery • Behavior

EXHIBIT 4.6 Ambition to Action

Ambition to Action has three purposes:

- Translating strategy from ambitions to actions
- Securing flexibility—room to act and perform
- Activating values and leadership principles

The starting point for Ambition to Action is the established strategy. Strategy is about making choices. Those who never say *no* do not have a strategy. So next time you listen to someone presenting their strategy, ask what they have said *no* to. If they can't answer, there is no strategy. No fancy slideshow can fix that. But saying *no* is not enough. We also have to be able to execute what we have said *yes* to. This is where Ambition to Action kicks in, helping to implement strategic choices through a *horizontal* translation at each organizational level:

- Where are we going, and what does success look like? (Ambition and Strategic Objectives)
- How do we get there? (Actions)
- How do we measure progress? (KPIs)

We ask these questions within each of the four standard balanced scorecard perspectives: Finance, Market, Operations, and People and Organization. We have added a fifth, Health, Safety, and Environment (HSE), due to the extreme importance of this dimension in our industry.

There is then the *vertical* translation between organizational levels. This shall ensure the necessary alignment throughout the organization, from corporate to frontline teams. We must, however, not use so much glue to secure this alignment that we lose what is also important: ownership and commitment and the autonomy and flexibility to sense and respond. Ambition to Action is also about helping frontline teams to perform and deliver in their daily operations. Finding the right balance between the two is important as they sometimes pull in different directions.

The process should be more about strategy *translation* than *cascading*, with each level interpreting and translating what other relevant Ambition to Action levels around them should mean for them. They need to look up to the unit above, and maybe further up, sometimes all the way up to the corporate Ambition to Action. It might also be necessary to look left and right if there are interfaces with neighboring units. In addition, each unit should run its own strategy process as necessary. This might add on themes and objectives that cannot be read out of messages from above. It can also bring out new strategic issues that might influence strategies above. It is critical for ownership and commitment that teams feel they are not just passive backseat passengers when their own Ambition to Action is developed. This is absolutely possible even with clear guidance and direction from above.

We have had many discussions about the right order for establishing Ambition to Action processes. Some argue for a stringently sequenced process, where no level starts before the level above is finished. Today, this part of the process is quite fluid, with little orchestration from the top. The more self-regulating the process is, the better. Moving away from annual versions in 2010 made the process even more continuous, as we will discuss later.

Ambition to Action is obviously focusing on important areas where we want *change*. There might, however, be important areas where we don't want change, because the situation is okay. Here, we have a monitoring section in MIS, outside of Ambition to Action, where we can monitor the development on "important but okay" issues. If any of these start showing a negative development and is turning into a problem, we can lift it onto Ambition to Action with corresponding actions until the problem is solved.

Some years ago we turned around the conventional order of the five perspectives. Most scorecards start with the Finance perspective on top. We now start with People and Organization, followed by HSE, ending with Finance. We switched because we saw what happened in business review meetings when the agenda is tight and time is limited. "Let us come back to People and Organization next time . . . ." There was no ill will behind it, but those are not the signals to send if we aim to be a people-focused organization. So we moved People and Organization to the top. Another small gap closed between what we say and what we do.

Lately we have made some further adjustments. We found that many used the Finance perspective for anything related to money, for instance, cost KPIs, which typically belongs in the Operations perspective. We therefore renamed Finance as Results. This is actually in line with the intention of a balanced scorecard: working cause-and-effect by addressing in the other perspectives what we need to be good at in order to create results and value. For profit centers this works quite well. As we have a value-chain structured organization, many units do not have a true bottom-line responsibility, like for instance our Technology and Project Development business area, which serves the other business areas. Any unit should, however, reflect on why it exists and what its contribution and results should be, even if these can't always be defined in direct bottom-line terms.

In addition, we have renamed Health, Safety and Environment (HSE) to Safety, Security and Sustainability and moved this first, without any intentions of downgrading the importance of People and Organization. Security was lifted significantly higher on the agenda after a terrorist attack on our operations in Algeria in 2013, where five Statoil employees lost their lives.

Exhibit 4.7 provides an example of an Ambition to Action, actually a screenshot directly from MIS. It is from a few years back, so it does not reflect these latest adjustments.

Each Ambition to Action starts with an ambition statement. At corporate level, this would be our vision of "Shaping the

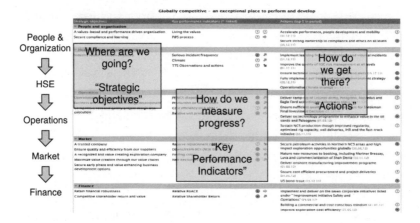

EXHIBIT 4.7 Ambition to Action Example

Future of Energy." The discussion about the correct use of *ambition*, *mission*, and *vision* pops up from time to time. I don't really care what we call it. What is important is that we state something meaningful about the overall purpose or direction, something that makes people tick and provides guidance for the rest of Ambition to Action. I believe the majority of employees could not care less about the distinction between mission and vision. They just want to be ignited and inspired! Today, there are around 800 Ambition to Action initiatives in the company. There have been more, but the business areas cleaned up some time ago as there probably were more than needed. Most organizational units of a certain size have, however, their own. The Statoil Ambition to Action is what the board approves instead of a budget. In addition, the board of course approves our largest projects, but continuously and not through an annual investment budget.

It is not mandatory to have an Ambition to Action. Managers often ask us if their team should have one. We absolutely recommend trying it out, but we advise yes only if the team itself experience this as a sensible and value-adding way of managing themselves. If not, they are better off without. The management job still has to be done, however: providing direction, planning and executing actions, and measuring that things are moving in the right direction. If the team prefers PowerPoint, Word, and Excel, it is their choice.

Some managers still believe they have to have one, often with low ownership as the result. The best indication of missing ownership is when Ambition to Action is updated only before business review meetings with the level above. We even came across a manager who believed he had to have one to participate in the bonus system. I can hardly think of a worse motivation.

There is, of course, a clear expectation that the concept is applied at the higher business area and business unit levels, but I do not think anyone here feels forced to do so. A number of staff units have also decided to use Ambition to Action. In Performance Management and Risk, the unit where I am based, we have had one for several years. We are a bit thin on KPIs, but it still works because we have clear and meaningful strategic objectives and actions.

All Ambition to Action processes are established, followed up, and maintained in the MIS system. We will discuss MIS and business follow-up in more depth later on.

As in most organizations, acronyms flourish also in Statoil. It didn't take long before *AtA* popped up. Then came *A2A*, and I have also seen *AtoA*. Personally, I feel that there are some things that deserve to be spelled fully out. No one has for instance abbreviated the Statoil values or our leadership principles. It is not a coincidence that the Statoil Book only talks about Ambition to Action. I used to point this out to people, but I gave up. You should pick your fights. Not all are worth fighting!

The Ambition to Action Process

Exhibit 4.8 shows how Ambition to Action is illustrated in the Statoil Book. Let us go through it step by step.

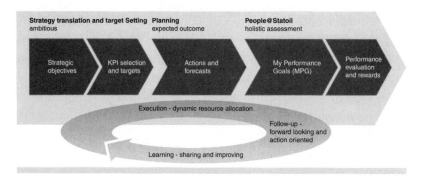

EXHIBIT 4.8 The Ambition to Action Process

Strategy Translation and Target Setting

STRATEGIC OBJECTIVES   The first part of Ambition to Action, the strategic objectives, are born in the strategy process and could in balanced scorecard terms be called our strategy map. The strategy process varies somewhat across the company. At group level it is more of a continuous and issue-driven process, where strategic themes are addressed as needed or at regular and longer Executive Committee strategy sessions, typically every sixth month.

Strategic objectives describe what success looks like on a medium-term time horizon. How long this is depends on the rhythm of the actual business. Once established, strategic objectives remain relatively stable unless there are major changes in strategic direction.

Here are some questions we recommend teams to ask when developing and testing the quality of their strategic objectives:

- Do they reflect ambition and strategy, and areas that are both important and need change?
- Do they provide clear guidance and direction?
- Are they written in a language that makes people tick, without too many buzzwords?

- Do they support each other (cause and effect through the five perspectives)?
- Is the time horizon right, reflecting a relevant delivery period?

The importance of tone and language used when formulating objectives is often underestimated. Strategic messages can easily be lost in too many words where "correct and precise" win over "makes people tick." The consulting language is full of words to be avoided, because they do not reach people the way we think they do. Take the popular *Excellence*, for example. It is a worn-out term that I believe turns more people off than on. *World class* may be in a similar category. Actually, many would probably be much more fired up by "Let's beat the s*** out of the competition!" Whatever language used, aim for the simple and natural, but paint big pictures that engage and that people can relate to and believe in. What kind of language is it that ignites yourself? Trust your instincts more than the buzzwords. Don't invite employees to play Bullshit Bingo. You got it right if people respond with a roaring "Yes, this is a journey I want to be part of!"

Some management teams get impatient when working on strategic objectives. They want to move on to KPIs and actions, which they feel are more concrete and tangible compared to the longer-term strategic objectives. It is, however, critically important to spend sufficient time developing strategic objectives, and it must be done together. These discussions, where strategies are sharpened and crystallized, often bring on the table different interpretations of strategic direction that otherwise might have been left unnoticed and unaddressed. BBI Core Team member Dag Larsson puts it like this: "Speed can never replace direction."

It is also much more difficult to identify good KPIs if the groundwork is not done on strategic objectives. Remember that the main purpose of a KPI is to measure that we are moving toward these objectives. If we jump straight to KPIs without being clear and agreeing on what these are, how do we know which KPIs to select?

From a group perspective, strategic objectives become more and more operational the closer to the front line we get. That is exactly what we want, a translation into something more concrete and "executional." Frontline units still see their objectives as strategic, providing guidance and direction. We once considered changing the name "strategic objectives" to something more operational in this part of the organization. But where should we switch, and how should we explain it? "You guys should focus on today and forget about direction and tomorrow." I am glad we did not act on that idea.

KEY PERFORMANCE INDICATORS: SELECTION AND TARGET SETTING   It is more than 20 years since we implemented balanced scorecards in Borealis, as one of the first European companies to do so. I can still recall the excitement of discovering this new management tool. I was especially intrigued by the KPI part. Finally, we would be able to understand all the true performance drivers in our business. We should have known that it wouldn't be that easy. Those perfect KPIs that revealed the full truth were quite difficult to find, at least when moving outside the Finance perspective. I can sometimes be stubborn, and my hunt for those perfect KPIs continued for many years. Today, I have given up, simply because they do not exist. Again, they are not called KPTs – Key Performance Truths. This does *not* mean they are not useful. We just have to remember their limitations.

Earlier, we discussed some of the characteristics of a good KPI. Here is the checklist we use:

- Do they measure progress toward strategic objectives?
- Do they measure real performance?

- Is there a good mix of leading and lagging indicators?
- Do they address areas where we want change or improvement (or is monitoring sufficient)?
- Are the KPIs perceived as meaningful at the level they are used?
- Can data be collected easily?

Many asked us about the right number of KPIs on an Ambition to Action. There is no right answer. It depends on how many strategic objectives there are, and how measureable the business is. It also depends on the quality of strategic objectives and actions. The clearer these are, the less dependent we are on also measuring through KPIs. People kept asking, and in the end we gave up and said "between 5 and 15."

When teams are selecting KPIs, they can chose between "automatic" or "manual" ones. We have several hundred pre-defined KPIs in MIS. If any of these are chosen, the team gets the reporting for free, as data automatically are pulled from the SAP data warehouse. If for some reason none of these are seen as good enough, teams can choose to define their own KPIs. Reporting must then be done manually by the team itself, who must judge if such a tailored and manual KPI justifies the additional workload.

As already discussed, *relative* KPIs can be very effective. There are two types of relative KPIs. The first is about input/output relations, focusing for instance on unit cost instead of absolute cost; the second is about benchmarking and comparing with others. The two can also be combined.

It can sometimes be difficult to find peers to compare with, especially externally but sometimes also internally. Input/output or productivity KPIs are often easier to define. The best ones are often a combination: benchmarked productivity KPIs. A Beyond Budgeting implementation does not, however, depend on finding such KPIs, as some seem to believe. They just make implementation a bit easier.

One thing must always be in place for benchmarking and league standings to work. They must be seen as *fair* and *relevant*. If this is not in place, forget it. There will be endless discussions about not being comparable. One reason can be structural differences between units being compared, where laggards coming out low never will be able to hit the top spot. Take production regularity, an important KPI for both offshore platforms and onshore plants. These vary in age, from brand new but past the startup trouble, to 30-year-old veterans. The latter will typically struggle more on their regularity performance. How can we then benchmark? One solution is "indirect benchmarking": comparing how well each unit improves their *own* performance. This gives everybody a more common and fair starting point (Exhibit 4.9).

Acceptance is key—two alternatives

Alt 1 - Direct		**Alt 2 - Indirect**	
Own performance vs. others		Own improvement vs. others	
Unit C	1.6	Unit D	+ 20%
Unit A	1.7	Unit F	+ 18%
Unit D	1.9	Unit U	+ 15%
Unit F	1.9	Unit A	+ 10%
Unit G	2.0	Unit C	+ 2%
Unit U	2.1	Unit K	– 2%
Unit M	2.3	Unit M	– 4%
Unit K	2.4	Unit G	– 6%

When easy to compare and high acceptance for direct comparison

When difficult to compare and low acceptance for direct comparison

EXHIBIT 4.9 Direct and Indirect Benchmarking

The two main financial KPIs on Statoil's Ambition to Action are both relative, the first being Relative Return on Average Capital Employed (Relative RoACE). Which return are we able to create on invested capital? And how does that return compare to our competitors?

Before 2005, this KPI was only relative in the first sense, being an absolute percentage number only. One year the target was 12 percent, adjusted for changes in the oil price. Finance loves such targets where monthly progress can accurately be reported. One year, the RoACE crept upward as year-end got closer: 11.5, 11.7, 11.9, before just passing 12 percent in December. Yeah! Great performance! Really? What if the competition delivered returns of 13, 14, or 15 percent? Or maybe it was more than great performance, because almost all peers came in lower?

We therefore established a league standings list of 11 other reasonably similar oil and gas companies. We compared our own RoACE performance with this peer group. The target is about where we want to be, and that is not at the bottom! We have done the same with the other financial KPI, Relative Total Shareholder Return (TSR), which is our dividend-adjusted share price development compared to the same peer group. These two KPI targets are the main financial targets the board approves. There is no need for a big annual exercise. We call them "evergreen" targets. They stand until there is a need to change them. We have done so only a few times since the introduction almost ten years ago. These two KPIs also drive our common employee bonus scheme, which we will discuss later. Everybody in the same boat; us against the competition. None of these KPIs are perfect; they definitely have their weaknesses. This is partly overcome through also having many other KPIs on Ambition to Action, and by having a holistic performance evaluation, as explained later.

Listed in Exhibit 4.10 is our peer group. They are not all identical to Statoil. Some of them have more so-called "downstream" activities like refining and also retail through their own gas stations. Such businesses typically work as a cushion and perform well when oil prices are low. Still, these are our competitors. Again, this is less precise than an absolute target, but ten times more relevant. This way of defining performance is also quite robust against a wildly fluctuating oil price.

I once spoke at a conference when someone in the audience insisted that something was wrong with this picture: "The math is wrong, it doesn't add up!" I just couldn't understand what he meant, until he pointed to the top of both rankings. Not everybody knows that Total is a French oil company! It is a coincidence that they are on top of both charts. Over time, it is actually a pretty dynamic picture, where Statoil generally has performed well against peers.

I recall our Investor Relations colleagues being quite worried when we first communicated these new metrics to the market. Would investors and analysts think we were trying to escape their tough scrutiny, by no longer committing to hardwired and concrete return targets, only promising a competitive return? They hardly blinked. This is what we do all the time, they said: Compare the performance of one company to that of other potential investment candidates. They probably rank us on more parameters than we do ourselves!

These relative financial targets are not cascaded mathematically to business areas, as doing so is not desirable or possible. They are instead translated in various ways. One business area once set its main financial target as having "RoACE at group level." Others have from time to time simply taken the corporate relative RoACE target as their own, as a measure of shared success. Others have no overall profitability targets as they aren't

Financial performance as we define it

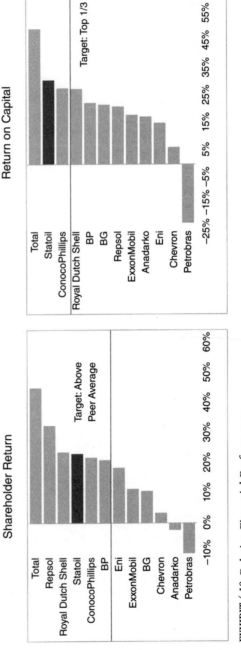

EXHIBIT 4.10 Relative Financial Performance

profit centers. But if they deliver on their own Ambition to Action, they will definitely contribute toward Statoil doing well and beating the competition.

Almost all our relative KPIs are internal and not external like the two just mentioned. As we discussed, some organizations believe they can't go Beyond Budgeting because they struggle with finding relative KPIs. So do we in many areas. The majority of our KPIs are actually in the "absolute" category. We simply try to use relative KPIs where it is possible and where it makes sense, but again, a Beyond Budgeting journey does not depend on these. If absolute KPIs and targets are used, *ranges* or *rounded numbers* are normally better than the decimal-loaded numbers. The more absolute KPIs and targets are used, the more important it is to also apply a holistic performance evaluation, where we also look at what measurement isn't picking up. More about this later.

As we have discussed, benchmarking can be an effective and self-regulating way of driving performance, because no one likes to be a laggard. We must, however, not forget the original purpose of benchmarking, which is *learning*. It is about identifying high-performing units that we can learn from. We should position learning as the most important purpose and regard the gentle but effective performance push as a nice and welcome side effect.

We constantly discuss how ambitious our targets should be, often quoting Michelangelo and his wise words about aiming high and missing versus aiming low and hitting, where the latter is the problem, not the first. We do this because it is easy to forget the *purpose* of goals and targets. The purpose is to motivate and drive, to secure the best possible performance, even when this turns out to be lower than targeted. What is best performance under equal circumstances (and high is good): delivering 100 against a target of 90, or delivering 105 against a target of 110?

Most would agree that there has to be a certain element of stretch in a target. The issue is how much. There is no simple answer. The more ambitious a target is, the less it must be perceived as imposed from above. Without ownership and commitment, ambitious targets become nothing but a numbers game. Unfortunately, the market and the external world do not always seem to appreciate this way of looking at performance and targets. Here, "aim low and hit" is often better received than not meeting a demanding stretch target. Sometimes it even seems like performance is about hitting the analysts' consensus expectation, because they do not like surprises. There are companies that have been able to leave this game, giving no promises, no guidance, and not holding any "Capital Market Day" for investors and analysts. Getting there is achieved only by consistently delivering good performance. The Catch-22 is that the singing and dancing around guidance and quarterly results might actually prevent companies from reaching the performance level required to quit the game.

A final reflection on targets. As discussed, a target is actually *not* the target or the goal. What we really want is *the best possible performance, given the circumstances.* Setting targets is one way of achieving this, but it is a medicine that often comes with a number of negative side effects. These include lowballing, negotiations and hidden (or not-so-hidden) agendas, and even more of it if a bonus is linked to target achievement. The rational (or cynical) manager has no reason whatsoever to set ambitious targets. On the contrary, it only reduces the chance of hitting the number and getting the reward.

What if we could find other ways of getting people to do their best without these side effects? Relative benchmarking KPIs without targets is one alternative. Those skilled in target negotiations are often very competitive people. I have yet to meet anyone stating that "I am perfectly happy being down in that fourth quarter." As discussed, some organizations do not set targets at all; they have found other and better ways.

Let us close this section with a few words on target-setting frequency and time horizons. When we started out in 2005, we separated target setting and forecasting in time. Strategic objectives and KPIs were reviewed and adjusted as needed before the summer. When that job was finalized, KPI targets were set, some before and some after the summer. The key point was to set direction and finalize target setting *before* moving into the planning phase of action and forecasts in the autumn. KPI targets were set for the coming year and for longer periods where relevant, such as for production.

When we later moved toward a more dynamic and more continuously updated Ambition to Action in 2010, we knew that we gave up this sequencing mechanism as a way of separating target setting and forecasting. It was a price worth paying, as we will discuss later.

On some KPIs we introduced rolling three-year averages. This was typically done where the business has a longer-term nature (exploration, for example). It takes several years to secure access to an area, shoot and interpret seismic, plan, drill, and analyze the results. One-year periods and targets do not make much sense here. The problem is that when being in the third year of a three-year average target, we know what needs to be delivered that last year. With a rolling average, we will always be in the last year, again knowing what has to be delivered. So in both cases we haven't been able to escape the annual target. If a longer-term target on the other hand is set for a fixed point in time, longer gets shorter and shorter as we approach the target deadline. For some KPIs we simply gave up and reverted to annual targets.

Planning: Actions and Forecasts

When we know what we are aiming for, it is time to plan how to get there. Planning is about:

- Which *actions* do we need to take in order to deliver on strategic objectives and KPI targets?
- What are the expected consequences of these actions, expressed as a *forecast*, either against KPI targets or in other financial or operational areas where we need to understand what lies ahead (e.g., financial capacity)?

Planning is not about target setting, because this lies behind us. Neither is it about resource allocation, because this is handled in a separate process.

Actions need to be ambitious, because what we aim for is challenging. The consequence of these actions, the forecast, must, however, reflect the *expected outcome*, whether we like what we see or not. We also forecast to reveal issues early enough to take required actions. It can be useful to distinguish between these two types of forecasts. The last category is about *outside/in* or external forecasting, trying to understand developments in our environment and what the implications are for us. These forecasts might trigger actions that we also need to understand the consequences of, and could be called *inside/out* or internal forecasting. In the following, both forecasting types are addressed.

It is quite natural to have *gaps* between ambitious targets and realistic forecasts. The goal is of course to close such gaps, as deadlines and delivery time are approaching. A gap is not necessarily something negative; it just shows that we are aiming high while at the same time having a realistic view on where we believe we will end up as things look today. The earlier gaps are identified, the easier it is to do something about them. Having no gaps sometimes is more questionable, especially if delivery time lies some time ahead. This might indicate ambitions that are too low or forecasts that are too optimistic.

Yet if targets are too ambitious, gaps can become too big. People might give up or do stupid things to deliver. We have therefore established a "target review" mechanism. This is an opportunity to have targets adjusted if gaps turn out to be too tough to close. It is not used very often, but the organization knows it exists and knows it is for real. It works both ways; ambitions can also be increased.

Setting targets before knowing how to get there can be uncomfortable, and even more so if targets also are expected to be ambitious. We therefore need mechanisms that can create *comfort*. The target review is one such mechanism. Another one is the holistic performance evaluation, where stretching can be rewarded instead of punished (and the other way around), and where changes in assumptions can be taken into account. We are sometimes asked which mechanism to use: a target review along the way or the holistic evaluation afterwards? Let us assume that a unit is halfway through and the forecast is showing that they probably will do much better than targeted. Should the target be increased through a target review? It depends on the circumstances. If the reason is positive events that gave irreversible effects, it might be okay to adjust halfway. If there is significant uncertainty about the final outcome ahead, it might be better to wait for the holistic evaluation. Motivation is another dimension to consider. If the unit is likely to lean back because the target has become a piece of cake, that is of course an issue. It is in any case always better if units adjust their own targets instead of someone else doing it for them.

The holistic evaluation approach is further explained in the "Performance Evaluation and Rewards" section later.

Although our forecasting principles are simple, the practice of them is not necessarily so for several reasons. The first has to do with our heritage from the budget days, which are not that far behind us. In the old process, there was "one number" only. This was optimized depending on the main purpose: a "high" number if the main purpose was to ask for money and a "low" number if the main purpose was target negotiation.

Now, a forecast should just be a forecast and nothing else. If you game your forecast, the only one you fool in the end is yourself. Even if most people understand and appreciate the difference, we still see skewed forecasts. As we learned about investment forecasting in Borealis, it takes time to leave old behaviors behind, much longer than we think. Some managers still let their forecast sway in the direction that would have paid off in the old system. We are seeing less and less of this, but it still happens. What we talk about here is *bias* in forecasting, conscious or unconscious. It is a systematic error. Bias is different from *noise*. Noise is random variations above and below the actual outcome, with no systematic patterns. Noise is inevitable, and we need to understand the difference between the two.

A forecast is *not* a promise, not something to deliver on. People using that expression have not understood the difference between a forecast and a target. Again, a forecast is what we think will happen, an *expectation*; a target is what we want to happen, an *aspiration*. Sometimes we definitely don't want to hit our forecasts. Assume we are out sailing. The target is clear; we want to reach the next harbor. Our radar screen provides us with forecasts of what lies ahead, and now it tells us that we are on course to hit a rock. That is definitely not a forecast we want to deliver on! On the contrary, we want to do whatever it takes to avoid hitting the rock. We use forecasts in our decision making to help us hit harbors and not rocks.

Some would call "on course to hit a rock" a bad forecast. Assuming it is true, it is a *good* forecast even though it contains bad news. The only thing that can turn a good forecast into a bad one is if we get it too late, leaving no time to respond. Leadership behaviors are often to blame for good forecasts becoming bad ones. What kind of reception do we usually see when people bring good forecasts with bad news? There is seldom applause; on the contrary! Such experiences hardly encourage anyone to do it again, or do it early rather than late, which often means too late.

Let us stay at sea. A supertanker needs a huge radar screen. It takes a long time to turn, so it is important to be able to discover dangers and obstacles early. A speedboat, however, hardly needs a radar screen. It can react and turn the very second something is observed. The speedboat is much more *agile* than the supertanker, which uses forecasting to compensate for its lack of agility. Maybe companies should put less effort into becoming better at forecasting, and more into becoming more agile?

Dynamic forecasting and dynamic resource allocation are closely related. What is the point of having the world's largest radar screen and the ability to sense and respond instantly, if there is no dynamic resource allocation ensuring that the necessary resources also can be instantly accessed or reallocated, instead of being locked up in a detailed annual budget?

Many try to measure forecasting quality or *accuracy*: "Was our forecast correct?" That question only makes sense when we *can't influence* the outcome. Weather forecasting is a good example. We can forecast the weather tomorrow and check tomorrow how good our forecast was. Here, it makes sense to measure forecasting accuracy, because we can't influence the outcome. If wrong, we should also try to learn and understand why.

The sailing example is very different. Hopefully we reacted and avoided hitting the rock. Measuring how much we missed and call it forecasting inaccuracy is meaningless. This was exactly what we wanted to happen, and it happened because we could influence the outcome.

The distinction we made earlier between external (outside/in) and internal (inside/out) forecasting is applicable here. Measuring forecasting accuracy is normally only relevant for external forecasting where we can't influence the outcome (oil prices, exchange rates, etc.).

Although forecasting (describing the future) is a science in itself, there is little of what accounting (describing the past) has loads of: international standards, thick manuals, well-documented procedures, and detailed audits to check the quality. An exception in our industry is found in construction projects, where regular updates of expected total costs, the "master control estimate," is a profession in itself. Also here we can observe the occasional gaming, the reluctance to lower cost estimates because it is perceived as giving back money that might be needed for a rainy day and that might have to be asked for again. In other words, forecasting is mixed up with resource allocation.

It is of course important to have correct and reliable accounting information. But it can be just as important to have high forecasting quality. Forecasting is the basis for decisions about new projects, new initiatives, and corrective actions: value-creating activities that later hopefully end up as profit that we accurately can account for. Forecasting is maybe more important than accounting when it comes to value creation.

We should however not turn forecasting into a new accounting industry. Not everything should be forecasted. Many parameters carry so much uncertainty that they cannot be predicted in a meaningful way. When I worked in Statoil's crude oil marketing unit, there was an impressive knowledge about the fundamentals of oil markets and the mechanisms that drive oil prices. Still, I am not sure if the average prediction hit rate on both short- and long-term price movements was very different from what a rolling dice would have shown. Of course, we need to make assumptions on oil price and other important parameters, but multiple scenarios, ranges, and what-if analyses are often more meaningful than one number only. The purpose of a price and currency forecast is, however, not only about trying to be "right." It is just as much about making sure that everybody uses the same assumptions, making projects and decisions comparable.

Many would argue that the bigger the decision, the more forecasting and analysis is required. The biggest decision many of us ever make, getting married, seems, however, to happen through a very different process, with no or little analysis taking place. I am not at all recommending to forecast implications and to make a business case out of this important decision! It is just another reflection on how different we tend to behave depending on which side of the company gates we stand.

Here are a few simple but important forecasting principles. Forecasting should primarily be something *you do for yourself* to help you manage your own business. If a lot of your forecasting is triggered by requests from above, asking for data you otherwise would not have bothered with in order to manage your own business, then something is wrong. Why do others need this information if you do not? Local ownership is key for getting good data quality. There is always better quality if those making the forecast depend on the quality themselves.

A forecast should also be *actionable*. If the information cannot be used to trigger any action, why do we forecast? Often requests from above seem to be on autopilot: "We have always asked for this." Such requests often come with little or no explanation of the underlying reason why the information is needed, which would be useful for both those asking and those being asked: "If this is what you're after, you should ask for this and not for that. And you already got some slightly different numbers last week that should be good enough for this purpose. Next time, maybe you should make a rough estimate yourself, instead of asking everybody below to submit forecasts for you to add up."

It is amazing how much forecasting takes place where these simple questions are not asked or cannot be answered very convincingly. The unnecessary requests often come from finance people without enough front-line business knowledge, too afraid to stick their necks out and make a roughly right estimate themselves. Another reason for unnecessary forecasting is "control" managers who ask for much more than they need, understand, or can do anything about. It is about requiring a million details just in case someone above should ask. More managers should have the guts to reply that "I don't have that information, but I can get hold of it if really needed."

What about relative benchmarking KPIs and forecasting? Even if own performance can be forecasted, how do we know how our peers will perform? Is this a problem? Not necessarily. It simply means that the main focus should be on trying to perform as well as possible and make forecasts on that. From time to time peer performance is available. If lagging behind, the result is hopefully an extra effort. And that is exactly what we want. The goal is good performance; a forecast is just something to help achieve this.

Some of you might have waited for a description of a rolling forecast process at Statoil. In fact, we did not implement what has now become quite a common solution. The initial reason for not taking this step was simply that we felt we had enough on the plate when we started out in 2005. We were, however, waiting for a natural opening to launch also this part. We are glad we waited, as we later discovered that rolling forecasting wasn't the right solution for us. In 2010 we instead introduced what we called "dynamic forecasting." More about that later!

People@Statoil—My or Our Performance Goals

The very first words in the Statoil Book read as follows: "At Statoil, *how* we deliver is just as important as *what* we deliver."

Ambition to Action defines, directly or indirectly, the "what": business or *delivery* goals for everybody in the company. (See Exhibit 4.11.) When a management team together has developed an Ambition to Action, they have also defined the delivery goals that the manager is accountable for. There is no second, private negotiation leading to a set of different delivery goals, as often was the case before. Such a double set of goals would completely undermine the credibility of Ambition to Action, even if the actual differences should be small. What kind of motivation and commitment does a manager create when rallying the team around common goals in Ambition to Action while everybody knows there is a private and secret piece of paper in the back pocket that says something else? If a bonus is involved, it

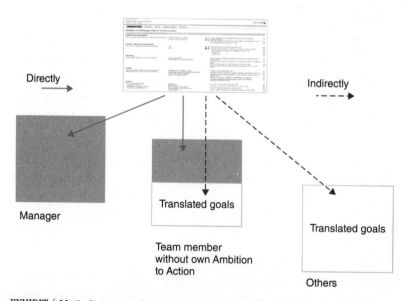

EXHIBIT 4.11 Delivery goals are based on Ambition to Action—directly or indirectly.

makes it even worse. Again, *transparency* is key. There might be exceptions where sensitive business or organizational goals can't be shared, but the general rule is transparency.

If you are a member of a management team with an Ambition to Action, but do not have your own, your delivery goals are sourced from that Ambition to Action. Some take it all: "As a team member I have a collective responsibility for us delivering." Others pick from strategic objectives, KPI targets or actions, or they translate and personalize. For those farther away from the nearest Ambition to Action, there is less direct copying and more personal translation.

Back to the Statoil Book. "How we deliver" is about values and behaviors. The purpose is to ensure that values and leadership principles are alive and applied when delivering on Ambition to Action. Behavior goals are based on the values most critical to Ambition to Action delivery, with emphasis on those with the largest improvement potential. If a team is facing a major change effort, behavior goals might, for instance, address involvement, communication, and motivation. We want to *activate* our values and leadership principles. They are all far too important to be left as well-intended words in the Statoil Book.

Not everyone fully understands the reason for the strong emphasis on values; they believe it is all about cozy "hugging and kissing." There is, however, a solid business reason behind this. If we want to keep our license to operate in an environment with increasingly higher expectations toward business and corporations, then we cannot ignore values and behaviors. CEO Helge Lund had a clear message when he started: Two things can break the back of this company—a serious integrity violation or a serious accident. The list of companies that are no longer with us due to integrity violations is longer than the list of those disappearing due to accidents. To make sure everybody understood that he was dead serious, he put the weighting between the *what* and the *how* to 50/50, driving promotion, base pay, and bonus. It was a brave decision, as not too many other companies have done something similar. On the other hand, it was an obvious decision. How can we say that we are trying to be a values-based company, if values are completely absent in our management process? That would have been a pretty big gap between what we say and what we do.

Some find it hard to set good behavior goals. I agree, I often struggle myself. Still, the 50/50 message is strong and something most people highly appreciate.

Goals can be set either as individual or team goals in the People@Statoil system. This is linked to MIS, so Ambition to Action can be copied, either fully or partly. It is possible to set also team behavior goals. Both delivery and behavior goals can be set as "open" for anyone to see. Goals can also be changed dynamically, although the appraisal dialogue still takes place on an annual rhythm. This increased focus on "Team, Transparency and Dynamics" was introduced when HR changed the People@Statoil IT platform in 2013. The inspiration actually came from Ambition to Action, where these have been key principles since day one. As part of that system change, Finance and HR again joined forces to design an even more integrated Statoil Performance Process, which we will return to later in this chapter.

Dynamic Resource Allocation

There is no doubt that what Statoil managers find the most difficult in Ambition to Action is to manage costs without a traditional budget. Cost budgets are definitely much easier, if that is the goal. But it isn't! The goal is an *optimal use of scarce resources,* and we need something much more effective than the annual, preallocated, and detailed cost budget. On the search for something better, many immediately start hunting for new KPIs or other tools and processes to replace the budget. We need to do that as well, but installing the most sophisticated Beyond Budgeting model is no guarantee whatsoever for success unless something else also is in place. There has to be a foundation of strong values and a responsible mindset. We need to foster a *cost-conscious* culture where *frugality* saturates every decision made. The better job we do here, the fewer tools and regulations are needed (Exhibit 4.12).

The mindset we need to move away from is the one expressed by "Do I have a budget for this?" as the main and sometimes the only question asked when a decision with cost implications shall be made. The answer is typically *yes* if there is budget money available; otherwise, it is *no*. I know that decision-making in a budget regime is somewhat more sophisticated, but there is still a big core of truth in this observation.

Instead we want people to ask, "Is this the right thing to do? What is good enough? How is this creating value? Is this within my execution framework?" If in doubt, a good test is to imagine that the answer was yes and the money was spent. If someone

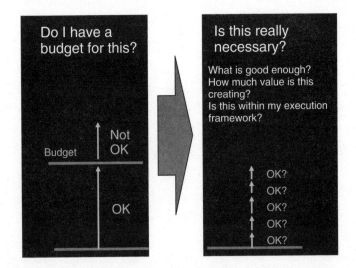

EXHIBIT 4.12 The Mindset Required—Cost-Conscious from the First Cent

later questions your decision, how comfortable will you be in defending it? If not, think again, or discuss with someone. Our ethics policy recommends the same kind of test when facing ethical dilemmas.

We want these questions to be asked all the time and on every cent spent. Such questions are heard also in a budget regime, but mainly in November and December and seldom in January and February. I know why. In the beginning of the year the budget bag is full. No worries! Toward the end, the bottom is visible as the bag is almost empty. Then, at least some cost consciousness emerges, but too little and too late.

There is an interesting parallel here to safety performance. Safety is extremely important in our business. In the early Statoil years, the focus was very much on the technical safeguarding of our operations. We did a good job, but we still had too many incidents and accidents. The root cause often turned out to be people's behaviors, circumventing technical barriers consciously or unconsciously. It was therefore decided to refocus our efforts. A massive Colleague Program was for instance launched, focusing on mindsets and behaviors. Slowly, it started to pay off. Today, the "Serious Incident Frequency" KPI (incidents per million hours worked) is now at 0.5, an unthinkable level back then when we thought a frequency of three or four was pretty good. Today, it is not only *accepted* but also *expected* to speak up if you see a colleague doing something unsafe.

We are aiming for exactly the same mindset on cost consciousness. We are not there yet. The social barrier for speaking up against unwise or stupid spending is still higher than what it is on safety. One day, however...!

A cost conscious mindset is *necessary,* but not always *sufficient*. At Statoil, more is needed, given our size and the capital intensity of the business. We do not believe we can secure the optimal use of scarce resources through the right mindset only, although there are definitely organizations where this is the case. We have therefore established a toolbox of alternative mechanisms. These tools fall in two categories: those applied for larger projects and capital investments and those applied for other costs like operating cost, administrative cost, and similar. Fortunately, the bigger the money involved, the easier it is.

Let us start with the last category, the most difficult one. What we want is a *dynamic* allocation of resources that is as *self-regulating* as possible. What we don't want is the detailed budget preallocation, where all units are given a bag of money divided into detailed cost items: salary, overtime, travel, consultants, and all the other cost types in the chart of accounts, often further divided into monthly budgets. This is what creates the millions of preallocated bags in big organizations. It should not be necessary to repeat why this is a problem. Exhibit 4.13 shows our alternatives to this outdated way of managing cost.

Starting from the left, the options the organization has available are:

- A *burn rate guidance* or an overall frame. There is still a number, but it says "around 1,000" and not "1,003.4" with a lot of smaller bags inside. This alternative is about guidance to avoid teams feeling completely in the dark about which activity level to operate within. The number can also reflect expected affordability if the income side is predictable. Within this overall constraint, the unit has full flexibility to act and optimize. The "1,000" doesn't have to be an annual number; it can also be a 12-month average target, valid until there is a need to change it, up or down. Dropping the details within the total number is definitely a step in the right direction. Some of the budget problems may still remain unsolved. If there is a lot of uncertainty ahead and if the revenue side is unpredictable, how do we know that 1,000 is the right number? Maybe it should be 800? Or 1,200?

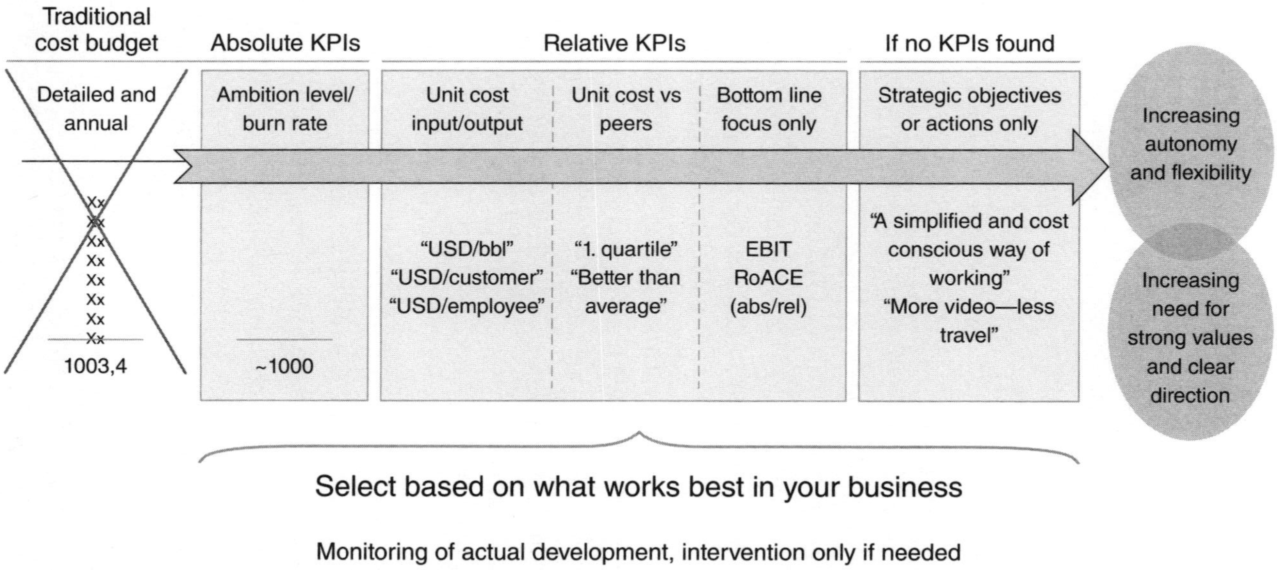

EXHIBIT 4.13 Dynamic Resource Allocation Tools

- This can be solved by moving from absolute to *relative* KPIs. A *unit cost* target is more flexible than an absolute target. The higher the output, the more can be spent on input, and vice versa. It is a self-regulating mechanism.
- *Unit cost benchmarking* is even more self-regulating. Targets can be set as "better than average," "first quartile," etc. Everybody tries to improve while changes in assumptions that affect all peers are neutralized, such as market fluctuations in demand or raw material prices.
- It is also possible to operate without cost KPIs at all, and instead rely on the self-regulating effect of a challenging *bottom-line target* on such as operating profit or RoACE, absolute or relative. You can spend more if you earn more, and vice versa. Good costs are okay; bad are not.
- Finally, it is possible to manage costs with *no targets* at all. Instead, we rely on the two other dimensions in Ambition to Action. Strategic objectives can, for instance, express what kind of cost mentality we want, such as "We spend company money as if it was our own." Actions can be more concrete: "More video, less travel." This can, of course, be said in combination with some of the above alternatives already discussed.

This is a menu, without one right answer about which alternative a unit should use. It depends on the situation, on the type of business, and also where teams are on their own journey. Some alternatives can also be used in combination. The farther to the right we move, the more dependent we are on a solid value foundation and on strategy and direction being understood and embraced.

In addition, we require that decisions meet our decision criteria and are within established decision authorities (most relevant for larger projects and major new activities) and that we have the necessary financial and organizational capacity.

The financial capacity comes out of our dynamic forecasting. Understanding our organizational capacity is something we still struggle with, as discussed in Chapter 1.

Independent of which menu alternatives are used, we always monitor actual trends and developments, looking at both actual and forecasted costs. If trends look okay, we do nothing. If trends start to move in what might be the wrong direction, we ask the necessary questions. Mostly, there are sound and good business justifications. But there will also be cases where our questions reveal the opposite: managers who unconsciously have lost focus on cost or, worse, consciously abused the autonomy they got.

The model is based on trust, on the belief that the majority of people are mature and can be trusted to spend money wisely. The only thing we know for certain when trust is shown is that someone will abuse it. In Statoil, it has happened and it will happen again. As in so many leadership situations, there is a simple (but wrong) response and a more difficult (but right) one. Simple and wrong is about putting everybody in jail because someone did something wrong. "This trust thing doesn't work! Now it happened again!" It can all be canceled with a simple, sweeping decision. No need to talk to anyone. The right, but also more demanding response is to have that very firm talk with those involved, and let it have the necessary consequences. Trust is not about being soft.

The staff unit I am based in is not a profit center, and thinking in unit-cost terms doesn't make sense. We have therefore operated on the far-right end of the scale for many years. No budget, no target. Costs did not explode. We often found it *more* difficult to spend money without being given a budget. We monitor actual cost trends and also do some simple forecasting. Bigger decisions would be checked with the CFO whom we report to, like for instance arranging a global network conference, which is quite expensive. The decision would be taken based on the need for such a conference and to the extent we felt we could afford it. It should actually not be too difficult for our CFO to trust us on costs. If we can't be trusted to manage our own travel cost, how can we be trusted when we advise and recommend on million- and billion-dollar projects?

Here is our former CFO Torgrim Reitan back in 2010 (he later moved on to head up our U.S. operations):

"We could easily put in place a cost program instructing all business areas to reduce costs by a given number. I believe this would work against our intention of building a cost-conscious culture. If we want to become more fit, a crash diet does not work. It takes a change of lifestyle. I believe Statoil is made up of competent, responsible, and commercially oriented people who will make the right cost decisions. This means always working hard to reduce bad cost while protecting good cost. You know better than me what these are and where they are."

Some would argue that what followed later contradicted these wise words. I disagree, and let me explain why. In 2011, Statoil did an extensive external benchmarking of cost and quality in staff and support functions. We scored very high on quality, but quality has a price tag. We were generally in the higher cost bracket compare to peers. The "dark forces" immediately showed up, blaming our management model. In addition to a high quality level, a main reason was less outsourcing. Many years ago we moved support and transaction-oriented work in Finance, HR, IT, Communication, and Facility Management to our shared service center. For different reasons, the big bulk of this work was still kept in Norway or in other higher cost locations like Houston. Our peers had been much more aggressive in their offshoring of these services to cheaper locations.

The benchmarking led to all functions being asked what it would take to reduce cost in the range of 30 percent. It was not a target, but a hairy ambition to make everyone think out of the box. One of the actions taken was more outsourcing and also more offshoring, for instance in IT. I hope these were the right decisions, and that the more invisible costs of coordination do not eat up the very visible savings. Luckily, we started out well before the oil price crash, when the need for such actions became even more pressing.

Another consequence was that most functions, including ours, introduced a "burn-rate guidance" in line with what we long had said in the Statoil Book:

> Cost targets are established if and when necessary. These are primarily set using relative KPIs (unit cost or league tables). Absolute cost targets may be set if a significant change in activity and cost levels is required, but must be set at the overall rather than the detailed level to secure the necessary flexibility. Even if no cost targets are set, both actual and forecasted cost trends are monitored and corrective measures taken as required. All entities should continuously challenge their own efficiency, level of activity and resource use.

So right now there is a number, but no details. No travel budget or similar. Still, this would not be the last time those not understanding our management model would say, "So much for Beyond Budgeting"!

A few years later our forecasts showed expected investment levels ahead never before seen in Statoil's history. It was partly a luxury problem. We had a huge and great portfolio of projects, new discoveries ready to be developed and put in production. But those high numbers were also the result of a cost explosion in the industry, on everything from the drilling rigs we rent to the services we buy. We all knew there was neither financial nor organizational capacity to execute all those projects. The CEO and CFO urged the Business Areas to review their investment plans. They all came back with somewhat lower forecasts, but capacity was still an issue. After a few more rounds several

Business Areas simply asked to be given a number based on what Statoil could afford. Both the CEO and CFO hesitated, even if they knew roughly what the total Statoil number needed to be. They were simply uncertain about the right allocation of that investment capacity between Business Areas. For a period there was almost a tug of war. Who would blink first? In the end they gave up, and a number per Business Area came on the table, under the condition that it would be kept at that level. This was no preapproval of specific projects, which would still take place in the Capital Value Process, described later. Such a burn-rate guidance is in line with our model, but my concern was a creeping distribution of those numbers below Business Area level. Exploration wanted, for instance, to take their number one level down to Business Clusters. We strongly advised against, but we couldn't veto it. You can't get rid of command and control through command and control. Half a year later they gave up. There was simply too many dynamics requiring a constant reallocation of capital between clusters.

How we talk and the words we use are important. "Frame" was often used when Business Area investment constraints first were introduced. Later, Eldar started to use "level" to underline that the number on the table was "in the range of" and no preallocation of funds and something subject to change at any time if needed.

Let us stay with Exploration and take a look at how this unit is managing its costs. It is a good example of combining tools on the cost management menu. Also, here there is a "level" or burn-rate guidance, currently around 3 bn USD. It is a capacity constraint, but less of a performance indicator. The main KPIs for managing this business are a volume KPI, a unit cost KPI, and a value creation KPI. The first one is about how much we need to discover of new oil and gas reserves in order to replace more than produced in order to grow. The unit cost KPI is about efficiency and how much it on average should cost to find a new barrel. Value creation addresses how much value each new barrel brings to the company. Performance is ultimately about how much value Exploration creates at an activity level of around 3 bn. USD. There is a huge performance difference between finding 300 million barrels at 10 USD/per barrel and finding 600 million at 5 USD, although both outcomes involve the same spending level.

In addition, all project decisions taken must be within established decision authorities and meet the corporate decision criteria. Finally, all big decisions are pressure tested by the Exploration Arena, an independent body that calls on relevant competence from across the company to assist in structured project reviews as projects pass predefined decision gates. These reviews address project risks from many angles: geological, technical, HSE, finance, HR, and political risk. The Arena has no decision authority, but few seek final approval of their project with a negative Arena recommendation. Similar arenas exist for investment projects and for information technology projects.

Let us close this section with what Beyond Budgeting means for investment management and capital projects, the "easiest part" as mentioned earlier. Project price tags can easily reach billions of dollars. "Johan Sverdrup," our biggest project right now, located in the North Sea just outside of our headquarters in Stavanger, will cost around 14 bn USD to develop.

Simplified, the process can be described as follows. Again, there is no annual preapproval of all projects. Approvals take place in our Capital Value Process, where projects are matured through decision gates. At "decision gate 3" the final decision is made. If yes, resources are allocated. A project can always be forwarded for DG3 approval. The bank is open 12 months a year. How high up it needs to go is regulated by an authority schedule. Yes or no depends on two things. First, does it meet our strategic, operational, and financial decision criteria?

Second, can we afford it? The answer is found in our latest forecasts showing free investment capacity within our self-imposed burn-rate guidance, which right now is around 15–16 bn USD annually.

What about portfolio optimization and project prioritization? How do we know, when we say yes to a project today, that there won't be a better opportunity popping up tomorrow? This dilemma will always be with us, but we are definitely not solving it by turning prioritization into an annual stunt. On the contrary, the longer we can wait, the better information we have, not just about the project itself, but also about our capacity to execute it.

The conflict between targets, forecasts, and resource allocation is present also in projects. Therefore, we no longer have only *one* single "budget" number approved. Instead, we have separated, and operate with three numbers also here:

1. The *project estimate* (e.g. 1,000) is the expected cost estimate used in the profitability analysis of the project. Being merely a forecast, this number will continue to live throughout the project.
2. The more ambitious *target cost* (e.g. 900) is the cost level the project team aims for.
3. The *resource allocation estimate* (e.g. 1,100) or the mandate to spend is set higher than the 50/50 project estimate, to avoid on average every second project having to come back and ask for more money.

As a consequence, the phrase "project budget" is no longer very meaningful and is slowly (but very slowly) disappearing from our vocabulary.

A final reflection on investments: I have always been puzzled by the fact that we decide on these projects using criteria that we more or less leave behind once we move beyond approval. Projects typically are analyzed and decided as they should be, with a value creation focus and with Net Present Value as a key financial criterion. When approved, the focus narrows. Now it is almost only about *time* and *cost*. The consequence is often no or little room for good costs or more time, even when this would have increased the value of the project. In Statoil's history, value creation and "do-the-right-thing" often won. Unfortunately, media and the external world seemed to understand "budget" and "deadline" only. For them, it was cost overruns and delays, full stop. We lost two great and brave CEOs because of such narrow-minded thinking. The projects that brought them down are today among the highest ranked in the Statoil portfolio. One of them was paid back in less than two years!

It is easy to cut activity levels. It is harder but much more sustainable to change the way we work. This was the background for the Statoil Technical Efficiency Project (STEP) initiative. During 2014 and 2015 this project helped the business areas achieve significant savings across a range of operational areas. The project is now closed but the improvement activities continue through the establishment of a COO (chief operating officer) role. The Lean philosophy is an important part of the way forward.

The increased cost focus, investment constraints, and STEP made some wonder if we now had abandoned Beyond Budgeting. We have spent quite some time reminding people that Beyond Budgeting does not mean that cost is not important, and that the constraints introduced are set at very high level. Some also needed a reminder that Beyond Budgeting is about so much more than cost management. There are actually 11 other principles!

We asked a student from NHH to investigate more thoroughly how line managers felt about the situation. Her master's thesis on the subject had an interesting conclusion. A clear majority said they still experienced that Beyond Budgeting was in good shape. This group also had the best understanding of what Beyond Budgeting is about. The less the understanding, the more likely the response was that the model was abandoned. I could clearly recognize the pattern from my own discussions with people throughout the organization.

Business Follow-Up

Business follow-up is built around monthly reporting and regular business review meetings, typically quarterly. Ambition to Action plays a key role. Many reviews are done live in the MIS system, supported by other sources only when necessary. In addition, a short weekly status report is made, also in MIS, built from business unit level.

A key principle in our business follow-up is "forward looking and action oriented." The KPI status (red/yellow/green) is therefore set by comparing *forecasts* with *targets*, instead of actual versus budget or target year to date. "Green" means forecast better than target, and "Red" the opposite. The purpose is to shift the focus forward, away from the past and from explaining historical variances. This does not mean that we do not focus on our actual figures. It is the comparison to an increasingly outdated year-to-date reference point we have skipped.

This focus triggers one of two questions:

1. If the KPI is green, which risks can jeopardize what looks okay, and how are these risks addressed?
2. If the KPI is red, which actions must be initiated to get back on track?

I must admit I am ambivalent to the use of KPI colors. It works well in teams which mainly see them as a simple way of sharing status with each other. It works less well when perceived as part of a top-down control-and-reward regime, sometimes triggering gaming and unethical behaviors to change reds to greens.

We are back to leadership again. The colors themselves are probably not to be blamed.

Where relevant, the KPI status is reported in rolling windows, typically covering 13 months, so that the current month can be compared with the same month last year. The purpose is to provide better trend reporting than what you get in a January–December picture, which on average is half empty. Compare the graphs in Exhibits 4.14 and 4.15. Which provides better information?

Business reviews do not only focus on KPI status but on the whole Ambition to Action. The strategic objectives stand there as a constant reminder of what we are aiming for longer term, something against which KPI results and actions must be calibrated constantly. Actions are also color-coded; is the action on schedule or expected to deliver the planned outcome? Actions are managed dynamically in the system. Completed ones are closed, ongoing ones are monitored, and new ones are established as necessary. All of this is done by the team owning the Ambition to Action, not by any central staff.

Performance Evaluation and Rewards

A key purpose of Ambition to Action is to provide a broader and richer language for describing and evaluating performance. The old language was quite simple. Good performance was about delivering on the budget, yes or no. Then we introduced KPI scorecards and got a new phrase in the performance vocabulary: "green or red KPI." When we dropped budgets, we were again left with one word, the KPI color. Again, the only qualifications required for evaluating performance were not being colorblind and being able to count the number of red vs. green KPIs.

Ambition to Action has given us a richer and broader performance language. First, evaluation of delivered results is

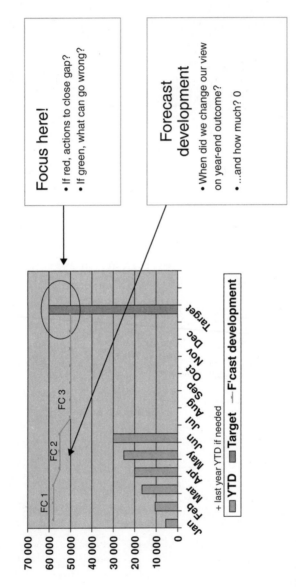

EXHIBIT 4.14 Report Example 1

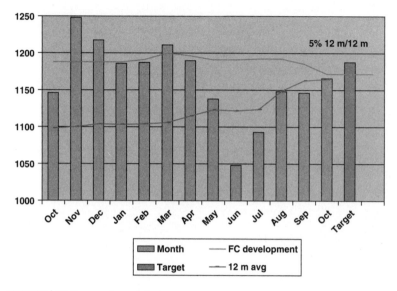

EXHIBIT 4.15 Report Example 2

no longer based on KPIs only, but on the whole Ambition to Action through a holistic assessment. Second, the introduction of behavior with a 50 percent weight provided us with a completely new dimension in our performance language.

Delivery goals are evaluated by *pressure-testing* of delivered results, which initially are measured as KPI results against KPI targets. These are now merely a starting point, not the end point, because KPIs are merely indicators (Exhibit 4.16).

We recommend these five questions to test measured KPI results:

1. *Did delivered results contribute toward the strategic objectives?* If we consider what the KPI was unable to pick up, how does it look? There is normally a lot of hindsight information available. The answer might confirm what the KPI indicated, or reveal a more positive or negative picture.
2. *How ambitious were the targets?* Imagine two teams. One stretched and set themselves an ambitious target, but just

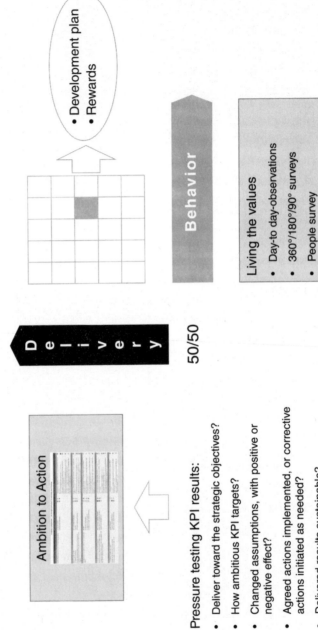

EXHIBIT 4.16 Performance Evaluation from Narrow Measurement to Holistic Assessment

missed. The other lowballed and negotiated and was able to get away with a much lower target, which they hit. We shouldn't punish the first team and reward the second.

3. *Are there changes in assumptions that should be taken into account?* Was there significant tailwind or headwind that had nothing to do with performance? Was there an earthquake in Japan, making it all more difficult? Was there a competitor going bankrupt, making that sales target a piece of cake?

4. *Were agreed or necessary actions taken?* Were actions continuously established and executed as needed?

5. *Are the results sustainable?* Or have there been suboptimization or shortcuts in order to hit the target?

The intention with these questions is not to create a long list of excuses for not delivering. The purpose is to understand relevant background information and then conclude on how much of this should be taken into account. It works both ways; it can just as well downgrade measured results. (See Exhibit 4.16.) There are several information sources available for establishing and evaluating *behavior* goals, like the organizational climate survey, where some of the questions provide direct feedback to individual managers. Day-to-day observations and sound judgment are important supplements. Many of the pressure-testing questions are also applicable when evaluating behavior goals. It is not easy to set and evaluate behavior goals, and we are learning every day. But we are convinced that this is the right thing to do. It wasn't easy when we started with KPIs many years ago, either.

The outcome of the delivery and behavior evaluation results in a score on a 1-to-5 scale in each dimension. The rating is used for next year's individual development plan, for base salary increases, and for individual bonuses. I will come back to the issue of rating, a concept many now are leaving for very good reasons. This discussion is also taking place in Statoil.

In Chapter 1 we discussed the difference between results and performance. The holistic evaluation is about using measured results as a starting point for revealing the true underlying performance.

As we also discussed earlier, combining development, reward, and legal documentation in one process is problematic due to the conflicting purposes, especially between the two first ones. HR is aware of this and is encouraging managers to try to keep these issues apart. The solution should be a much clearer separation, just like we did with the budget. That would enable us to radically improve each one. Feedback and development should not be an annual stunt and could be more peer-based. Colleagues have often a better picture of a person's performance than the manager has. Annual bonuses could be replaced or supplemented with spot bonuses, which are not dangling "do this/get that" carrots. Base pay adjustments could still be an annual exercise but decoupled from feedback and development. Finally, the legal side could be secured by simply issuing the necessary written warnings only when there is a

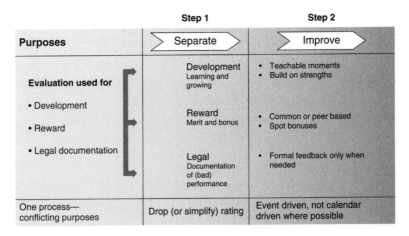

EXHIBIT 4.17 Performance Evaluation—One Process with Three Different Purposes

need for it. These are examples of improvement opportunities available once the three purposes are separated (Exhibit 4.17).

I have already shared my view on individual bonuses. Statoil does have such bonuses, although they are quite modest on both reach and size, at least in Europe. The bonus area is still one of the few areas where we follow mainstream performance management. I can't help thinking back on all the great performance and outstanding achievements in the company when it hit the ground running in 1972, and before individual bonuses were introduced in 1998. The conditions created and levers pulled to motivate during those pioneer years all had something in common; it was all about great leadership! It is, however, important to remember that we have neutralized some of the negative bonus effects. We have broken the fixed performance contract, the mechanical link between target and reward, by using relative KPIs where possible and by introducing the holistic performance evaluation.

There is also the collective bonus scheme for all employees, based on how the company is performing against competition. The maximum bonus potential here is 10 percent. In addition, there is a very popular share savings program, where all employees can buy shares for up to 5 percent of their base salary each year and receive one free share for each one bought. Shares must be kept for a minimum of two years.

In 2008 it was decided to split the collective bonus in two, with up to 5 percent on the group level and up to 5 percent on business area performance. I was skeptical. We have a value-chain-based organizational model in which interdependence and the need for cooperation between business areas are high. I argued that the dissatisfaction among those coming out low would completely outweigh any positive motivation from those coming out high. Fortunately, the mechanism was never used, and after a few years it was quietly abandoned. Today, the discussion about team bonuses is again on the table.

The challenge remains how to fairly reward differently teams who depend on each other.

As we discussed earlier, some managers struggle with the subjective assessment in the holistic performance evaluation. They prefer a clear target number only and no discussions afterwards. Hit or miss. Very simple. It is leadership versus management, once again. But as we discussed earlier, a performance evaluation can never be entirely objective. There will always be subjectivity, and the reason is uncertainty. First, there is the *definition uncertainty*: How well do the chosen KPIs describe performance? How big is the "I"? This uncertainty is constant and with us all the time and requires pressure-testing of measured performance indications, which can only take place afterwards. Already here, total objectivity is lost. Then there is the *target uncertainty*. Target setting is about trying to describe what good performance looks like at some point down the road, for instance at next year-end. The more uncertainty there is, the more difficult it is and the more assumptions we have to make. We are forced to be subjective, whether we like it or not, as we are deciding on which assumptions to go for: prices, exchange rates, market developments, competitor moves. When it is time for evaluation, all this assumption uncertainty is gone. We know whether we were right. We also know if other unexpected events influenced performance. Why on earth should we ignore all these insights just because we want to be 100 percent objective, which isn't possible anyway? (See Exhibit 4.18.)

A Dynamic Ambition to Action

The first edition of this book closed the Statoil chapter with a section called "What Is Next?" The fixed calendar rhythm was seen as one of the main problems. I shared thoughts we had

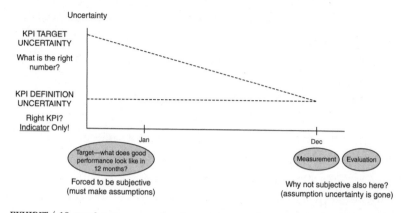

EXHIBIT 4.18 Performance evaluation can never be 100 percent objective.

at the time about making Ambition to Action radically more dynamic, way beyond the dynamic resource allocation already introduced. These were ideas we had already back in 2005. We decided, however, not to pursue them at the time, as we were afraid that these changes on top of everything else would be too much for the Executive Committee, ending with a *no* to it all. With the Hydro merger finally behind us, we picked up the discussion again. In 2010 we went back to the Executive Committee with our proposal. Not only did we get a loud-and-clear *yes*. As we left the room, one of the executives whispered to us: "Closer to a standing ovation you will not come in this room." It was a good day, and time to roll up our sleeves again!

We were actually not that surprised. We didn't expect that great comment, but we had expected a *yes*. Like everyone else, the Executive Committee had become braver along the way. What had been a bit scary in 2005 was no longer so. It had worked, and actually very well.

What we proposed was to introduce *Dynamic Forecasting* and also abandon *annual* versions of Ambition to Action in favor of a more dynamic and event-driven process. Let us start with Dynamic Forecasting.

One of the problems on the "budget problem list" we discussed in Chapter 1 was "The world stops December 31." One consequence is "forecasting against the wall," or *accordion forecasting* as it deserves to be called. During budgeting time in the autumn we want to understand all of next year, 12 months ahead. As we move into next year and pass the first quarter, a nine-month horizon is enough. We can still see till year-end. Midyear, six months is enough, then three months, before we suddenly get interested in 12 months because it is budget time again. When it comes to longer term planning, however, there are no accordion horizons. Here, we find a *rolling* process. It is typically done once a year, and always with the same time horizon of, for instance, 3, 5, or 10 years.

Many companies going Beyond Budgeting solve this inconsistency by introducing *rolling forecasting*. The forecast is typically updated every quarter, and always with the same time horizon of, for instance, five or six quarters. This is definitely much better than accordion forecasting. As you will recall, this was also the solution we went for in Borealis. When we separated target setting, forecasting, and resource allocation in Statoil, we did not change the forecasting rhythm at the same time. For us, the separation was most important. We believed, correctly, that this alone would significantly improve forecasting quality by making it less biased. The intention was to address the rhythm issue at a later stage. Along the way, we began to hesitate whether quarterly rolling forecasting really was the right solution for us.

As mentioned when discussing the rhythm problem, many of the Statoil businesses run on a very different pace with, for instance, oil trading being very different from exploration or production. Why should we force them all into a fixed and common frequency and time horizon? A key purpose in forecasting is to get issues on the radar screen early enough to act. When is the right time to check the screen: at fixed and predefined intervals, or more based on the situation? Does sailing in narrow and busy waters and not at open sea make a difference? And a supertanker definitely needs a larger radar screen than smaller ships, right?

The solution became *Dynamic Forecasting*, with no fixed and predefined frequency or time horizon. Units update their forecasts when events occur or new information becomes available that they deem important enough to justify an update (external forecasting). An event can also be an action taken that will have a forecast impact (internal forecasting). We did not issue any instructions defining exactly what an event is and how big it should be to trigger a forecast update. Actually, we couldn't, even if we would have wanted to. Units, therefore, decide for themselves. What is a big dot on a local radar screen would often be an event that corporate can ignore, but seldom the other way around. We also keep reminding the local businesses that they are not doing forecasting for us at corporate level; they do it for themselves in order to manage their own business.

Some were concerned about having to do more forecasting. Dynamic forecasting does not necessarily mean more *often*; it means at the *right time*. For some, it could actually mean less often. Another benefit is a more even workload, although rolling forecasting also would have helped.

On the input side, forecasting data keeps flowing into our SAP system. On the output side, there are still regular milestones where we tap into the latest forecast to provide data to internal or external stakeholders, such as the Executive Committee, the board, authorities, partners, and others. In addition, there are situations and important events that may trigger unscheduled analysis of financial capacity or the bigger picture. These milestones should not lead to a frenetic rush to update the numbers. The job should be more about doing some final checks and quality controls. It has been fascinating to observe how the expression "tap in" that we invented for this process now has become an established phrase in the Statoil vocabulary.

Let us make a comparison with what happens on the accounting side. We do not stockpile orders, invoices, and payments and register all of them at month-end. We register these continuously, and anyone with a need for more frequently updated information can get it. There is a wealth of information available for us in the system during the month, from order status to cash positions.

Another reason for hesitating on quarterly rolling forecasting was the quarterly "buckets" that forecasting data is put into. For many of our units with a slower pace and longer horizons, quarterly numbers seemed too granular. For most of our units, it works quite well sticking to annual buckets. What is important is *how often* a bucket is updated, and *how many* at a time. As for time horizons, Statoil typically needs to look a minimum of 10 years ahead and sometimes much longer. Some of our fields are producing for 40 years. But why should we force all those with much shorter horizons to fill those outer buckets with forecasting data when they have no need whatsoever for that information themselves? We therefore encourage the levels that need the longer horizon to fill the gap themselves with more generic numbers, using their own knowledge of the business. Again, we can't bring the accounting mindset of precise bottom-up consolidation into a process like this.

Dynamic Forecasting was an important step toward making the entire Ambition to Action more dynamic. Having annual versions where everyone made an almost new one every year was, however, a major obstacle. As discussed, January to December or any other fiscal year period is often an artificial construct from a purely business point of view. Even when there are seasonal variations in a business, the winter season is always cut in two.

"What if we organized ourselves around business cycles instead of calendar cycles in the rest of the Ambition to Action process as well, not only in forecasting? What if we left the calendar year behind at every chance possible? What would our processes look like?" Those were the questions we asked ourselves back in 2010. Here is what we now do:

- Our *strategy* process was already quite continuous and issue driven. *Strategic objectives* can now be updated as needed, when strategy changes so much that new or revised objectives are required.
- *KPIs* can be replaced at any time if strategic objectives change, or if we simply find better ones.
- Even *KPI targets* can be changed if they have lost their meaning by becoming impossible to reach. Such targets don't work. They don't motivate and inspire. They have only one function left: punishment. It could also be the other way around; the target has become too low with no stretch whatsoever. We already had the "target review"; this was about strengthening this mechanism.
- The *target horizon* can vary, depending on the type of business and what we aim to achieve. We want more natural target deadlines, driven by urgency and complexity. The more relative targets we use, the less need there will be for annual targets. "First quarter," "above average," and similar targets do not need to be reset every year.
- *Actions* were already meant to be continuously updated, but more dynamic strategic objectives and KPIs now make this even more obvious and natural.
- *Forecasting* is more continuous and event driven, as described above.

- *Performance evaluation* in People@Statoil is still done on an annual cycle, but it is now easier to change team and individual goals, as described later.

Although teams now are able to in principle change whatever they want whenever they want, it is not an anarchy. We introduced a simple but effective control mechanism. If a change is *big*, approval at one level above is required. If the change is *small*, it is enough to inform to the same level. Big or small, teams need to inform other teams affected by their changes as part of a more continuous coordination. We leave it to teams themselves to sort out with the level above what is big and what is not. This is not something we can or should define from corporate. If someone in one part of the organization ends up with a small/big definition that is different from someone else's, this is no problem as long as it works both places. The MIS system keeps a log of all changes.

As already mentioned, a key principle since day one has been to create alignment between our many Ambition to Action processes more through *translation* than through *cascading,* because heavy top-down cascading easily destroys ownership and motivation. Instead, we want each unit to translate from other relevant Ambitions to Action, like the one above, or further up, or left and right if there are interfaces with other units. If such a translation should go wrong and end up with unacceptable ambition levels or wrong direction, the level above should, of course, intervene. This is not a big problem, however. One reason is transparency. All Ambitions to Action are open and accessible for all employees, except for share price–sensitive information, which we need to restrict access to. There is no place to hide with a stupid Ambition to Action. We have left it to each unit to decide which information needs to be closed to access. Unfortunately, we do see some applying more restrictions than strictly necessary. It is the trust issue again.

The translation approach does not mean that we never cascade. There are situations where top-down cascading is both necessary and appropriate. It should, however, be the exception and not the rule. This makes cascading also more accepted when it takes place.

Leaving annual versions of Ambition to Action had positive effects also in this area. When every unit made a new one every autumn, it was tempting and in some cases almost an invitation to cascade from above. With fewer of these annual start-from-scratch stunts, and with Ambition to Action content now being updated more continuously and organically, massive top-down cascading has become more difficult and also less natural.

Another aspect of cascading in annual stunts was the hunt for the perfect sequencing. Who goes first and who is next? For Finance people with a strong need for structure and control with regard to budgeting and planning, this is an important question. In a complex matrix organization like ours, a perfect sequence is very hard, if not impossible, to design, given all the interfaces. These discussions about "the right order" have now more or less disappeared. Units synchronize and coordinate between themselves in more self-regulating ways, with limited orchestration from corporate. It isn't perfect, but good enough.

The more continuous and self-regulating we can make the whole process, the better. The less we need to do from corporate, the better. This doesn't mean that we abdicate. We support when necessary, and intervene when necessary. But just as in the roundabout, our main job should be more about creating conditions for the business to manage itself and less about managing the business.

There were, however, some concerns about the new principles, especially around the possibility to adjust targets. Would it be abused? We therefore formulated a few questions that we recommend teams to ask themselves when considering changing a target:

- *Does the target still have a motivational effect?* If tougher but still inspiring and motivating, consider keeping it.
- *What is your track record on changing targets?* If it is always about lowering ambitions and never the other way around, that is something to reflect on before doing it once again.
- *Can the holistic performance evaluation be used instead?* Can changed circumstances be handled in the holistic performance evaluation?

There has, however, been little abuse and no explosion in target changes. Most teams stick to their targets. Having the *possibility* to change is still important. It creates comfort around stretching and a feeling of fairness in the process.

Some would argue that the organization needs the imposed discipline of a fixed and regular cycle: "If not, things simply will not happen." I can accept that small children and some adults need the order and the predictability. If this is a major problem in an organization, I see it more as a symptom of something else, as a lack of mature and independent leaders and employees taking the initiative as needed. Is the situation really that bad, or could it be again the trust issue at play here?

Lack of updating discipline might also be a symptom of lack of ownership of the management process itself, which we too often try to compensate for through discipline enforcement instead of addressing the underlying causes. If teams operate their Ambition to Action for themselves more than for others, then updating discipline becomes less of an issue because the root cause problem is removed.

Is the calendar completely eradicated at Statoil? Absolutely not. Everything related to statutory accounting and reporting still runs on monthly, quarterly, and annual cycles. There are also areas where these periods make sense even if we could have chosen differently. Still, we are not as continuous and dynamic as we could and probably should have been. Again, things take time. Our journey to become more dynamic probably resembles a group of horses that have always been chained to a pole and can only walk in a circle. One night, somebody sneaks in and cuts all the chains. Some horses immediately discover what has happened and take off, thrilled about their new freedom. Others take a few cautious steps outside the circle. "Can it really be true?" they ask themselves as more and more steps outside are taken. But there are also horses that continue to walk in the circle as they always have done, even if they know that the chain is gone.

We can't force anyone to take advantage of these new possibilities, and we shouldn't be surprised if it takes time, given how dominant the calendar has been and still is in so many aspects of our lives. We shouldn't become fundamentalists. In the same way as we can't forbid anyone from making budgets, we can't forbid the calendar year. Again, we can't get rid of command and control through command and control.

What Could Be Next?

I keep reminding anyone interested in Beyond Budgeting that implementation is a journey and not a project. The direction is clearer than the destination, if there is one. Thinking back to those early Borealis days, I could already sense something bigger, something more agile and more human. I had, however, no idea what that would mean in Statoil 20 years later. Thinking ahead, I am convinced that what we do 10 years from now will be both different and better than what we do today. In some areas I feel rather certain about what might be next. In other areas visions are more blurred.

When in the first edition I described what could be next at that time, I was convinced that it was just a question of time before we had a more dynamic Ambition to Action, including Dynamic Forecasting, up and running. I feel the same now about the integration of performance and risk management, which is high on our agenda right now.

Statoil has long been in the forefront of developing enterprise risk management, just like the company has been ahead of many on performance management. The two functions, however, operated quite separately. Although both were based in the CFO organization, it was two different units that were also located separately. It had long been clear for both that there were important links and interfaces between the two. This was even more evident and obvious for all frontline teams where risk and performance sit together on the management table every day.

In 2011 the two corporate functions merged, and Risk also moved in with us. This significantly strengthened the dialogue between us. It became even more obvious that we needed to think more in terms of one than two processes. We got the same message from many line managers. At the same time we started working on upgrading the system solution behind MIS. We decided to use this opportunity to try to integrate risk management into Ambition to Action.

Risk management is not only about identifying and quantifying risk. It is just as much about identifying and executing mitigating actions, or *risk-induced* actions. These are currently kept and followed up in separate risk systems. Actions have long been an important part of Ambition to Action. Their purpose was to secure that we deliver on Strategic Objectives and KPI targets, and could therefore be called *target-induced* actions. We saw, however, many overlaps between the two types of actions. Some were actually triggered by both risk and targets. Another observation was that a too-narrow KPI focus often represented a risk in itself, by causing sub-optimizing and risk-increasing behaviors among managers.

The need for something more integrated was obvious. We therefore designed a new Ambition to Action template, letting the two principal objectives of our business become more visible: *avoiding incidents* and *creating sustainable value*. We added a risk column after strategic objectives, letting risk also drive actions. The plan is to also move our risk maps and risk radars into MIS. Maybe we will have this up and running even before this book is published.

Now to another integration effort, this time toward HR and the People@Statoil process. As I will elaborate on later, Finance and HR in Statoil have for many years worked closely together in designing an integrated process connecting Ambition to Action and People@Statoil. Still, there were two different systems that spoke together but were separate. As mentioned, the MIS system needs upgrading. HR was in the same situation, as the tailor-made People@Statoil SAP solution turned out to be quite cumbersome and also expensive to operate.

We both saw this as an opportunity for a much stronger integration, maybe even with one common system solution, supporting a truly seamless process with no traces of the two of us being organized in separate functions. We did not start by going system-hunting; we started with spending a lot of time together designing what such a truly seamless process could look like. We agreed it would not be called a performance *management* process. We named it *The Statoil Performance Process*.

We saw a number of improvement opportunities. First, we wanted the very first words in the Statoil Book to be more visible in the process: "At Statoil, the way we deliver is as important as what we deliver." This emphasis on *how* and not only *what* is, in our current process picture, only visible when we arrive at performance evaluation.

We also wanted to address important inconsistencies between Ambition to Action and People@Statoil related to *team, transparency,* and *dynamics.* Ambition to Action is per definition about teams and their business deliveries. People@Statoil was almost solely about individuals and their goals and development. Ambition to Action is highly transparent, with almost everything open and accessible for all employees. People@Statoil information was only accessible to the employee and the manager in addition to HR. Finally, People@Statoil was a strictly calendar-driven process, with no or very limited possibilities for changing anything during the year. We all agreed that more team transparency and dynamics was desirable also in People@Statoil.

As with Risk, People@Statoil operates with actions. Delivery and behavior goals were typically formulated as actions, so were short- and longer-term development goals. We saw an opportunity for developing a more generic action term, covering both these types of actions and actions from Ambition to Action and Risk. (See Exhibit 4.19.)

We were all excited about the result, which we felt illustrated the totality of our leadership and management thinking in Statoil in a much better way. Then reality hit. A new IT strategy recommended off-the-shelf solutions instead of more costly

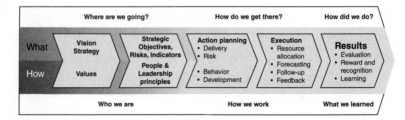

EXHIBIT 4.19 The Statoil Performance Process

in-house developed solutions. We started looking for software packages that could support such a process. We found nothing. It was actually not a big surprise. We had long suspected that our thinking was way ahead of software suppliers. They can provide great stuff, but it is either in the enterprise management area or in the HR area. No one seemed to think much about integration across the two as we did.

HR was in more of a hurry for a system replacement than we were. Shortly after they went for SuccessFactors, a product in the SAP family. Fortunately, they were able to implement most of our thinking around team, transparency, and dynamics, although we had hoped for something even more integrated. Personally, I have not given up. I am convinced that we one day will have a system solution that can handle what we designed.

The Finance/HR interface is important. So is the interface between Finance and the new COO (chief operating officer) organization, including the team working with operational performance analyses and the "Management System" team, responsible for work process requirements.

A few years ago it was concluded that these requirements had become too extensive, and that the process owner/line matrix was challenging. One problem was dilution of line accountability when global process owner set operational standards. There was a need for something that would strengthen both line empowerment and accountability. It was therefore decided to limit global and common requirements to a minimum by establishing a much leaner set of "corporate fundamentals." The business areas were given the freedom to define and develop what was needed in addition. The process owner role was also dissolved, and the responsibility moved to the line.

Earlier in this chapter we looked at a key illustration in the Statoil Book, "The Execution Framework" (Exhibit 4.3). This picture was developed several years ago to illustrate the new

boundaries around the increased empowerment that had been
introduced. The two walls we mainly focused on at that time
were those at the left and right, Ambition to Action and financial
decision authorities.

The management system simplification that followed later
used exactly the same figure to illustrate the kind of further
empowerment and "bigger room to move" that now was
pursued. This time, the focus was on simplification and decen-
tralization of work process requirements, a wall that we back
then had found hard to move in any significant way. Decision
authorities were also addressed, but now more in operational
than in financial terms, as we had focused on. This initiative
complemented very well what had been achieved earlier, making the "room to act and perform" even bigger (Exhibit 4.20).

It could, of course, be argued that such a simplification of
work process requirements should have been an integrated part
of the Beyond Budgeting implementation from day one. I don't,
however, believe that the company was ready for these steps

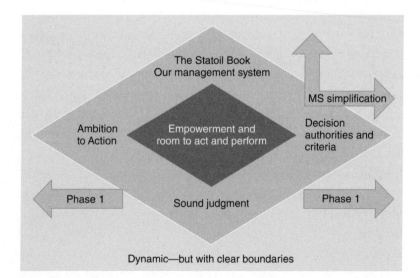

EXHIBIT 4.20 Expanding the Room to Act and Perform

back in 2005. For me, this is another example of the evolving journey we are on. Also, it doesn't matter whether the umbrella is called Beyond Budgeting or something else. The main thing is that things are moving in the right direction, inspired by a shared vision of more autonomy and agility.

The Management System team has historically focused more on documenting and administering work requirements with a special emphasis on safety. I find their new direction and their more holistic approach very promising, and I look forward to working more with this team. The same goes for the Lean initiative that is being launched, which I also look forward to following.

Target setting is another area that needs to be addressed. I firmly believe there are too many targets around. We are too often on autopilot: "If there is a KPI, there has to be a target." This is not true. When we have good strategic objectives providing direction, and when we know roughly what good looks like, it isn't always necessary to spell it out further with decimal-laden targets. As discussed earlier, what we want to achieve is the best possible performance, given the circumstances. Setting targets is not the only way to achieve this, and often not the best way.

A few years ago, my colleagues, Arvid Hollevik and Toralf Rugland, developed a great operational dashboard as a supplement to the Operations perspective in Ambition to Action. Here, they made a very conscious decision not to allow for any place to enter targets. They wanted the system to be used for *learning*, not for *control*.

Many years ago, before I started to reflect on this issue, I attended a conference where the CFO in Handelsbanken Norway gave a presentation of their management model. The slides were in Norwegian. On one of them I noticed something that had to be a typo. It said *målestyring*, or "management by measurements." I had expected to see *målstyring*, or "management by objectives (or targets)." The additional *e* was no typo. As we know, Handelsbanken doesn't set targets. But they do measure in order to compare and to ensure that things are moving in the right direction.

I hope to see Statoil moving in this direction, too, with fewer targets than what we have today. There is, of course, a big difference between targets set for you and those you set for yourself. I am less concerned about the latter, as they cause much less damage. Still, we should aim for more *målestyring* and less *målstyring*. If we in addition could kick out the individual bonus, I might be satisfied. Or maybe not. There is always a better way!

Finance and HR: Time for a New Partnership?

Finance and HR are traditionally not the best of friends in companies. Having worked in both functions, I know too well how they talk about each other. It is not very nice, either way. They talk a lot *about* each other but not much *with* each other; they hardly communicate, and when they do they seldom understand each other. Some might see this somewhat hostile relationship as nothing but an innocent and given reality in company life. The consequences can, however, be serious. When HR preaches leadership while Finance pushes management, and the two point in completely different directions, the contradicting messages undermine each other and confuse the organization. Many HR people appreciate and preach the importance of autonomy, trust, and transparency. The problem is that they seldom seem to make a reality check against actual management processes in the organization. Budgeting is a prime example. The HR messages become hollow and theoretical. Everybody knows the rules of the game and what really counts. The hard finance processes almost always win over the more fragile but well-intended HR messages when the two collide.

This story from Borealis illustrates how differently Finance and HR is viewed both by managers and by themselves. Shortly after I had moved to HR, Borealis entered into merger discussions with a large European competitor. Such deals are typically preceded by a "due diligence" phase, where the parties investigate each other's financial situation to avoid any surprises. The main reason why mergers and acquisitions fail is, however, not financial surprises. The main reason is culture, or lack of cultural fit. I therefore proposed that we also should do a *cultural due diligence* in order to understand where the cultural challenges would be, so that these could be addressed and prepared for. My proposal raised a number of questions, both in Finance, among managers, and even among some in HR. This was something no one had heard of and many couldn't understand the need for. I insisted, and we did the survey, using an external provider who applied Hofstede's culture framework. The results revealed quite compatible cultures, but still with more differences than expected. Soon after, however, the merger discussion was closed. I am still convinced that the results would have been very useful for us in an integration process. To my knowledge, doing a cultural due diligence is just as unusual today as it was 20 years ago.

Becoming a "business partner" has long been high on the HR agenda. The ambition is fair enough, although one could ask how many partners business really needs. In most companies, Finance is already at the table, with loads of numbers and measurements. HR should, however, be careful in believing this is what will secure them a place, given the warnings about the limitations of measurement discussed earlier. It is almost as if Finance is meeting HR in the doorway: HR on the way *in* but Finance on the way *out* of the measurement room because it is too small. Maybe HR simply needs this detour to fully appreciate Einstein's wise words about counting.

Historically, the two functions have had very separate responsibilities and few interfaces. The Finance history is about statutory accounting, taxes, cash management, and so on. HR's legacy is recruitment, employment contracts, union relations, welfare, pensions, and the like.

This is changing. In both functions, transactional tasks are being moved over to shared service centers, allowing for more focus on a process that has been growing into perhaps the most important one in both functions: *performance management.* The problem is the Berlin Wall that obstructs a process that must run seamlessly all the way from Strategy and Finance into HR territory. I believe we are reaching a point where Finance and HR should join forces around a common process in a much stronger and more formal way, as illustrated in the Statoil Performance Process. There are three reasons for this: The organization and the process need it. Finance needs it. HR needs it.

I will elaborate on all three when discussing implementation in Chapter 6, because involving HR has been one of my very positive implementation experiences. In Statoil, Finance and HR are working much more closely together than what is normally the case. It has not always been like this. Although the two functions are located close to each other at the headquarters, the level of cooperation and mutual respect used to be similar to that found in most companies: not much to write home about.

Direction and business targets were formulated in a strategy- and finance-driven process. When it was time for individual goals, HR took over, sometimes starting almost over again instead of building on what already had been done. The HR chapter in the annual business plan was often a last-minute effort, with great words but varying substance and few implementation thoughts behind it all. I hope my good friends in HR do not feel I am being too hard, but this is how I recall it. Finance and top management were, however, as much to blame as HR.

Most of this is now history. The reason is twofold. First, CEO Helge Lund was crystal clear when he joined on his intentions of lifting HR and people and organization issues high up on the business agenda. Second, a Finance–HR channel was opened. I dare to take at least some credit. Heading up HR in Borealis radically changed my view on this function and on the formidable potential available for both functions in a stronger cooperation. I spent many hours in the HR corridors in Statoil when returning from Borealis. Perhaps some were skeptical, but most were curious about this finance guy familiar with their own language and being so interested in their own issues. Whatever the reason, today there is a much better climate and a clear recognition in both functions that stronger cooperation is the only way forward.

I hope and believe this cooperation will grow even stronger in the years to come. Personally, I have a dream about this common ground one day developing into something even firmer. Could we foresee a new function, with people from both camps responsible for the entire performance process (Exhibit 4.21)? I would not be surprised to see a number of

	Yesterday	Today	Tomorrow?
HR	Transactions administration People & leadership	People & leadership Performance management	
			Performance—people, leadership, and business
FINANCE	Transactions administration Business management	Performance management Business management	
SHARED SERVICES		Transactions administration	Transactions administration

EXHIBIT 4.21 Performance—a Growing HR/Finance Interface

strategy people knocking on that door—and also some IT colleagues understanding the power of Agile. What a great place to work that would be. Count me in!

The Beyond Budgeting Research Program

In 2008, the Norwegian School of Economics (NHH) embarked on a major Beyond Budgeting research program, with Statoil as a key sponsor. CEO Helge Lund opened the program. "What we are trying to achieve is increased autonomy for managers and employees, a more dynamic management model, and less gaming around key processes in the company," he said in his opening speech. As mentioned earlier, he also revealed his initial hesitation about getting "one more thing on the to-do-list." There were no regrets to be heard that day—on the contrary.

Professor Trond Bjørnenak followed and described how academia typically is slow in discovering new trends and ideas, and how their focus typically is on describing these long after they have happened: "This time, it will be different. This time we are coming in early, ready to study the development of these very exciting ideas."

Professor Katarina Kaarbøe has been heading up the project, and she presented one of her key research questions: "A part of the research will be dedicated to studying how the new management system creates learning within the organization. Is it perceived as a tool to create learning or more as a new control system?" She mobilized an international team of researchers and students. We gave them free access to the Statoil organization. Our only requirement was that the team should have a broad composition. Kaarbøe is based at the Institute of Accounting, Auditing and Law, but she engaged colleagues from Strategy and Management and also researchers with a strong leadership and organizational behavior focus. The team has over the years met for several workshops and has produced a number of papers and case studies, not only on Statoil but also on other companies. In 2013, the project work resulted in the book, *Managing in Dynamic Business Environments—Between Control and Autonomy.*

One of many useful activities for us has been all the master's theses written about different aspects of the Statoil implementation. Sometimes we proposed the topic; sometimes it came from the students themselves. I am really impressed with the quality of these papers (especially compared to the rubbish I produced in my own 1983 "thesis"). It has been amazing to observe how our managers opened up in these interviews, providing us with very clear and unfiltered messages about the situation. Although we normally were not surprised about findings and conclusions, they gave us very useful verification on what the real issues and challenges were. If we or our internal audit guys had done the same interviews, I am convinced we would have heard much more polished stories.

The cooperation with NHH continued through the FOCUS program, where a number of other Norwegian companies participated. This program included research topics like "dynamic control systems" and "leading knowledge workers." FOCUS was followed by a program that will study the effects of the management system simplifications that we introduced in 2016.

It has been a great experience to be observed from the outside by such wise people, bringing new perspectives and valuable knowledge to all of us working inside of our own implementations for so long. I believe that academia also needs these interactions. Hopefully, there has been learning both ways.

How Are We Doing?

Everything discussed in this chapter, whether implemented or ahead of us, has only one purpose: to improve the performance of the company. That point should be pretty obvious, but it is easy to become blinded by all the bells and whistles in our management processes and forget the underlying reason for it all. Russel L. Ackoff used a wonderful metaphor in an article in *Wharton* magazine back in 1977. He compared all the efforts put into planning and budgeting in companies with a ritual rain dance, where finance functions seem more interested in improving the quality of the dance than on having any impact on the weather. We should ask ourselves the same question: Does it work, or is it just better singing and dancing? Are we performing better?

The question is just as difficult to answer as it is fair to ask. To be honest, we do not fully know, although we have some very positive indications. We have probably not been on this journey long enough to draw any final conclusions. It is changes in leadership behavior that yield the largest benefits, not the process changes, whose main purpose is to drive these leadership changes. Sustainable change in leadership behavior does not and shall not happen overnight. We know, however, that we have a better management process. We have solved much (but not yet all) of the quality and efficiency problems. We set better targets and make better forecasts, and we have a more effective resource allocation. We spend less time on number crunching and historical variance explanations. All of this indirectly supports better performance, but it is hard to track it directly back to the bottom line. If we define performance in relative terms (as we do), then our main challenge is about holding the fort, as we have been performing pretty well against the competition for many years on growth, profitability, and value creation.

We did not spend much time trying to prove the business case for our Beyond Budgeting journey. There are some things we should do simply because we know it is right. I seldom hear the bottom-line effect of improving ethical or safety standards being questioned, simply because we know those effects exist, although the contribution often is about prevention of negative effects. As we say in the oil business, if you think safety is expensive, try an accident. The same is true for ethics.

We are also scoring high on transparency. Transparency International keeps ranking Statoil among the most transparent listed companies in the world. Corporate Knights, who rates companies on sustainability, just ranked Statoil as number four globally and number one in our business. On Fortune 500, we some time ago came out as number one on social responsibility and as number seven on innovation, again across all businesses.

The ultimate judge is the Statoil organization. All the positive feedback we get here is what really counts and is what gives us the energy to climb that next hilltop. At the same time, we are careful with too much victorious celebration. We are still implementing. There are still people in the company who do not believe in the model. We still see managers paying lip service to the new principles. Those are more dangerous than the openly critical ones, with whom you at least can have a discussion. And there are still those who claim that this is all nice theory, because they have not seen much change in their own manager's behavior. So there are still many hilltops to climb.

When we started out in 2005, we did not position the case for change and our proposals as a radical organizational turnaround like Handelsbanken did in 1970. Our problem description and proposed solutions mainly addressed quality and efficiency problems and the obvious consequences: replacing traditional budgeting with better processes. For most people in the company, this was still seen as a radical step. Since then, our focus and agenda have broadened. The budget discussion is still there, but much less heated than in the early days and now much more about understanding and improving than about protesting and rejecting. The leadership implications are emerging as a much more natural part of the model. When today we are invited into management teams, we always position Ambition to Action as a leadership philosophy as much as a management process.

The leadership messages resonate well in the organization. Many of the Beyond Budgeting leadership principles are actually quite obvious for us, a young company born and raised in a Scandinavian culture. The power distance in the company is short. The actual distance has always been shorter than what it might look like on the organization chart. Hearing the CEO addressed by his first name is as natural as seeing him without a tie. The value orientation has always been strong, which is seen in the intensity of discussions when value statements have been updated. The score on the annual employee survey question asking if people are "proud of the company and would recommend Statoil as an employer to friends and family" has consistently been high. The same goes for whether you "have the necessary influence over your own job." Our local autonomy has always been higher than that of our competitors. At least, that is what people tell us when they join us from these companies. Some might say it has been too high during heated discussions about harmonization of local back-office processes, which has little to do with the local business freedom Beyond Budgeting advocates. Innovation and challenge has been the bread and butter of the company. The transparency mindset has been there all along, and it is now supported by new and better information systems such as MIS and others. The company has a long tradition of working through processes and networks that runs across the formal organization chart.

Some people will claim that the characteristics I have just described were even stronger in earlier days. This is probably true and not any nostalgia trip. Something did happen along the way. Some of it has, of course, to do with size. The company is much larger, more complex, and more international today than it was in the 1970s and 1980s. But much also has to do with strong influences on management and leadership, especially from the United States. These have come dressed both as leadership philosophies and as tools and processes. There has been great stuff in both categories, but also the opposite. The Scandinavian culture has been strong enough to resist many of the more questionable leadership influences, but the armor has been thinner on the tools and process side. Maybe the reasoning has been that here, even though we could see potential negative side effects, our strong culture could handle it. Sometimes we were right, and sometimes not. Process influences and drives culture and behavior more than we think.

Addressing the leadership side of Beyond Budgeting just as vigorously as the process side is critical for achieving real change. Yet our initial *process* focus actually may have been the right place to start. Our cultural background provides us with a better starting point on the leadership side than many other companies born and raised in different cultures. Maybe job number one is to ensure that our processes are organized *on* and not *against* the culture we are coming from and the leadership style that we naturally lean toward.

In 2015 we ran a survey on how the organization experienced Ambition to Action. A key question was to which extent Ambition to Action "helps your team perform." More than 80 percent said "Good," "Very Good," or "Excellent." Another important question was how well Ambition to Action translates Statoil strategies and ambitions. Here the score was even better.

The feedback on whether respondents had observed sub-optimal behaviors due to KPI targets was, however, more worrisome. Almost 50 percent said yes. This strengthens my belief that we need more KPIs used for measurement only, with less target setting than today. When measurement is used for learning more than control, the risk of suboptimal behaviors is much smaller.

We all have our bad days. I cannot count many, but there have definitely been occasions when the "dark forces" came out of hiding; or I listened to someone I thought was onboard but whose words or behaviors indicated the very opposite. Fortunately, I have a simple and effective remedy for those days: I just think back on where we stood ten years ago and compare it to where we are today. In that time perspective we have done great. If we make equal progress over the next ten years, we will have moved mountains. For me, that medicine normally provides instant and effective relief. If not, I just think back on all the organizations I have visited who still haven't started and where traditional management still runs the show. Compared to these, we are way ahead!

A comparison with what we aim for on values and ethics might be relevant, because this is very much about change in leadership and behavior. From time to time, and perhaps more often than we like, we all observe colleagues who cross the lines set out in our values and ethical principles. How should we react to this? Should we give up, or should we rather roll up our sleeves and work even harder on what we believe in? For me, there is no question about the right path to take.

We are on a management innovation journey where I am certain about only two things: We are heading in the right direction, and what we do tomorrow will be different and better than what we do today. The direction is clearer than the destination, if there is one. Maybe this journey has no end. There is always a better way.

A New Start for Statoil?

When Helge Lund left Statoil in 2014 to head up BG (British Gas), he had, of course, no idea that his new company soon would be acquired by Shell. I really felt sorry for him, as I am sure he would have done a great job. Maybe he even would have embarked on a Beyond Budgeting journey?

I recall one of his first promises when he came to Statoil: "The next CEO will be internally recruited." This would, of course, not be his decision, but he was the one who could and should ensure that there were internal candidates for the job.

Eldar Sætre was asked to step in as acting CEO. He was, however, very clear about not being a candidate for a permanent job. Many were disappointed, but we could also understand the hesitation about taking on such a tough job with constant pressure and intense media attention.

Torgrim Reitan was still in the CFO role. Both Eldar and Torgrim had played key roles in securing the *yes* back in 2005, and both were firm Beyond Budgeting believers and supporters. What a special situation with the two of them together at the top! Media speculated about other internal candidates, but with Eldar out of the picture most of us assumed it would be an external recruitment. As the hunt for a new CEO started, I recall telling myself: "This is as good as it gets. Enjoy it as long as it lasts. Whoever is recruited, it can only be for the worse compared to having those two in charge."

Eldar quickly filled the CEO role. After a month or so he met with investors and analysts. His opening remark, made with a smile, got me wondering: "I could get used to this job!" Was there still hope?

The announcement came some months later. Eldar had changed his mind. I will never forget that day. The mood was electric. Everybody was smiling and everybody knew why. Throughout his 35 years in the company, so many had experienced a direct or indirect work relation with him. I can't recall anyone ever having anything negative to say. Compared to an external recruitment, he was not someone to play games with. He knew the business, and he knew the organization, inside and out.

Eldar was crystal clear when sharing his views on leadership: "Empowerment is key. Create meaning and direction, but don't tell people what to do. By empowering instead of instructing, you get a better sense of people and their capacity for ownership and accountability."

He quickly moved on to establish a new vision and strategic platform for the company. "Shaping the future of energy" was built around three strategic pillars:

- *Competitive at all times*. "When we put a platform offshore, we don't design it just for sunny days and calm waters. We make sure it can stand a storm."
- *Transforming the oil and gas industry*. "The time has come to radically change how we work as an industry. We are recognized as one of the world's most innovative companies. Let us use that to reinvent the way we work."
- *Providing energy for a low-carbon future*. "The future has to be low carbon. In addition to becoming the most carbon-efficient oil and gas producer, we will use our technology and competence on new energy solutions."

Statoil definitely recognizes climate change and global warming. The scientific evidence is overwhelming, and our industry is part of the problem. Oil and gas will, however, still play a significant role in the energy mix for many years to come, on the way toward a low-carbon future. We therefore believe that we also can be part of the solution. We are Europe's second largest supplier of natural gas. We can produce even more gas, an energy source with significantly lower CO_2 emissions than all the coal that Europe also burns.

We can also contribute by ensuring that we have the lowest possible carbon footprint from our own production of oil and gas. We are already the most CO_2-efficient producer globally, but we have set ambitious longer-term targets to ensure that we will continue to stay ahead of our peers.

Statoil is also involved in renewable energy. We have used our offshore operations experience to become a major player in offshore wind. In 2015 we embarked on the next phase of this exciting journey, by building the world's first floating offshore wind park. Our renewable activities are now organized in a new business area reporting directly to the CEO.

Climate change is a stark reminder of all the VUCA that the world and especially our business is surrounded with. New technologies and paradigm shifts can definitely change the energy picture as we see it today. That makes the need for business and organizational agility even more pressing, and our Beyond Budgeting journey even more relevant.

CHAPTER 5

Beyond Budgeting and Agile

"Responding to change over following a plan."

From the Agile Manifesto

M y IT career was short, but it provided great learning. As you might recall, I headed up the implementation of the accounting system Horisonten in Statoil back in the late 1980s. It was a system ahead of its time. You could play around and model to make it fit your own business, instead of the other way around: the system forcing a design solution on you. I was still based in Finance, but IT was, of course, an important player even if we could do much of the programming ourselves. How to run the project became a hot topic. IT required for instance a detailed user specification from us. We protested because of the great iterative interaction the system invited us to. We wanted to experiment and learn and not be tied to one solution too early. We had no name for what we wanted to do instead, but I recall we had a word for what we didn't want: a *waterfall* approach that was sequential with no turning back. We quarreled for almost half a year before we won and could run the project our way. The new system was a success, but I was exhausted and said to myself, "Never again an IT project." I have kept that promise! It would take more than 20 years before I realized that we were trying to go agile long before Agile came along.

I have lost track of how many conferences I have spoken at since the Borealis case started to attract external interest in the nineties. In the beginning, it was only Finance conferences. Then invitations to speak at HR conferences started to come in. I could understand why, given how Beyond Budgeting is emphasizing leadership.

Then one day I got an invitation to speak at an IT conference. I was a bit puzzled. Maybe these guys thought I would share the magic trick of how to get fatter IT budgets! I went to Finland and did my presentation. Afterwards, one of the organizers, the amazing Pekka Abrahamsson, came over and gave me a bear hug. "You," he smiled, "you will speak at our XP (Extreme Programming) conference in Sardinia!" It sounded more like an order than an invitation!

Those were the first of many invitations from the Agile community that came from all over the world. I quickly understood where the interest originated.

In 2001, 17 practitioners from various programming communities came together and drew up the *Agile Manifesto*. This group of wise people developed a radically new vision for how to develop software, rebelling against what was the traditional approach at the time, an approach IT many years earlier had copied from manufacturing project management. It was exactly what we experienced at the start of the Horisonten project. When users asked IT to develop new software, they first had to produce a very detailed requirement list, spelling out exactly what the new system should do. These specifications would be signed in blood and handed over for programming, with a stern warning from IT that no changes would be accepted after this point in time: waterfall, no turning back! No wonder the user specs were thick. They did not merely contain "need to have" but also lots of "nice to have," just in case, as there would be no second chance. Just like with budgets! IT then started the huge work of programming and testing it all, with a project team of specialized resources all doing their own bit, supervised by an almighty project manager. The much later handover back to the user was seldom a success: "This isn't what we had in mind!" No wonder up to 70 percent of functionality in software developed under this approach is never used.

This was the flawed concept the 17 rebelled against, and you can see their *Agile Manifesto* in Exhibit 5.1.

We are uncovering better ways of developing
software and doing it and helping others do it.
Through this work we have come to value:

Individuals and interactions over processes and tools
Working software over comprehensive documentation
Customer collaboration over contract negotiation
Responding to change over following a plan

That is, while there is value in the items on
the right, we value the items on the left more.

EXHIBIT 5.1 Manifesto for Agile Software Development

These four main values are supported by 12 more specific principles:

- Our highest priority is to satisfy the customer through early and continuous delivery of valuable software.
- Welcome changing requirements, even late in development. Agile processes harness change for the customer's competitive advantage.
- Deliver working software frequently, from a couple of weeks to a couple of months, with a preference for the shorter timescale.
- Businesspeople and developers must work together daily throughout the project.

- Build projects around motivated individuals. Give them the environment and support they need, and trust them to get the job done.
- The most efficient and effective method of conveying information to and within a development team is face-to-face conversation.
- Working software is the primary measure of progress.
- Agile processes promote sustainable development. The sponsors, developers, and users should be able to maintain a constant pace indefinitely.
- Continuous attention to technical excellence and good design enhances agility.
- Simplicity—the art of maximizing the amount of work not done—is essential.
- The best architectures, requirements, and designs emerge from self-organizing teams.
- At regular intervals, the team reflects on how to become more effective, then tunes and adjusts its behavior accordingly.

A colleague of mine explained what Agile is about in the following way: Imagine a project assignment where the task is to develop the world's best soup. Obviously, there is quite some uncertainty here: which ingredients, when will it be ready, and at what cost? Innovation, experiments, and creativity are key for success. Then imagine a second assignment. The recipe is ready and the task is to produce 100 identical portions of the soup. Would we apply the same methodology for these two projects? Obviously not! This is where it went wrong for IT many years ago, when opting for the manufacturing or replication approach for software development. This kind of work is not about replication; on the contrary, there is significant uncertainty and all variables—content, time, and cost—can't be closed upfront. At least one must be left open. While Agile should be the process for developing the soup, Lean can be a great concept for the manufacturing process as the uncertainty is gone and the outcome is defined.

A leading Agile method is called Scrum. The name comes from the circle that rugby players form shoulder to shoulder when starting to play. Scrum is an adaptive process with short time-boxed development iterations (called "Sprints" that typically last two weeks). In each Sprint, the highest-priority (small-size) goals are pulled from a product backlog and developed. At the end of each short iteration, there is a formal inspect-and-adapt step: Business sees the running, tested product increment; talks with the team; reprioritizes, adds or deletes on the product backlog based on the latest information; and repeats the cycle. Transparency; early delivery of tangible, high-value goals; time-boxing; and inspect-and-adapt are key themes. In addition, Scrum is based on cross-functional and self-managed teams with no traditional project manager; the team decides how to best meet the Sprint goals and time-box deadline. The team may also "descope" a goal if it is discovered to be more work than estimated, but the time-box is never extended; the process consists of fixed time periods of variable scope in short cycles. Scrum embraces flexibility and responding to change rather than following a plan; business can change priorities at any two-week Sprint boundary as they learn new insights, though never within a Sprint. Another theme is to favor close collaboration over hand-off of voluminous documents; the short cycles, feedback loops, and closer interaction between development teams and businesspeople typically allow for a big reduction in detailed written user specifications.

It didn't take long before I learned that the Statoil IT function also had embraced Scrum. The Finance–HR alliance now has a new partner. I have enjoyed many great discussions with wise IT colleagues working with Agile.

Agile has now become the new way of developing software. IT people are rightfully frustrated about how this great way of working doesn't influence and inspire more work outside of IT, including how the enterprise itself is managed. Scaling Agile upwards has therefore been a hot topic in the community. I don't believe, however, that Agile can be scaled using the Agile language and framework exactly as in a software development context just because it worked so well here. This is where Beyond Budgeting can help, as it is about agility also at enterprise level. Beyond Budgeting offers a language and framework that executives and line managers understand and can relate to.

The similarities between the two concepts are striking, like for instance, "responding to change over following a plan." The idea of *continuous delivery* and dividing bigger tasks into smaller batches addresses the same problem that dynamic resource allocation does. Deciding in detail about all costs to be spent next year is a way-too-big "batch." We need smaller batches through a more dynamic process, replacing the single big budget decision with more continuous and smaller decisions, reflecting the latest information we have, with as many decisions as possible taken by those closest to the situation. It is about "continuous delivery" of resources. Also the view on people, values, and leadership is very similar. Trust and transparency are important in both concepts.

The community often refers to "doing agile" versus "being agile," actually the same distinction Beyond Budgeting makes between the six management process principles (doing) and the six leadership principles (being).

I love speaking at Agile conferences. The community seems to understand Beyond Budgeting better than many Finance people, who often tend to become very interested in their shoelaces when the discussion moves from KPIs and rolling forecasts to people, values, and leadership. If up on stage I ever should be in doubt about which community I am addressing, I only need to look for the flashing IPhones. The first time it happened I simply couldn't get it. They all knew I would share the slides afterwards. What I didn't understand was that "afterwards" was too late. Sharing was about now, not later. When my wife is able to join me, watching from the back, she can in addition also look for the ponytails. I never saw one of those at a Finance conference!

CHAPTER 6

Making the Change: Implementation Advice

"If you want something you never had, you must be willing to do something you've never done."

Thomas Jefferson

"People don't resist change. They resist being changed."

Peter M. Senge

We are often asked why Beyond Budgeting adoption has been slower compared to many other popular management concepts out there. Take for instance Scrum, which we just looked at. As you will recall many, maybe most, IT organizations have now adopted Scrum although it has been around no longer than Beyond Budgeting. Lean is another hugely popular method that has entered new territory outside of manufacturing where it originally was developed. How come Beyond Budgeting is not yet there? I believe the answer is quite simple. You can't compare Beyond Budgeting with these and many other concepts for two reasons: *granularity* and *scope*.

Most of these concepts are high on granularity compared to Beyond Budgeting. They are very specific in how they should be implemented and operated. You can buy hundreds of books explaining in detail how to do Scrum or Lean, describing the concepts very explicitly. There are also thousands of consultants out there willing and sometimes able to help. A lot of training is being offered, sometimes with costly certification schemes attached. Six Sigma is a good example with its white, yellow, green, and black belt levels. Some of these concepts seem to be feeding an entire consulting industry.

Beyond Budgeting is no management recipe high on granularity. On the contrary, as discussed earlier, the 12 principles represent more of a philosophy: guiding principles that must be adapted to each organization's activity, history, and culture. Some find this frustrating, as recipes obviously are simpler to relate to. There is, however, no lack of specific Beyond Budgeting practices, but these are found in organizations on the journey more than in the principles themselves, and they vary from company to company. It is the implementing community that keeps giving Beyond Budgeting a richer and richer content, not the other way around. This is why the BBRT has such a critical role in connecting companies and sharing cases and practices.

As for scope, Lean and Scrum were never intended and designed to address the full management agenda. They can, however, still be great concepts for the areas they were developed for. Lean has, for example, no view on resource allocation, forecasting, or incentives. Beyond Budgeting addresses all of these and almost everything else from both a process and a leadership perspective.

Being low on granularity and high on coverage, it should be no surprise that a Beyond Budgeting implementation is harder and takes longer. But it also means that the end result normally is more robust and sustainable.

A final reflection on the success of Agile and Lean: Things get harder for concepts when they try to grow out of their original birthplace, in this case software development and manufacturing. The Agile revolution has gone almost completely under the radar screen of most corporate executives, at least where software development is not the core business. Agile has so far threatened none of these executives' beliefs or practices. The same probably goes for Lean as long as it is a manufacturing thing only. It is when such concepts start to touch executives and require changes in their own practices and behaviors that things get really tough. This is what Beyond Budgeting has experienced from day one, as the concept goes straight for the throat of so many executive beliefs.

I have often wondered where the consulting world stands on Beyond Budgeting. After so many companies have embarked on the journey and after academia got interested, I had expected the consulting business to grab the idea, wrap it, and market it as "the next big thing," and of course charge accordingly. For some reason, this has not happened, at least not yet. There are definitely indications that something is brewing, as all of the big consulting firms have approached us. It is in any case late, as the budget criticism and Beyond Budgeting have been with us for a long time now. Is it because Beyond Budgeting is too big? Is it too provocative? Is it challenging too many accepted truths? Is it too difficult to box and wrap? Is it the combination of management process and leadership philosophy that confuses? Perhaps the consulting companies have organized their management and leadership practices under separate responsibilities, as it typically would be with their customers? Or is the hesitation simply about fear of cannibalizing other products and services they offer?

I am convinced that one day the consulting business will wake up, and with some hesitation I hope they do. We need their muscles and their marketing channels to reach the many top management teams that seem to trust new ideas only when they come from these guys. So I welcome the consulting business to

Beyond Budgeting. We must, however, help them understand and embrace the full depth of the idea, so they do not reduce it to a narrow and mechanical concept when their impressive slideshows are rolling in front of nodding executives.

The more specific implementation advice that now follows is based on lessons learned in both Borealis and Statoil. You will probably recognize some from previous chapters, as most have addressed various aspects of implementation. These advices are mainly about what we got right, but also about mistakes we made and things we now realize we should have done differently. I do not claim to have all the answers on the right way to go Beyond Budgeting. I doubt if anyone has. Every company is different and has to choose its own way. The advice that comes next should still be relevant for many. I have grouped it as follows:

1. Create the case for change.
2. Handle resistance.
3. Design to 80 percent and jump.
4. Keep the cost focus.
5. Don't start with rolling forecasting only.
6. Involve HR and Agile IT.
7. You can't get rid of command and control through command and control.
8. Do not become a fundamentalist.
9. Balanced Scorecard pitfalls.
10. Revolution or Evolution.

Create the Case for Change

There are a number of change formulas out there, describing in detail the steps required to achieve sustainable change. My own experience leaves me skeptical. No formula can solve this huge task for us. Real change is never a sequential and straight line from A to B. Change is messy, often accidental, and always easier to explain in hindsight than to plan up front. Dave Snowden nails it with the Cynefin approach of understanding what kind of situation you are in and what kind of problems you are facing. If we are into "complex" or "chaotic," compared to "obvious" (I know what to do) or "complicated" (the experts know what to do), there are no recipes and predefined cause-and-effect; only experiments can help us understand what works and what doesn't.

I still have some sympathy for the "Formula for Change" created by David Gleicher and later refined by Kathie Dannemiller. It says little about sequence but highlights critical elements for change to take place. It reads as follows:

Dissatisfaction × Vision × First steps > Resistance

For organizational change to take place, there must be *dissatisfaction* with the current situation; there must be a *vision* of something better; and there must be some *first tangible and credible steps* toward it. The *product* of the three must be bigger than the *resistance* to change. If any of the three is low or zero, the resistance will normally be bigger and kill the change. Remember that it is always more fun and more effective to work on the left-hand side. The levers available on the resistance side are fewer. Shooting people is not an option!

The case for change is critical. If an organization or a management team does not understand the fundamental problems with traditional management and the damage these cause, there will be limited appetite for understanding what the alternatives might be and for trying out any. Everyone knows that *something* is wrong. But these glimpses of problem understanding alone are normally not enough to create the dissatisfaction level necessary for radical change.

In Chapter 1, we reviewed a number of problems with traditional management. Many of them are different in nature and therefore require different implementation strategies. We can group most of them in a problem cluster we could call the "performance" problem, because the damage they cause impacts performance much more severely than, for instance, the waste in the efficiency problem. The performance problems include problems related to trust, cost management, target setting, evaluation, control, rhythm, and bonus. They all have a lot in common. We are left with the "efficiency" and "quality" problems, which both are in a somewhat different category, more indirectly and less seriously affecting performance.

The efficiency problem is the easiest to describe and get across. Anyone with a minimum of experience from corporate life knows that budgeting and budget follow-up consume much more time and effort than deserved. If even this obvious fact should be disputed, it is relatively easy to document. Remember the Hackett Group's finding that the budget process on average consumes 25,000 man-days per billion USD turnover.

The problem with building a case for change around the efficiency problem only is that it is by far the *smallest* problem. If solutions and new processes are designed just with this problem in mind, there is a risk that the two other and far more important problem areas will be left untouched and the enormous potential they represent will remain untapped. Often, the efficiency problem is just a consequence of the other problem areas.

In the ideal world, we would be able to create a full and thorough understanding and acceptance of all problem areas before moving on to solutions and implementation. Everyone would grasp the full problem and also the full scope of what we are aiming for, even if this endgame can make "big hairy goals" look like a walk in the park.

Unfortunately, very few companies enjoy the luxury of such a starting point, although there are some great cases in this category. Until the consulting world and academia move in full scale, I am afraid it will still be an uphill battle, a guerrilla war with a small but committed and hard-fighting group of freedom fighters up against an overwhelming army of tradition, skepticism, and aversion to change.

Should we then surrender if people are able only to get their heads around the efficiency problem? Absolutely not, but I strongly recommend trying to broaden the initial case for change to include at least some parts of the other two problem areas. Which one to go for first depends on what kind of organization you are with.

I often recommend to start with the quality problem, with the separation of the three budget purposes, especially if the organization is dominated by engineers, finance people, and a lot of rational thinking and problem solving. The simple fact that an ambitious target cannot be the same number as a 50/50 expected outcome forecast has a mathematical ring to it. That a cost forecast that doubles as a request for resources seldom will be a good forecast is quite obvious and most people get it right away. Both are simple to explain and can be illustrated easily with concrete examples from actual budget and planning practices in the company. Remind people that separating and improving only can make things better, and that we are not stopping what the budget tried to do for us. Add on some calendar examples from the rhythm problem. The light will most likely go on, and people will see something they have always sensed but not fully understood.

The performance problem is, however, by far the most serious one and *must* be addressed at some point, but it can be more difficult to get across. When you explain that traditional management and budgets stifle innovation, prevent rapid response, and block good performance, many managers are likely to nod in agreement but think you are wildly exaggerating.

There is an interesting pattern in the responses to the performance problem. Leaders and managers respond differently. Leaders typically buy into this one, while managers more easily embrace the quality problem and also put more emphasis on the efficiency problem compared to their leader colleagues. If you are lucky enough to have many true leaders in influential positions, it might be wise to front-load the performance problem. Unfortunately, in most companies they still do not make up the majority, and this problem often ends up as the last one to be addressed. But you must not and cannot ignore this problem, even if it is the most difficult one to get across and to do something about. Because it is the most serious problem, it also has the highest payback once addressed and tackled.

Whichever strategy you choose, you will find that the process and leadership principles are closely interlinked and cannot be addressed entirely separately. Process change drives behavior change and vice versa. The effect is often strongest if process changes are introduced and explained not in isolation, but with a strong emphasis on the underlying intentions and implications for behaviors and leadership. What seldom works is communicating leadership changes only, without any supporting process change. Principles like transparency and autonomy cannot just be declared, without immediate, visible, and credible support from corresponding process changes. Abolishing travel budgets or limiting expense claim controls merely to spot checks are powerful examples of giving content to trust and autonomy.

Whichever order you go for, in practice the exercise will never be a nicely structured and sequential one. Assume that you start out with the efficiency and quality problems. You separate the three budget purposes but do little beyond simple improvements on each one, including spending less time on it all. When a critical mass is onboard and understands the separation, you move on with more radical design change. How can we set better targets? How can we design a leaner and better forecasting process? What does it really mean to manage scarce resources in the most optimal way? Involvement is critical in this phase.

The organization must own the solutions. Blind copying from theory or other companies can easily backfire.

This is where you start planting the seeds of the performance problem. Do it gradually and cautiously, using examples from your own organization whenever possible. Start with the most obvious ones, whether that is about trust, transparency, cost management, or any of the others.

When moving into solutions, be careful not to oversell. That will only lead people to expect too much too soon. Remember the change formula. Balance your vision and the next steps with the resistance you face.

A green light from the board is often seen as a must for getting started. I do not necessarily see it that way. It depends, of course, on what kind of board you have and on the size of the company. In a large company, with a professional board that understands its governance role (which is not about micromanagement), initial board blessing may not be that critical. At some stage, however, a board buy-in is required. Board members need more or less the same journey as any other manager: understanding the problems with the current way and the basics of the new way, as well as the very limited downside risk and the huge upside potential. Fortunately, we are starting to see some peer pressure building up among board members as more and more companies get started. That was nonexistent for us in Borealis back in 1995.

As you will recall from the Borealis case, every autumn we simply chopped out the calendar year from the five-quarter rolling financial forecast and shipped it off to the owners, providing them with the numbers they needed for their own budget process. This created a bit of extra work in later reporting, but fortunately not on a very detailed level. Many board members were actually quite intrigued by what we did, although they all came from budgeting companies.

In Statoil, for several years we provided the board with scorecard-type information in addition to budgets and budget reports. The transition to a "budget-less" reporting was therefore less of a big deal for the board members. I am, however, still impressed with how they welcomed and understood the new concept and how disciplined they were in not falling back to budget-type questions. This is especially true since approving budgets and asking difficult questions about budget variances is what makes many board members feel they are part of the action, with a hand on the steering wheel.

In December 2007, a few months after the merged Statoil-Hydro started up, the board approved the new company's first Ambition to Action. Even though there were a number of new board members, not a single budget question was asked. In 2008 Svein Rennemo was elected chairman of the board, a role he held until 2015. That was definitely no disadvantage!

Handle Resistance

What follows is learning from years of doing exactly the opposite of what is recommended here. It is about how to tackle all the skeptics you will meet. There will be many. They are convinced that anarchy will follow, costs will explode, and people will abuse their new freedom to run off and do lots of stupid things.

As I think back on all my discussions with these guys, a clear pattern emerges. Again, almost without exception, they all belonged firmly in the *manager* camp. I can hardly remember having these discussions with anyone from the smaller *leader* camp.

In the early days in Borealis, we spent a lot of energy trying to convince these guys that they were wrong. The problem was that we had no evidence, so our discussions were not very constructive. I have now stopped, even if I probably forget myself from time to time. I have stopped simply because it does not work, and it is not worth it. If people are fundamentally skeptical, you cannot talk them into changing their minds, at least not before going live.

Here is a different and better strategy. Tell the skeptics that they may be right. It might not work. Costs might increase. We might lose control. It is a possible scenario. Accept that it might happen, but only if they accept your scenario, where it does work and often in great ways. They will, of course, regard the probability as close to zero.

Then move on to the risk and consequences of each scenario. Start with the failure case. If we fail, totally and miserably, what are really the risks? We can go back to budgeting overnight! Not a single soul will have forgotten how it was done! We do not need to burn or delete procedures and instructions before we jump. Maybe the next job will not be that interesting for the few who stuck their necks out. Most skeptics will probably not count that as a negative consequence, but rather the opposite! But beyond this, what is really the big risk for the organization?

Then ask the skeptics to reflect on risk and consequences of the success case. If we should succeed, although they will insist the chance is slim, are there any benefits? How does it look in companies that have succeeded? How do these great benefits compare to the negative consequences of a failure? It is a very compelling risk picture, with so little downside risk and such a huge upside potential. This line of argument tends to calm at least some of the skeptics. "But I still don't think it will work!" some will insist. Do not worry. Let them have the last word and move on.

Sometimes you realize that you have reached these guys more deeply than you thought. I will never forget a meeting with a new team shortly after the 2007 merger. Naturally, there were a few skeptical comments from some ex-Hydro managers who by then had heard little but the Beyond Budgeting headline. I was explaining dynamic resource allocation when an ex-Statoil manager suddenly took over, passionately describing and defending the new way of managing costs. I could hardly believe my own ears; this was a guy I had spent hours together with trying to convince. Now I could just lean back and leave the floor to him. He was great; I could not have explained things better myself!

The skeptics typically fall in one of two categories. Fortunately, both groups are getting smaller. The first is the biggest one. These guys are simply skeptical because they are confused. Beyond Budgeting is new and different and can for some be hard to comprehend before tested in practice. My experience is that they simply need time to try it out and practice it themselves. They also need the important experience of having it applied from above, and not just once. So time is on our side.

The second group is smaller, but this is where we find the real skeptics. They are not confused at all. They understand perfectly well what Beyond Budgeting is all about, and they simply hate it. They are strong Theory X supporters, and they believe that tackling VUCA is just a question of more detailed planning and more top-down commands. I stopped wasting my time on these people years ago. Fortunately, time here is also on our side. It is partly a generational issue; some retire and some leave. Some are asked to leave, not because they are critical to Beyond Budgeting, but their beliefs and behaviors tend to spill through into other areas.

Design to 80 Percent and Jump

The only thing certain about implementation is that there will be challenges and there will be problems. The only thing uncertain is where and when. Of course we need to plan, design new processes, and try to think through where the risks are and what might happen. But we also need to apply a Beyond

Budgeting principle onto the Beyond Budgeting implementation itself. When entering new and unfamiliar territory, there will be surprises. Not everything can be planned. What is needed is the ability to experiment, to sense and respond, to act fast and do the right thing when the unexpected hits. This is actually not that difficult as long as the Beyond Budgeting philosophy is understood and the direction is clear.

As you will recall from the Borealis case, we put a lot of design efforts in the cost management area, because we were convinced this was where the problems would occur. Instead, these popped up within forecasting, through resource applications disguised as inflated investment forecasts.

Another risk of spending too much time on process design up front is that it detracts from the time you could have spent on creating problem understanding and sharing the underlying leadership philosophy. The more the organization understands the case for change and what we really aim for, the better platform and guidance they have for behaving in the right way and making the right decisions in areas where the new process is not fully developed from day one.

I would have loved to try out a Beyond Budgeting implementation where almost everything related to traditional management and budgets was removed and nothing else put in place, and then just go for it. No targets, no forecasts, no calendars, no micro-instructions, no bonuses, no nothing. After a year we would take stock and see what we really missed. I would not be surprised if that list turned out to be pretty short!

Keep the Cost Focus

As already mentioned, one of the biggest misunderstandings about Beyond Budgeting is that cost is less important than in a budget regime. This is so wrong. Cost and how we spend scarce resources *is* important, which is why we need more effective and intelligent ways of managing than what the detailed annual budget can offer. There will always be capacity constraints, and often (but not always) it is money. The issue is how we best optimize these scarce resources, whatever they are.

In Borealis, cost was always high on the agenda, simply because petrochemicals is a low-margin commodity business where your own fixed costs are among the few things you can fully influence. In our business, cost is of course also important, but success has been just as much driven by innovation, creativity, and quality in business development, exploration, construction, and production. Technology and great people make a big difference. Already before we embarked on our Beyond Budgeting journey, the main focus in the industry was on production volumes and growth, especially in the period when the oil price was well above $100. This was also what the market prioritized and rewarded. Cost was on the agenda, but lower down. The consequence was a disturbing cost creep, not just in oil and gas companies, but also on the supplier side. The activity level was record high as the industry had to enter increasingly remote and harsh environments to maintain or grow their reserve base.

Eliminating the traditional cost budget probably strengthened the impression among some at Statoil that cost was less important. Looking back, we should have been even more clear and explicit that this was not the case. We should probably also have put more effort into designing better and more self-explanatory cost reports. The way the industry captures and allocates cost for later charging to joint ventures is not always as transparent and simple as in many other businesses. The low number of true internal profit centers didn't help either. Still, I strongly disagree that Beyond Budgeting was the reason for a slipping cost focus. Volume and growth over cost and value was a conscious strategic choice. The entire industry had the same priorities and experienced the same problem, and everybody else had traditional cost budgets. In Statoil, we were actually very happy that we didn't enter 2015 with a detailed cost, revenue, and investment budget based on the autumn 2014 price level of +$100 oil, as the price already in February had fallen below $50.

Today, cost is high on the agenda in all oil companies, also Statoil. I only hope it isn't too high and the pendulum hasn't swung too far in the opposite direction.

Don't Start with Rolling Forecasting Only

Many want to start their Beyond Budgeting implementation with rolling forecasts. It may seem like the easiest way to get started, jumping the fence where it is lowest. My question is then always how the other two budget purposes will be handled: target setting and resource allocation. If the answer is through the rolling forecast, there is trouble ahead. What you end up with is nothing but a rolling budget. Almost none of the budget problems will be solved, and the price is a lot more work. There *must* be new and clear processes in place at the same time, describing how target setting and resource allocation also will be handled. It is, of course, possible to continue to run the two in a traditional budget process. The only problems solved will then be the "accordion" forecasting horizon and the forecasting bias, but none of all the other budget problems.

I also recommend reflecting on whether the granularity of quarterly buckets for forecasting data is needed. As mentioned earlier, at Statoil we decided to stick to annual buckets. Forecasting then becomes an issue of how often to update, and how many buckets ahead.

It is also important to rid the conversation of the "deliver on forecast" expression. It is *targets* we want to hit, and we use forecasting to help us. A "good forecast with bad news" is definitely something we don't want to hit. I would much rather have good forecasts with bad news than a bad forecast with good news.

Involve Human Resources and Agile IT

One of my regrets in Borealis was that HR was involved too little and too late. For different reasons this was not an issue at the time. I had not yet had my debut in HR. Also, my understanding of what kind of journey we had begun was narrower and more financially oriented than it is today. I am convinced that both the model and the implementation would have benefited greatly from having HR onboard earlier.

Some of my finance colleagues cannot understand why I bang on about involving HR. They probably believe that I am sympathizing just because of the four years I spent in the function. I do sympathize. I learned a lot that you do not learn in finance roles, not even in leadership roles. I got to know a lot of great HR people, and also a few who perhaps should have done something else—just like in the finance function. But that is not the issue. As you will recall, there are three other more important reasons why HR must be onboard:

1. The organization and the process need HR involvement.
2. Finance needs it.
3. HR needs it.

The first point has to do with *integrated* performance management. Ask any finance person for a definition of performance management. I guarantee the answer will include words like *strategy, budgets, business plans, KPIs, reporting and variance analysis,* and the like. An HR person will respond very differently, listing *individual goals, development plans, coaching and feedback, motivation, and rewards.* They are both right, but they only see their own part of the process. They both address performance management issues, but these have to connect from strategy to people. If you are based outside of Finance and HR, as most people in organizations are, you do not care who is responsible for what. You simply want things to hang together, to be consistent and reflect the same management and leadership philosophy.

So HR must be onboard to ensure that the new performance management process is integrated and consistent, all the way from strategies and business goals to individual goals and rewards.

The second reason for HR to be involved is that Finance needs it. Beyond Budgeting is a massive change project, where we need to go much further than merely changing management processes. We must also find our way into people's hearts and minds. We are seeking deep and radical change in leadership attitudes and behavior. The change is about much more than taking away a budget and implementing a scorecard or a forecasting process, which is where the finance community has its core competencies. When moving out of this comfort zone, help is needed from people with skills and knowledge in all those other areas we are trying to reach with Beyond Budgeting. These people are often found in HR. It happens to be their job!

The Norwegian bank SpareBank1 Gruppen went Beyond Budgeting several years ago. Their CEO, Eldar Mathisen, was the strong driver. I will never forget a session with 100+ of their top managers, with Mathisen on the first row, eagerly involved. Sadly he passed away the year after, but people around him moved on and secured a great Beyond Budgeting implementation. Initially, Finance took the lead, but later HR took over. The bank realized that leadership and culture were the key issues and the main stumbling blocks.

The third reason is important for HR. As discussed, most HR functions aim for a business partner role. This will not happen before HR becomes more interested in what happens in the performance management process *before* it reaches traditional HR territory. The business partner ambition might in itself be an argument for HR to join forces with Finance. How many business partners does the business actually want and need?

Whatever cooperation we talk about, it has so far been more of an exception than a rule. In most companies on a Beyond Budgeting journey, HR has not woken up, and Finance has not been ready to open the door. We are clearly in the very early phases of something that I strongly believe can grow into a powerful partnership.

As we discussed in Chapter 5, IT also deserves an invitation. The Agile enthusiasts found in most IT functions these days can be great contributors. Their role should not only be about bringing Beyond Budgeting into IT. They can help across the organization, fertilizing Beyond Budgeting design and implementing Agile inspiration and ideas. I promise my HR friends that they will find this community an easier partner than Finance!

You Can't Get Rid of Command and Control through Command and Control

Going Beyond Budgeting sometimes feels like conquering the mountains around my winter cabin in Norway. You aim for a peak in the distance and work hard to get there, only to discover that there is another higher one behind it. You make it to that one as well, only to see another one and another one. When we got the green light from the Executive Committee in 2005, I was very much aware that this was only the beginning. It was an important milestone but far from any victorious end.

It was not difficult to climb the immediate next hilltop, to implement the new principles between corporate and the business areas right below. They all welcomed the new model with open arms. It gave them more autonomy and flexibility, a more meaningful performance language, and less work. But despite the warm welcome, it was hard for some of them to pass on the newly won freedom farther out in the organization: "*We* can of course be trusted. The guys below, though . . . ."

In Statoil, for radical change to happen, an Executive Committee decision is necessary, but seldom sufficient. Implementation has been a long and hard climb despite the backing of a clear decision, and from time to time it was tempting to resort to a little dose of command and control. But it works poorly. You can instruct people to make budgets and practice traditional management. You cannot instruct them to stop.

Most large companies suffer from change fatigue. And no wonder. Constant waves of new corporate projects and initiatives roll over organizations. They all have fancy names and well-structured implementation schedules, backed by armies of consultants and a few business "hostages" as project managers and steering committee members.

You always get a warning. May 12 at 11 o'clock they will knock on your door. The implementation locomotive has reached your unit. They expect you to be motivated and prepared, drop everything else, and make *this one* your number-one priority. Forget the fact that the last team just left, and you are still digesting the changes those guys rolled in. I am sure you can name a project or two like this that has hit your own unit over the last couple of years.

In Statoil, we chose a different approach, based on two simple principles:

1. No fixed implementation schedule: We will go where the pull is.
2. No consultants: We will do it ourselves.

The decision to go without consulting support was, of course, helped by my previous experience from Borealis. But here we also had the same strategy. We did not ask Gemini Consulting to help; we knew they had little to offer. We simply wanted to do it ourselves.

I am not saying that consultants never should be used. A good consultant working behind or alongside you, and not in front of you, can absolutely make a positive difference. As we have discussed, so far the consulting business has not been very visible in the Beyond Budgeting arena. When they wake up, and if you want help, make sure you choose someone who understands the full picture and is not only in the box-pushing business. Watch out especially for those who wrap it as being all about rolling forecasts.

A good alternative is to talk to other companies that are ahead of you. The Beyond Budgeting Roundtable is a great place to make such contacts. An increasing amount of literature—books, articles, and case studies—is now also available.

Our implementation schedule did, of course, include the important milestone of getting the green light, but it wasn't planned long in advance. We simply asked for that "yes" from the Executive Committee when we were ready and when we believed they would be, too. Beyond that, we basically followed a strategy of going where the pull was, where there was an appetite for change. This included asking for units that wanted to volunteer as pilots. Three pairs of hands went up fast: our Shared Services unit, our Exploration unit, and a downstream unit called Nordic Energy.

After these pilots had started, more hands went up. We got invitations from an increasing number of management teams, finance teams, and eventually HR teams. We advanced on the battlefield every day, but more in a guerrilla style than with massive forces. There was no detailed master plan. We went where hands went up and there was an opening. We did not spend much time going for the enemy strongholds. Our strategy was to surround the resistance, not start with it. There was always enough demand to keep us busy. The openings sometimes came as positive surprises, in places we had expected to be closed for quite some time. This approach also allowed us to experiment. Units that wanted to go early could try out things and advise those following about what worked and what didn't.

I have lost count of all the management teams we have visited. We talked ourselves onto the agendas of leadership development programs, management conferences, and other arenas where leadership and management were discussed. One year I was only a guest at the annual HR conference; the next year I was a speaker.

The process probably looked somewhat messy and unstructured from the outside and maybe from the inside as well. The route might seem like a longer one than a more conventional and structured implementation approach. Yet I am convinced that this is a better way of anchoring both the philosophy and the process, making the new model more robust against the unavoidable counterattacks from the "dark forces." Do not be fooled just because they remain still and silent. They will be there for a long time.

One final piece of advice: Bury the word *rollout* in a place where it can never be found again. When you say "rollout," the organization probably hears "roll over," and probably for good reasons. You also may want to bury *cascading* in the same place. Out there it might sound like a bucket of water is about to be thrown at you.

Do Not Become a Fundamentalist

People often ask if the word *budget* now is forbidden. Of course it is not. We still have joint venture budgets, because we have to. But beyond these, we do ask people to try to avoid using the word, simply because it can confuse. If we say "budget," what do we actually mean: a target, a forecast, a resource allocation? Nor is it forbidden to keep a piece of paper in a drawer or a spreadsheet on a PC that looks like a budget. If people need this safety net in a transition period, then it is not a problem. But be clear that those numbers will not be reported against or consolidated. Over time, people will find out that perhaps it is not worthwhile spending time on creating these safety nets. But they have to find this out for themselves.

Balanced Scorecard Pitfalls

In both Borealis and Statoil, balanced scorecards were high on the list of tools and processes that replaced the budget. I like the concept, because it helps us to make connections: long term and short term, cause and effect, financial and non-financial, line and support, strategy, finance, and HR. It provides us with a better performance language than perhaps any other management concept out there. If you are unfamiliar with the concept, I recommend checking out the many books written by the inventors Robert Kaplan and David Norton.

One reason for the huge popularity is the impressive packaging and marketing of the concept. Nevertheless, there is a solid concept behind all that nice wrapping. However, if the balanced scorecard is implemented and used in the wrong way, its full potential will not be realized. In the worst case, scorecards can do even more damage than budgets. In this section we look at some typical pitfalls. There are enough balanced scorecard success stories out there; I believe there is more to learn by understanding where things can go wrong.

There are many ways of getting it wrong. Here are seven classic mistakes. There might be more to watch out for. Some are more dangerous than others, especially the command-and-control one. In combination, they are almost guaranteed to make you fail. None of these pitfalls should be read as an argument against the balanced scorecard. On the contrary, I point them out in order to help you get the maximum benefit out of the concept. You will already have heard about some of my concerns, like the KPI addiction.

The pitfalls are:

1. A new box on top of old boxes.
2. It is all about KPIs.
3. Just another command-and-control tool.
4. Only one scorecard at the top.
5. A paralyzing balance.
6. It is a finance thing.
7. It is a manual thing.

These are all based on own experiences in Borealis and Statoil, and on observations made in the many organizations I have advised over the years.

A New Box on Top of Old Boxes

It is so much easier to add on than to take away. You can implement a lot of highly acclaimed management concepts without really having to threaten any of the old processes or those responsible for them. You buy a new box and just put it on top of your other boxes.

Look at the huge number of companies that have implemented balanced scorecards. Almost all of these have simply added the scorecard on top of existing management processes, including budgeting. It is definitely the simplest way. No threats, no conflicts. Everybody is happy, except those who worry about even more to do.

But budgets and scorecards represent two fundamentally different approaches. Scorecards are rooted in strategy and in longer time perspectives. They focus on non-financial drivers that lead to financial performance and value creation, all the way from people and learning. Budgets are very much the opposite: They have weak strategy links and short time horizons, and are about money only. The balanced scorecard was actually invented as a response to the narrow, financial-only focus that dominated business management for decades.

Many argue that the combination of scorecards and budgets is an uncomplicated marriage. They claim that the budget can represent the targets in the financial perspective in the scorecard. The other perspectives are established and operated as the theory prescribes, defining and measuring the non-financial levers to pull in order to deliver on the budget numbers in the financial perspective. It sounds simple. There are, however, major challenges with this solution. First, defining good financial performance through fixed and absolute budget numbers is not very smart for reasons already discussed at length. There is, however, a second problem. If the scorecard works well, it should quickly pick up internal or external radar signals when assumptions change or the unexpected happens. The right response often is to adjust the course. Revised tactics and new actions are quickly put in place. People are ready to move, but there is a ball and chain around their legs: *the budget*. To ensure delivery of the fixed budget number in the financial perspective, it was cascaded down into every single unit with rigorous detail, spelling out not just profitability targets or the like but also which activities to execute and at which cost. The conflict between scorecard and budget is suddenly real and tangible. And the winner is . . . .

These two opposites collide more often than we think. When they do, the budget wins, again and again. The budget is familiar, it has a track record, and it often carries the bonus money. No wonder the scorecard so often loses out, even if everyone thinks it is great. But we keep the scorecard. It is hard to drop, even when we feel it does not work as promised. Everyone else has it.

The answer is not to drop the scorecard but to drop the competition: the budget. We never got this insight in Borealis, because we never experienced the conflict. We dropped the budget and introduced scorecards in one big bang.

Statoil, however, had been running scorecards in parallel with budgets for many years. Although the second bottom-up process was successful, it was removing the budget in 2005 that turbo-charged it all. It quickly became clear to the organization that the rules of the game had changed. The fact that the board no longer approved budgets but only Ambition to Action was tangible evidence of a new focus.

It Is All about KPIs

Kaplan and Norton were almost too successful with the KPI part of the balanced scorecard. Although their first book was rather KPI focused, later books have repositioned the scorecard more as a *strategy execution* process, with KPIs as just one part of the model. But the initial KPI success seems to stick too well in many companies. KPIs are now all over the place—not just in business, but increasingly also in public organizations. The New Public Management ideas, first developed in Australia and New Zealand in the 1980s, where KPIs play a key role, have now spread to many parts of the world.

There is nothing wrong with KPIs. They can do great things for us. The problem is that we need *more* than KPIs. They cannot do the job alone. As already discussed, we seem to have forgotten that the *I* in KPI stands for *indicator*. They are meant to measure and give us an *indication* of whether we are moving in the right direction. This works quite well in the finance perspective of the scorecard. Here, the link between strategic objectives and KPIs is normally strong and quite obvious. If a strategic objective is to increase shareholder value, and the KPI is share price development including dividends paid, the KPI is providing much more than an indication of delivery against the strategic objective.

The more we move from the financial perspective to the non-financial ones, the more indicative this relation becomes. Take the example of safety, very important at both Borealis and Statoil. A strategic objective might be to achieve a step change in safety performance. Is it a given that this is taking place just because the number of safety meetings held is moving in the right direction? A high fever is an indication that something is wrong, but it seldom gives us the full diagnosis. We cannot expect KPIs to always tell us the full truth and the whole story.

As mentioned, my scorecard and KPI journey started in 1995. For way too long I searched for the perfect KPI. I gave up many years ago, simply because it does not exist. There are many good KPIs, and combinations of KPIs can make them even better. But the perfect one? Forget it.

We need something else in addition to the indications we get from KPIs. When making decisions and evaluating performance we need to also make other observations and use these in a more holistic assessment. Again, don't forget Einstein's wise words!

Just Another Command-and-Control Tool

The budget is an effective tool for micromanaging an organization. Still, it is limited to *financial* micromanagement only. For executives wanting even stronger and longer whips, the balanced scorecard offers many more control opportunities. Not just strategic objectives, KPI targets, and actions, but also additional perspectives in addition to the financial one. On all of these, corporate can instruct and cascade much more effectively than through a budget. Unfortunately this is exactly what happens in a number of organizations. Corporate functions such as HR and HSE often join in, demanding that "their" objectives, KPIs, and actions on the corporate scorecard should be found all the way down to ensure "corporate delivery."

A top-down approach does not cause serious damage only to motivation. Wrong decisions might also be made, and good ideas lost, especially when the distance to the front line is long, maps are outdated, and there are surprises hiding around every corner.

As the name states, *balance* is key in a scorecard. I believe there is one balancing act that has not gotten enough attention in the scorecard theory, the right balance between:

- Alignment, from strategy to people, from center to front line
- Autonomy, flexibility, ownership, and commitment, helping local teams to manage themselves

These two purposes often pull in opposite directions. If the alignment purpose always wins and local scorecards become nothing but a landing ground for instructions from above, with no room to move and with no place for local focus and initiatives, then the scorecard risks losing its standing and relevance. The result is a feed-the-machine perception, something done for the layers above only. The classic symptom is again when scorecard updating takes place only when it is time for the next business review with the level above.

Of course, a scorecard cannot be local only and disconnected from the rest of the company. It has to be a combination of the two, but the *perception* should still tip in favor of local ownership. One way of achieving this is a broad and involving scorecard design process that reflects both purposes. It feels local but has a central origin. This is what the Statoil translation approach aims for, as described earlier.

Only One Scorecard at the Top

Some companies have only one or just a few scorecards. In a small company, this might be fine. In larger organizations, this is seldom enough. It might seem sufficient for top management, describing overall direction and spelling out corporate targets and initiatives. But beyond this, what does the scorecard really mean for each of the business areas and for units in the front line? All of these probably have their own budgets. With a budget but no scorecard, the result is a simple walkover.

I am not saying that all frontline units and cost centers necessarily should have their own scorecard, although it can work well for many. The nearest scorecard must, however, be close enough to provide clear guidance and inspiration. It must be perceived as relevant and meaningful. That will seldom be the case if people need binoculars to see it.

As we discussed earlier, managers operating without a scorecard would still need to do most of the scorecard job. They still need to think and talk about tomorrow and not only about today. Some kind of measurement of whether things are moving in the right direction is also necessary, and so is some kind of action planning. The scorecard systematizes and automates such information. This can be done in different ways, but the management job must always be done.

The analogy of an airplane cockpit sometimes is used to describe the balanced scorecard. I am not sure if I like this metaphor. It triggers a number of traditional management associations in me. The captain and the copilot—the CEO and the CFO—are both in the cockpit, surrounded by measurements. They are constantly fed updated information. They watch, analyze, and take decisive actions when lights flash and alarms ring. Back in the cabin, the passengers eat, sleep, and kill time waiting for the pilots to bring them safely to the destination. They have limited information beyond what they can see through small windows and hear in a noisy cabin. Business-class passengers are a bit better informed, as they sit closer to the cockpit door, which from time to time is open. They also find the trip more comfortable than those back in economy class.

Some passengers react to all of the instructions from the cabin crew, from those with less impressive uniforms than the guys up front in the cockpit. There seems to be a sharper edge in their voices the farther back in the cabin they move, passing on messages from the cockpit and issuing instructions about seatbelts and luggage.

Don't misunderstand me. I still want the guys in front to fly me safely home. I am just questioning how applicable the metaphor is. In today's organizations, people no longer accept being passive passengers, leaving their destiny completely in the hands of a few guys at the top. People want to be informed and involved. They do not accept being intimidated by middle managers who believe authority comes from stars and stripes.

A Paralyzing Balance

A scorecard is a much bigger and better radar screen than a financially oriented budget and business plan. The broader focus includes other stakeholders: employees, customers, shareholders, and society at large. We formulate cause-and-effect relationships between the different perspectives and stakeholders. How does the organization's learning and development impact our operating processes, which are necessary for the satisfied customers we need in order to create revenues and value? There might still be conflicts between different stakeholder interests. Employees might want higher salary levels, customers might want lower prices, and taxes or restrictions imposed by society might conflict with shareholder interests.

If we want to create sustainable value, we cannot ignore any stakeholder. At the same time, we cannot aim for simultaneous short-term maximization of all stakeholder interests, as this might cause a paralyzing balance. When a scorecard does not sufficiently address choices and priorities, and does not distinguish between today and tomorrow, we risk sending the message that everything is equally important. This might leave the organization in limbo, trying to run after everything at the same time. Again, strategy is about making choices. If you never say *no*, you do not have a strategy. Choices must be made and reflected in the scorecard.

A final reflection on balance: Sometimes it is actually lack of balance that brings movement and progress, like the human body walking. Each step leaves us out of balance, which we handle by taking another step, and another one, and the result is that we keep moving forward.

It Is a Finance Thing

The majority of scorecard projects and operating responsibilities sit firmly in the finance function. One reason is probably that Finance is the main number collector and also the reporting and control function. In many companies the scorecard process is about just that, so Finance is the obvious candidate for the job. Could other functions take it? What about the strategy function, or HR?

This is the wrong discussion. The main issue is not where to place the responsibility but how the responsible function works together with other functions. Whoever the owner is, a close coordination across traditional functional borders is required. The scorecard process must involve Strategy, Finance, and HR. It is about *integrated* performance management, from overall strategies and strategic objectives to KPIs, actions, and forecasts; and further to team and personal goals, evaluation, and reward. There is in fact no perfect candidate for the scorecard job within the traditional functional structure in companies. Obviously, it is a line responsibility, but so is everything. You need a clear owner who drives, coaches, and ensures a continuous development of both process and system. Finance is probably best positioned for the job, simply because it sits in the middle between strategy and people. It requires, however, a different mindset and competence than we typically find in Finance, including a holistic perspective and a broad understanding of strategy and organizational behavior, on top of the necessary business and financial competence. Add on communication skills beyond the ability merely to read out the numbers.

Some companies have set up a dedicated unit, as suggested by Kaplan and Norton. The "Office of Strategy Management" holds an overall responsibility for the strategy execution process. It is an interesting idea, but it also introduces an additional interface to manage. On balance, I believe a more sustainable solution is to take the longer and more demanding route of growing Finance into this role. Or maybe a Finance/HR alliance could be a solution, as discussed earlier.

Sometimes the context in which a scorecard is introduced can do something with the perception of ownership. When a big PC producer introduced scorecards several years ago, it also made changes to its bonus system, including a tight link to scorecards. For several years, people talked about scorecards only as "the bonus system."

It Is a Manual Thing

An active and pulsating scorecard process, living from the boardroom to the control room, cannot be based on a manual collection and publication of data. Some kind of system is needed.

Whatever your system choice is, it is important not to let the system become a straitjacket for your process design. It might be wise to start out manually on a small scale, maybe with a few pilot tests to learn and improve before a more permanent model is automated. The manual period should not be too long, though, as manual scorecards are demanding to operate and often do not provide the best data quality.

A number of scorecard packages are on the market, ranging from standalone systems with varying integration possibilities to scorecard modules in larger enterprise performance management (EPM) solutions. Beyond all the IT-technical issues that someone else must help you with, my advice is to pressure test the system candidates with these questions:

- Does the package focus on KPIs only, or does it also have good functionality for handling strategic objectives and actions and other free-text information?
- Is the user interface simple and intuitive, a no-brainer for managers who still have their secretaries print all their e-mails?
- Can you easily add on information that teams need in their daily jobs, so that the application becomes more of a management information portal?
- Can the system follow you on your scorecard journey? Can you adjust and improve without mobilizing armies of IT people?
- Does the system vendor understand performance management from an organizational point of view or only see it as a mechanical drill-down data-collecting and reporting exercise?

It goes without saying that the final decision must lie with the scorecard-responsible function and not with IT.

Revolution or Evolution?

Implementation as a revolution or an evolution is often debated in the Beyond Budgeting community. Former Handelsbanken

CFO Lennart Francke used the following metaphor on Beyond Budgeting implementation choices: "Picture a busy London street. Could you imagine the UK changing from driving on the left to driving on the right by starting with buses one month, trucks the next, and finally the cars?"

It is a nice metaphor, but I am afraid it isn't that simple. The ideal starting point is, of course, a full and unanimous support for the entire Beyond Budgeting model. Getting the whole management team onboard is a huge task, though. Even when top management understands it all and wants it all, implementation will still be a long and phased journey. And even if it is possible to synchronize all process changes in a common launch and a big bang, the implementation will not be over before the understanding and acceptance of process changes have been translated into a corresponding change in behaviors throughout the organization. This is a long-haul change, not a quick fix. Even if the revolution is roaring on the management process side, the required change in leadership, behaviors, and culture will always be an evolution.

So, even if we switch traffic from left to right overnight, as Sweden did in 1967, we will still see people driving on the wrong side of the road for many years to come. Some will do so because they simply disagree and refuse to change. Others simply forget themselves, without any bad will involved. As long as they are few, these ghost drivers are not as dangerous as those in real traffic. Over time, this kind of driving is of course not acceptable, and such drivers must be brought in line or have their driver license confiscated. But it is unavoidable that there will be a transition period where things will look messy. Many will be confused because there are old and new behaviors on the street every day. But remember, if there is no mess and no confusion, we are not seeing any real change, just a bit of singing and dancing to the latest music in the charts.

As discussed earlier, organizations embarking on a Beyond Budgeting journey often get braver along the way. What seems scary when starting out almost always becomes less scary and sometimes even blindingly obvious at some point down the road. This not only increases the appetite for more, it also tends to stimulate the creativity and innovation needed. The result is typically an evolution through a number of mini-revolutions in management processes over time. Each one requires their own, sometimes slow, digestion in the organization before resulting in the desired change in leadership and behaviors.

This should not prevent us from thinking like revolutionaries, every single day. At the same time, we need to watch out for the counter-revolution. The dark forces have long lives in most organizations. Sometimes they get outside help. All those great new, simpler and better processes developed over many years can be terminated by a new CFO or CEO, typically externally recruited. Unlike the more step-wise revolution, the counter-revolution can easily be a big bang, a sweeping decision as part of those dangerous "100 first days" programs. The way back to the old processes needs no experiments, no testing and no learning. It is all too familiar. Many will remember, most with horror. The corresponding change in leadership and behaviors back to the sad old way will however be slower, even if the counter-revolution banned all the great stuff overnight.

Fortunately, we have seen very few counter-revolutions so far, on the contrary. Almost all organization that has started out seems to continue. Some very cautiously, though, but discussions are still more about how to improve and move forward and not about going back. Maybe because going back is nothing but a dead end.

Closing Remarks

When we started out in Borealis way back in 1995, before Beyond Budgeting even had a name, I was convinced that what we had discovered was so brilliant that it could only be a question of time before this would become *the* new way of managing organizations.

It has not happened on that scale, not yet. The adoption has been slower than for many other concepts, for reasons already discussed. I feel, however, that we are approaching a tipping point, given the huge interest not just from organizations around the world, but also from academia and the consulting business. It can only be a question of when, not if. The uncertainty and pace of change in our business environments is not slowing down. People's expectations toward their employers and leaders keep increasing. Beyond Budgeting may be the most important new idea out there addressing the totality of these radical changes, due to its broad scope and coherent approach. A number of other management innovation concepts and communities are also attacking traditional management. The more we join forces, the stronger we will be. I don't care what we end up calling it, as long as it helps organizations to become more agile and more human. One day, we will all smile about how we used to think about leadership and management. Just like we now smile about the time before the Internet.

An indication of the strong interest is all the requests for keynotes and workshops that keep coming in. Personal highlights include addressing GE's top 600 managers at their legendary Boca Raton gathering, speaking at Harvard, and keynoting at the world's largest Agile conference. A *Harvard Business Review/McKinsey Management Innovation award* was also a great experience.

I have throughout the years helped a number of companies get started on their own journey. Nothing beats being part of something like that. My employer, Statoil, has recently opened for select consulting work to meet a massive demand. As retirement from this great company is slowly approaching, I think I know what I want to do next, beyond the writing and the speaking.

In the early pages of this book, I warned that I would do some shouting and make things as black-and-white as necessary to get my points across. My apologies if I sometimes got too loud, passionate, and emotional. It is hard not to on such big and important issues. If I did, I hope you were able to hear through the noise. I hope you found something to get you started or something that can help if you are already on the move. Thank you for listening, and farewell on your own journey, wherever you are coming from and wherever you are heading.

And remember, if you want to travel far, travel together.

Index